KU-161-519

REDISCOVERING
MASCULINITY

By the same author

Kant, Respect and Injustice:
The Limits of Liberal Moral Theory,
International Library of Philosophy Series.

With Lawrence Blum,
A Truer Liberty: Simone Weil and Marxism.

REDISCOVERING MASCULINITY

Reason, Language and Sexuality

VICTOR J SEIDLER

HAVERING COLLEGE
OF FURTHER & HIGHER EDUCATION
LEARNING RESOURCES
CENTRE

London and New York

52487

305.31

First published 1989
by Routledge
11 New Fetter Lane, London EC4P 4EE

Reprinted in 1990

Simultaneously published in the USA and Canada
by Routledge
a division of Routledge, Chapman and Hall, Inc.
29 West 35th Street, New York, NY 10001

© 1989 Victor J. Seidler

Typeset by J&L Composition Ltd, Filey, North Yorkshire
Printed and bound in Great Britain by
Mackays of Chatham PLC, Chatham, Kent

All rights reserved. No part of this book may be reprinted
or reproduced or utilized in any form or by any electronic,
mechanical, or other means, now known or hereafter
invented, including photocopying and recording, or in any
information storage or retrieval system, without permission
in writing from the publishers.

British Library Cataloguing in Publication Data

Seidler, Victor J. (Victor Jeleniewski, *1945*
Rediscovering masculinity: reason, language
and sexuality,
1. Masculinity
I. Title
305.3'1

Library of Congress Cataloging in Publication Data

Seidler, Victor J. 1945–
Rediscovering masculinity: reason, language, and sexuality
Victor J. Seidler.
p. cm.
Bibliography: p. 221
Includes index.
1. Men–Psychology. 2. Masculinity (Psychology) 3. Men–Sexual
behavior. 4. Power (Social sciences) I. Title.
HQ1090.S44 1989
305.3'2–dc19

ISBN 0-415-03199-0

For Anna

CONTENTS

PREFACE AND ACKNOWLEDGEMENTS

This work touches on nearly twenty years of men's responses to the challenges of feminism. Men have responded in very different ways, partly depending upon class, race, and ethnic background. Heterosexual men have had to respond to the phenomenon of gay liberation, so learning about the power men share both in relation to other men and to women: this has often produced fear and guilt, as many reacted defensively, unable to listen or to hear. The response to feminism has been a slow and difficult process, in which many men have sought to identify with feminism rather than to change themselves. In the 1970s it was easier to think that men getting together to share their experience in the context of consciousness-raising had to be a consolidation of men's power in relation to women. It was easier to learn to say the right things, than to explore the contradictions of our experience as men.

Men have been slow to meet both the personal and the theoretical challenges, for feminism has challenged not only the ways that we use our power in relation to women but also the ways that we experience ourselves as men. It has also challenged the forms of our knowledge – our moral and political theories as much as our theories of knowledge. Unlike so much orthodox Marxist theory, feminism has also challenged the relation of learning to experience, the relation between the personal and the theoretical. Our personal experience can no longer be so readily dismissed as 'subjective' or 'biased', but must be recognized as opening up ways of locating ourselves within a shared experience of power and subordination. So it is that feminism has implicitly challenged both the methods and the theories that we had inherited within social theory and philosophy, as well as the institutional relationships of teaching and learning within which they were embodied.

In the early 1970s there was a widespread feeling that we could change our lives as part of changing the larger institutions of society. The ending of the Vietnam war, over which so many people had struggled, seemed to prove the possibility of individual and collective change. But instead it was to prove a watershed, for we have grown used in the 1980s to living in a very different world, in which it is hard to expect change – even to hope for it. It is as if we have grown used to an idea that our deepest needs are reflected within the commodities of a consumerist culture. The tension between what we might want for ourselves, and the fragmented identities that we are offered, is in danger of disappearing, for it has become difficult to imagine or dream of alternative ways of living.

The social theories which have come to dominance resonate with these cultural feelings and with the disappointment of early hopes. Structuralism, and the post-structuralist theory that followed a partial reaction against the writings of Althusser, Lévi-Strauss and the psychoanalytic work of Lacan, marked a profound shift in our sense of the place of individuality and subjectivity. We have lost a sense that we could shape our own lives, even if not in circumstances of our own choosing. The attempt to theorize feminism within a structuralist tradition threatened what had been learnt about the significance of felt knowledge. Yet this had been part of the challenge to relativism and the way that feminism had challenged traditional epistemology. It was what people had experienced and embodied that allowed people to distinguish between information that could be accumulated as some kind of commodity, and knowledge that has the power to touch and transform us.

Within a structuralist tradition the dialectical relation between what people were struggling to become within themselves, and the prevailing relationships of power and subordination, got lost. There was no longer any tension between human agency and social structures, nor any sense that social structures were themselves outcomes of social relationships. The individual was taken to be an effect of various structures, and 'experience' was taken to be an effect of discourse. Though it has been heralded as a strength of Althusser's work that ideology was not to be conceived in orthodox Marxist terms as a veil that should be removed to reveal underlying material relationships, but was rather a lived reality that would still be necessary within a socialist society, its vision was essentially fixed and static. It could give no account of this lived quality, as it could give no sense of socialism as the embodiment of a more humane and equal society, rather than simply as a more advanced mode of production.

The strength of Althusser's work lay in its challenge to orthodox Marxism as a form of economic determinism and in the possibilities he offered to challenge its pervasive reductionism and to recognize the relative autonomy of state institutions and the media. But its categorical distinctions still haunt the post-structuralist work that has followed. We inherit an abiding hostility to 'essentialism', to any notion of there being fixed human qualities that exist prior to society. Yet essentialism is a confusing term that combines a multitude of issues that are rarely separated out. It has made it difficult to talk of human qualities as anything other than the outcome of a particular form of social relationships. It has weakened our critical traditions, for issues of gender are assumed to be issues of ideology. In part, feminist theory is disempowered as it loses grasp of its early awareness of the tension between the needs and desires that women were identifying for themselves and the definitions of their reality provided by the dominant masculine culture. This was not to assume a unified conception of identity, or to underestimate the reality of fragmentation.

But it is important to recognize that these insights are not exclusive to post-structuralism. The development of Critical Theory by Horkheimer and Adorno in the 1930s had already broken with Marxism as a form of economic determinism. They recognized a shift in the terms of power by which the state, bureaucratic enterprises, the media and advertising came to exert enormous power to fragment and disorganize individual experience. It made no sense to presuppose the integrity and unity of the individual. It was a strength of Freud and psychoanalytic theory that it showed how our sexualities and identities are fractured. They develop out of the quality of contact and relation we experience in early childhood. Our identities are not given, but there is a constant tension between who we are struggling to become, and the indignities and humiliations we often endure as children. It is this tension which is so often flattened out within a structuralist tradition, so it is difficult to explore the tension between the experience of men and the dominant forms of masculinity, in terms of which men are constantly judging and comparing themselves.

At the same time it is a strength of post-structuralist theory that it rejects any false consolations and promises of unification. It breaks with the Hegelian reconciliation through history, but at the cost of undermining the importance of a historical consciousness. Too often, history is reduced to a theoretical construction, with little sense of experience or reality existing beyond, or independent of, our theoretical constructions. So it is that the crucial tension between theory and experience is lost, for experience is nothing but the discourses through which we choose to articulate it. Critical Theory was also suspicious of the guarantees of history. It saw little evidence for the notion that history would deliver progress: our century has known too much cruelty for such a vision to be sustained. But the crucial difference is that it attempted to sustain a sense of morality and justice. It challenged a relativist conception of truth which leaves us bereft of a moral language with which to judge the atrocities, say of Hitler's attempted genocide of European Jewry. If we can no longer put our faith in the idea of history or progress, we have to be careful not to commit ourselves to theoretical positions which threaten to deny the importance, or even the possibility, of learning from history.

If history is reduced to a series of discourses in terms of which we constitute the past, the atrocities of the past can so easily be forgotten. Our sense of history, even our own histories, gets attenuated. Again, this is to reject a false polarity, that often remains implicit, that history is either given or else it must be a social construction. It is true that as we learn about oppression and suffering in the present, so we begin to understand the past in new ways. We learn to ask different questions. But this is to redefine the nature of objectivity and historical truth, rather than to abolish it. We are left with more than a series of interpretations. It is because the task is also to change the world that this theoretical vision is flawed. If we are sceptical of any claims to truth, we capitulate to a commodity culture, for we are bereft of any moral language in terms of which we can evaluate our experience.

To restore some of the history of personal and political change can serve a theoretical task. The object is not to reinstate a different vision of masculinity that can be rationally defended. We are searching for different questions that can illuminate the quality of our experience and relationships. But it is hard to begin the process of learning from our experience if we assume – as does so much phenomenology and post-structuralist theory, when presented within a rationalistic framework – that experience itself is constituted through discourses. I will argue that this is a false grasp of the relationship of language to experience, and that Wittgenstein's work, which is so often invoked to defend this position, is in fact a sustained challenge to it. This is crucial work if we are to challenge the idea that it is the categories of language which provide us with the categories of the social world. As our experience is contradictory, so is our relationship to language. Wittgenstein was centrally concerned to challenge the idea of language as some kind of screen that can be set against the social world. His vision of language provides us with a new starting point, that potentially challenges Saussure's vision of language that has provided the underpinning of so much recent work.

Many people are rightly suspicious of moral language, because they remember the moralism of so much in the field of sexual politics. In a period in which people have given up hope for change, people ask for their theory to be fun or playful. We learn not to take things too seriously, and we are suspicious of the intensity of those who would have things differently. It is as if consumerism is all that we can believe in. Its satisfactions seem to be the only things that we can trust. Steve Taylor, a member of *Arena*'s editorial group, expresses a widespread feeling when he says:

'Sexual politics doesn't appeal to any of us. For our generation – I'm thirty-five – that discussion was blown. It was no fun. We don't want to go back to it. It think it would be really yuck to have a Cosmo man style. Talking to men about their feelings would be a commercial death wish' (quoted by J. Rutherford in 'Who's that man?' in *Male order: unwrapping masculinity*).

This is the voice of commercialism that we have grown familiar with. Sometimes it can feel as if radical politics is to be remade in its image.

It is important to learn from the moralism of sexual politics for what it can teach us about the socialist culture that we inherit. Too often we assume that it is a matter of replacing one set of ideals by another, as if there is a single path to follow. We have rightly learnt to challenge these pretensions. This has helped to set the terms for a genuine pluralism in which we can genuinely begin to respect the differences between different cultures, histories and ethnicities. In the past we have learnt to listen to others only to guarantee that we have had the last word ourselves. It is this vision of truth as the exclusive possession of a single group that has needed to be challenged. Without it, our understanding of democracy would be sham. This remains different from a vision of a liberal pluralism, because it is informed by an understanding of the workings of class, ethnic and gender relations of power and subordination.

We inherit a sexual politics that has been prescriptive and judgmental and I attempt to explore some of its sources in the rationalistic culture of masculinity that we inherit. It has been the failure of sexual politics to address the crucial issues of masculinity and the ways that it has been embedded in the theoretical and political culture that we inherit, that has made it so difficult to remake the relationship between socialism and democracy. It has been the writings of Foucault, Derrida and others who have allowed some of these questions to be raised, but often at the cost of moving beyond morality and beyond politics: it seemed to be the only way of acknowledging that people want different things out of life and have different needs and pleasures. The bias towards self-denial and self-rejection is so deeply embedded within a socialist culture that it has seemed to many that it is only beyond that tradition that pleasure, joy and sexuality could be reinstated. It was part of the project of *Achilles Heel* in the mid 70s to challenge men who sought to renounce their masculinity as a way of assuaging the guilt they felt for the power they wielded: this is a dead end that led many men to renounce their anger, strength and vitality, as if these qualities themselves were essentially oppressive to women.

It has been important for men to learn that we can have their vulnerability as well as strength, anger as well as tears, reason as well as feelings. But this is something that men have to learn for themselves, for it is not simply a matter of intellectual conviction. One of the things I try to show is that men have inherited false conceptions of change, thinking that change can always be achieved through will alone. For too long, men have learnt to live within the narrow boundaries of reason alone, threatened by feelings and emotions that they have had so little relationship with. Defined by reason alone, these other qualities were not part of what men were, but a self-indulgence that men had learnt to live without.

Many people have helped me on this path. You do not learn without making mistakes. Many of the ideas that I share were born in discussions and encounters with other men. In America there were the first tentative steps of consciousness-raising, with Larry Blum, Joseph Pleck and Jack Sawyer, as well as the first traumatic steps in collective living in the Cameron Avenue Collective with Ed Englander, Janet Kaplan, Shira Karmen, Susan Bloom, Ellie Goodale and Joel Dwek. This period in the early seventies is part of another era – a moment of excitement and learning – that can still be learnt from. In England there were different men's groups, in which some of these ideas were shared with, amongst others, Paul Atkinson, Trevor Evans, Paul Morrison, Andy Metcalf, Steve Turner and James Swinson. Along with Steve Gould, this was the nucleus of the early *Achilles Heel*, which was an attempt within a socialist context to share what we were learning about men and masculinity. It is still worth reading.

More recently some of these ideas have been tried out on the Masculinity Research Group at Goldsmiths' College, University of London. Along with others there were Trefor Lloyd, Ed Mason, Peter Lewis, Dave Phillips, Julian Wood, Mike Falk, Tony Eardley, Bob Connell. I have also shared some of these ideas with David Boadella, Sheila Ernst, Lucy Goodison, Patti Howe, Anna Ickowitz, Tom Monk, Terry Cooper, Rex Bradley, Tony Skillen, Sally Inman, Mary Stiasny, Caroline Ramazanoglu, Sheila Rowbotham and Tony Seidler. Karl Figlio, Anthony Giddens, Carol Gilligan, Jeffrey Weeks and Robert Young provided encouragement at various crucial stages. I would also like to thank Janet Ransom whose intelligence, clarity and enthusiasm for ideas have been so supportive to this project. Paul Atkinson and John Tosh gave some useful suggestions at a late stage and Rob Senior and Terry Cooper helped with the title when I was despairing of it. Anna Ickowitz has lived with me through the difficult period of rewriting, and knows more than most the gulf between my theory and practice. Our son Daniel, now 6, has helped me grasp the difficulty of growing into boyhood without forsaking a sense of self. He insists that the title should be 'For all the people'. Hopefully he's right.

Chapter One

INTRODUCTION: MASCULINITY, LANGUAGE AND SEXUALITY

This is both a personal and a theoretical book. It is a contribution to an understanding of a particular masculinity in its social and historical formation. It is also the experience of a particular man and his growing up into masculinity. It attempts to share some of the pain and confusion of that education. It does not attempt to talk for all men, though I sometimes talk in terms of 'we' to encourage some form of mutual recognition and identification where it might feel appropriate across differences of class, race and ethnicity. In some ways it is also a reflection on some of the difficulties created for heterosexual men with the challenges of feminism. This calls us as men to think again about who we are and who we would want to be as men.

To begin to confront the character of our historical grounding, and to respond to the challenges that feminism has presented us with as men by thinking through our potential to become more who we want to be, involves, I believe, necessarily both a personal and a theoretical exploration. This is not to argue for two radically distinct forms of exploration. Rather, this work is concerned with the interrelationship of these levels. Social theory has provided different accounts of the relationship between them, and part of my focus is to consider the sense in which these accounts have been limited.

Broadly, I want to argue that the rationalism which social theory has tended to build on and retain is itself at the basis of many of the problems we face, as men, when we try to change. If it is important to recognize in this process that our identities are historically forged, it is also important to retain the substance of our individual experience as a theoretical resource. I want to

1

show that our experience is forged and fragmented in particular ways and that our social theories often feed into and sustain these fragmentations, rather than offering us ways in which we could develop a more transcendent vision. Our established traditions are not merely intellectual in their consequences; rather they consolidate and sustain particular ways of thinking about ourselves and experiencing ourselves. They are often implicit in the ways we live our lives.

This means that as men we need to engage both with our own experience and with the historical and cultural sources of our experience of masculinity. These are facets of the same project. Yet it is a project made difficult in part by the institutionalization of men's power itself, which has made it hard for us to distinguish particular masculine voices or experiences. We have acquired a sense that we can speak for all; this has been part of the consolidation of patriarchal power. To take this on critically, then, is to seek to reclaim the particularity of heterosexual men's experience. It is to reinstate ourselves and our histories into our own theorizing. This becomes crucially an issue of method.

So, rather than divide this work into a personal quest and a theoretical investigation, and thereby reinforce a radical distinction of levels or discourses, I have sought specifically to relate these categories as an issue of method. Feminism has brought into focus the importance of establishing a different kind of relationship to our experience, which our established traditions of social theory have had difficulty in grasping or illuminating. This is because many of our traditions have sustained a rationalist inheritance, which has cut across both radical and conservative understandings. We have inherited a historical identification of masculinity with reason and morality. This identification was central to Kant's moral and political theory; it is an identification with which it is crucial to come to terms, if we are to grasp what it means to grow up as a man in modern western culture. Kant's philosophy offers us an account of the human subject as split irrevocably between reason and desire, in which it is our reason, and not our inclinations – that is, our desires, emotions and feelings – that guarantees our capacity for morality. It is our reason that allows us to calculate the rightness of action, through a process of abstracting from particular situations and working out whether our action is in principle universalizable.

Yet the claim to objective rightness, as well as the fragmentation of the self on which it is built, and the shifting of questions of morality into a realm of abstraction, can be argued to be itself a normalization of a particular kind of masculine experience. This is to take the question historically. When we consider the historically-emergent character of this fragmentation, we can come to see that it constitutes both a source of the damage that, as men, we do to ourselves, and a facet of our patriarchal power.

This means that it becomes an issue of political practice to understand the historical sources of our abstracted moral theory, as well as its connection with and formative power in terms of the experience and identity of men. This raises questions about how we might develop a different grounding for our sense of our moral selves. Relatedly, I argue that consciousness-raising, psychoanalysis and therapy can mediate the relationship between personal experience and theory, in liberating ways.

I am, then, exploring masculinity as a historically-emergent experience. Little sustained attempt has been made to do this, despite the challenges of feminism; yet this is a precondition for thinking about whether it is possible for men to change. I argue that men can and should take responsibility for these questions themselves. This means men learning to speak for themselves, rather than constantly falling back into speaking for others in the supposedly neutral and impartial language of reason. Reason has its place, but it is a place that has yet to be properly discerned. It is not the only voice, and too often it has shut out the more personal and individual voices of men. It has been the historical identification of masculinity with reason and progress that has led men so readily to speaking for others, creating a blindness around the particular experience of heterosexual men. I want to investigate the implications of this for theory and for men's experience.

One reason that it is important to think about masculinity in these terms, is the normalization of a certain development in men's experience: it becomes a norm against which others are to be judged and found wanting. Because society has taken as its self-conception since the Enlightenment a version of itself as a 'rational' society, and because reason is taken to be the exclusive property of men, this means that the mechanisms of the development of masculinity are in crucial ways the mechanisms of the development of the broader culture. This makes masculinity as power invisible, for the rule of men is simply taken as an expression of reason and 'normality'. This constitutes, at the same time, a source of women's subordination, and a loss of quality in the lived experience of men. So it is that men become strangely invisible to themselves. They become estranged from the personal aspects of their experience, as they learn to think of themselves in terms of the neutral standards of reason. Feminism has shown that women have been rendered invisible in the public realm. A theory of masculinity[1] has yet to show how men are rendered invisible to themselves.

The Enlightenment has established rationalism as the common sense of a liberal moral culture. This defines freedom in terms of rational choice, so that we extend our freedom by extending the ranges of choices available to people. It identifies freedom with reason, for it is only when we act out of an autonomous reason that we can be free. This fosters the fragmentation of people through the division of reason from desire. Our emotions and feelings are seen essentially, at least by Kant, as 'inclinations' which are attempting to determine our behaviour externally, and so as sources of unfreedom.[2] Only when we act from the inner voice of reason are we acting independently of influence and determination. It is this sense of the relationship between reason and freedom that has operated as such a powerful force in liberal consciousness.

In thinking about the organization of our consciousness and our experience, it becomes crucial to understand the force of language in shaping and giving form to that experience. Language and available conceptual frameworks, partly in the form of our inherited cultural traditions, necessarily mediate our experience. But recent developments, particularly under the influence of structuralist and post-structuralist theory, have undermined potential critical insight by making it impossible to think about the relationship between language and experience.[3] This is because language or discourse is seen here to be prior to and constitutive of experience, so that language and experience are at some level conflated. Personal experience is undermined as a theoretical resource, as we are presented with the idea that the 'individual' is a category constructed through the working of socially-grounded discourses which are essentially external to, and therefore in a sense independent of, individual identity. This mode of collapsing one level into another, and its consequences for our vision and our understanding, will form a core focus of this work. It has made it difficult to ask questions about how language is used to establish a particular relationship to experience. In so far as it is blinded to the differences in our relationships to language, a structuralist tradition becomes part of the normalization of a masculinist model.

I am looking at ways to reclaim language as a facet of experience, and also thinking about what our assumptions about language, or theories about it, tell us about the quality of experience. This involves looking at the ways rationalism continues to structure even what appear to be radical traditions of theorizing. The philosophical writings of Wittgenstein, particularly the development he makes from his earlier to his later writings, can help challenge the intellectualism inherent in those traditions. A real challenge draws on diverse sources. It is the weakness of a rationalist method to imagine that you can dispense in total with a theory or tradition when you can establish its inconsistency or illogicality. What we are challenging are not simply theoretical connections, but certain ways of living and relating as men. It is our experience and relationships as men that must be changed.

It might be useful to set out the main structure of the argument as a series of central themes which will be approached in different ways. I shall work through these themes, drawing on different theoretical traditions, and try to illuminate what is at issue by shifting to a personal voice in many sections throughout the text. Centrally, my argument is that there is an emergent historical relationship between a particular conception of reason, progress and masculinity, and that this relationship has consequences for the categories in which modern philosophy and social theory is couched, as well as for our sense of gendered identity. One of the clearest sources of these connections is in the Enlightenment, particularly in the ethical writings of Kant.

These consequences for identity are not grasped by structuralist and post-structuralist modes of asking questions about them.[4] Whilst distinctions between structuralism and post-structuralism can be drawn, for the purposes of my argument their significance resides in a key shift of conceptualization, in which the subject is displaced from the centre of his or her own experience and reconceptualized as a category constituted through essentially external forces. Broadly, I use the term 'post-structuralist' to refer to that predominantly French tradition most clearly represented in the work of Michel Foucault, which combines Saussure's notion that meaning resides in the relationship between categories, or, for Foucault, discourses, with a Nietzschean theory of power as prior to and constitutive of morality. Put simply, it is not an issue of establishing how discourse constitutes identity, but rather of the damage done to people's (here particularly men's) experience of themselves and the world. A crucial facet of this damage within a post-Enlightenment tradition is that we inherit a relation of domination to self that gets set up through the fragmentation of identity and knowledge into reason and unreason. Kant crucially established reason as an independent faculty which is separate from our emotions, feelings and desires, which can in no sense be genuine sources of knowledge. But it is crucial to recognize that this is not simply an intellectual distinction that can be dealt with purely theoretically. It is a distinction which permeates and organizes the character of what we take to be reason and what we experience as desire. Only when we have grasped how, in our individual lives, these distinctions have organized our experience, can we hope to challenge them theoretically. It is only then that we grasp what is at issue.

I want to show that within social theory, structuralism and post-structuralism embody this fragmentation which is part of Kant's inheritance. These traditions echo Kant in precluding people from grasping emotions and feelings as sources of knowledge or as an integral dimension of political possibilities and change. Kant's categories are replaced with a constitutive conception of language which assimilates experience into language and eradicates any critical ground from which to grasp the tension between them. This tradition thereby loses the moral ground of politics and precludes itself from understanding the different relationships people have to language or the ways that people's relationship to language reinforces and expresses their relation to themselves. This is crucially an issue for sexual politics, since the fundamentally contemplative relation to the world assumed in social theory and philosophy, and particularly in post-structuralism, mirrors the relationship men have to their own experience, but this remains invisible.

It is important to recognize that at a level of personal experience and engagement in relationship, the invisibility to themselves that results from men's power and propensity to impersonalize and universalize their own experience tempts them into constantly talking for others, while presenting themselves as the neutral voices of reason. This constitutes a limit to men's experience, for it precludes them from grasping the particularity of their experience and its social and historical sources. This could be a source of learning and the basis of the development of a different relation to self and individuality, which would involve drawing on the insights of a psychoanalytic tradition which has too often been dismissed as essentialist in contemporary, and particularly post-structuralist social theory, and which can help us to understand that masculinity is an essentially negative identity learnt through defining itself against emotionality and connectedness.

This core negativity gives men's experience a particular character. An internal hierarchy is set up which takes the form of a relation of domination, whereby that part identified with reason dominates emotions, feelings and desires. This builds a consequent distancing from feeling, often in the form of a propensity to admit feeling only in so far as it can be assimilated into rational categories. This is to distort feelings through intellectualizing them, and to suppress feelings that do not fit into a model of instrumental action. An instrumental–purposive model of action comes to structure men's lives, including their sexual activities and relationships, and defines a particular relationship to language so that language comes to be used as a weapon for the defence of masculine identity, rather than a mode of expressing connectedness with others, or honesty about emotional life.

This instrumental relationship to language and to feeling is ultimately expressive of an instrumental relationship to self which grows from the denial of particular realms of human experience. It is not adequately grasped as a discourse or discursive practice, because such a conceptualization blinds us to the character of the process of men's development of an identity built through negation. An internal dynamic is set up whereby men set goals for themselves to which they then relate externally, and in terms of which men judge themselves. This means it is hard for men to relate to or to articulate their needs in terms of their emotions or capacities, but rather that they will use an externalized standard against which to measure and evaluate themselves. It is important to recognize that what is at issue here is a particular social and historical experience, in which the processes of damage and distortion of identity (rather than simply its construction) are central theoretical and personal questions; the point, in other words, is that what is significant is not the category of 'masculinity' *per se*, but rather the ways in which the category normalizes a distorted life experience, and creates a distance from men's capacity for a fuller experience.

It is important not to lose sight of the fact that there is a principle of non-identity between the institutionalized power of men as a sex, and the experience of particular individual men. This means that, whilst acknowledging the force of its contribution on other levels, we need to see that the radical feminist assumption that the world is organized to the unconditional benefit and fulfilment of men, is inadequate as an analysis of the relations between men and women. This has consequences for the development of a sexual-political understanding of language. To see that the culture's dominant language encodes and validates a particular masculinist version of reality is to develop an important insight; but a sexual-political theory of language has to push further, to raise questions about the relationship between this language and men's experience of the world, at the same time as it acknowledges the intensity of oppression which the implicit assumptions of this language constitute for women. Thus, whilst acknowledging that issues of the terms of discussion are political issues, and that feminism has brought this into focus, I would argue that the radical feminist theory of language, which we see for example in Dale Spender's work, is inadequate to the extent that it sees language simply as a one-way mechanism of domination. Whilst significantly challenging the rationalist basis of masculine terms of discussion, a radical feminist theory of language has failed to grasp the full sense in which language is a site of struggle. Men do not necessarily feel that the terms of the dominant discourse are adequate to their experience; the insight that this discussion is part of the institutionalization of men's power has to be kept distinct from the claim that reality, as drawn in these terms, provides in some all-encompassing way for each man's fulfilment. This is to leave the substance of men's power unexplored, or to see 'benefit' merely as the power to dominate. It is partly because language is a site of struggle that sexual politics challenges empiricism, helping us to see the importance of engaging critically with the terms in which our experience is presented to us through retaining a sense of the tension between the truth of our experience and the pressures exerted within a particular culture to contain it within a given framework, and to divest us of the power to bring our experience into closer conformity with our experienced needs.

A post-structuralist tradition has drawn our attention to the difficulties of referring to human needs as an unproblematic category; this can be useful in so far as it challenges a mechanical conception of need as something core, given and uniform. However, when the critique is pushed, as a post-structuralist tradition has wanted to do, to the claim that all reference to need is invalid because it is necessarily essentialist, we become divested of a language in which to make crucial differentiations within our experience of our lives, and are left, at best, with a bald utilitarianism. Rather than define the concept of need as a commonsense construct outside the terms of academic debate, we should recognize the urgency of renewing this discussion. This again brings into focus the importance of reworking our sense of the relationship between the personal and the theoretical. Defining our needs is at the same time a reworking of our identity.

Psychoanalytic traditions and therapy help to restore a critical ground for exploring the dialectic between social relations, knowledge and identity. This dialectic gets lost in some of our most powerful theoretical traditions. Structuralism and post-structuralism bypass the dialectical character of this relationship by regarding 'experience' as an empiricist category, and assimilating experience into intellectualized categories and language. Through a different but related process, a Marxist-Leninist tradition precludes itself from grasping the importance of the struggles through which identity is forged, by incorporating an ethic of self-denial and self-subordination to duty. It thus remains within an essentially Kantian moral tradition. Action is goal-oriented; emotions and feelings are not the reference point of political activity. Knowledge is seen essentially as a matter of replacing one world view with another, 'individuality' is lost as a critical concept, and personal experience cannot be conceptualized or acknowledged as a political resource.

Yet if structuralism, post-structuralism and Marxist-Leninism carry a rationalistic inheritance in marginalizing or defining as illusory the force of individual experience, the difficulty is not overcome in traditions which would take the individual as somehow *a priori* the social. This is to retain the problems of the dichotomy, whilst shifting to the other side. These traditions embody a Kantian rationalistic inheritance in a different way: by assuming the integrity of the individual, liberalism precludes itself from developing a sense, as feminism has done, of the damage done to the individual through the workings of relations of power and subordination. Rather, it conceives relations between people as private and voluntaristic, and sees power as having to do merely with access to goods, thereby becoming tied to distributive conceptions of justice.[5] Liberalism, then, cannot begin to explore the relationship between personal identity and social oppression, because it operates with a reified conception of personal identity and an impoverished conception of social oppression.

I want to contribute to the development of a position which can acknowledge the damage people sustain without losing the category 'individual' and without imagining that their integrity is guaranteed in a transcendent realm. This is to refuse the post-structuralist rejection of 'humanism' without falling into an oversimplified claim that it is possible to identify a set of core human characteristics that do not change or are inviolable. It is to problematize our relationship to our experience and crucially to grasp it as a process. To move towards this we need to shift our focus of concern from the humanist-versus-social-constructionist framework of debate, and to attempt a grounding in reality of our theory, whilst retaining a critical relationship to that reality.

Psychoanalysis alerts us to the fragmentation of the person that relations of power and subordination bring about, and to the importance of emotions and feelings, which have their own inner logic, in grasping the damage done to people. Therapy can help reinstate a dialectic between personal experience and social relations by drawing on psychoanalysis to illuminate the social and historical core of privatized experience. Therapy, then, can be a means whereby moral issues become central to politics and personal experience is reinstated as integral to politics. This is part of what men can learn from the challenges of feminism.

I am arguing, then, that the polarity which appears in Marxism, structuralism and liberalism between individualism and collectivism, is a false one. Rather, learning to define our individuality can be part of a crucial moral and political process in which this polarity itself is undermined. This means learning that we do not have to choose between theories which see either the individual or the social collectivity as ontologically prior, but that it becomes both a theoretical and a practical task to reclaim individuality as a critical concept.

This is to set out theoretically the central themes of the argument, but it is difficult to grasp what is at issue if it is expressed in purely theoretical terms. Throughout this piece of work I have drawn on my own life experience to suggest how a renewed sense of the relationship between theory and practice might begin to be developed. This has involved a shift in voice at particular stages throughout the text, hopefully to show the sense in which we live our particular images of ourselves in our day-to-day lives, and come to learn to negate particular kinds of knowledge in favour of externalized forms. I have wanted to show how our validation of ourselves as men comes to be focused outwards, and how experiences like consciousness-raising and therapy can help in reclaiming a connection to the parts of our experience which our culture marginalizes and compells us to negate. I have also drawn on the lives of other people who shared these experiences with me, to bring out the force with which rationalistic commonsense assumptions can shape our consciousness and limit the fulness of our experience.

This means that the examples I have used are not intended to be read as instances of theoretical principles, in the way that they might in the context of traditional philosophy. They are intended to convey an expression of life process and not an acting-out of a theoretically established tenet. Thus it is that we learn to define our needs within different levels of a context of meaning;

we can begin to question our histories and the modes of understanding and moral frameworks our society makes available to us. In this process we can become more of ourselves, recognizing that we have a dialectical relationship to a context which is both enabling and negating. The movement within the examples is the process of self-definition against a context which would negate the integrity of the self; and these selves are in a process of trying to forge their individuality.

In sharing some of my own experience and some of my attempts to change, I want to draw attention to the dangers of a certain form of moralism, strong in the sexual politics of the 1970s, that seemed to offer a single path and pattern of relationship.[6] We have had to learn that it is not a question of replacing one ideal with another; rather it is this structuring of masculine experience through externalization that has to be challenged. As men are so locked into intellectualizing their experience, it can be difficult to learn from consciousness-raising. It can be difficult to sense the possibilities that we have disowned for ourselves. Social theories which deny the possibilities of a politics of experience for men are appealing, partly because we are so used, as men, to using language as an instrument with which to defend ourselves. Structuralism fails to identify the issue, since for it language is supposedly working to organize whatever sense of 'experience' we have.

A Protestant tradition, as Weber grasped it, makes self-denial the fulcrum of our inherited moral theory and conception of self.[7] It is in this context that we grasp the importance of learning to define what we need and want for ourselves individually and collectively. Crucially, for men, this means learning how we have become the men that we are. In this way we can begin to subvert power as domination within relationships in both the private and public realms, through the empowerment that develops through a more authentic individuality. This is a crucial insight of feminism, though it is an insight which is lost if the experience of feminism is solely theorized within a structuralist framework.

In arguing for the reclamation of masculinity as a social and historical experience, I am also recognizing the existence of different masculinities. At the same time the historical conception of reason in the Enlightenment and its association with an emerging sense of masculinity brought about a fundamental reorganization of sexual relations of power, and set the terms for what we might call a 'modern' conception of masculinity. This gave enormous institutionalized power to a particular conception of masculinity, normality, and relationship that left a profound mark on the experience of women, gay men and lesbians. It established the standards against which their behaviour was to be deemed irrational and pathological. It was the Enlightenment which universalized a particular morality, premised on a radical division between reason and emotion. It still casts its shadow over the visions we inherit of ourselves, even on the terms in which we supposedly reject prevailing definitions of sex and gender.

We are educated into these visions of masculinity along with particular conceptions of personal and political change. For many years now, feminist theory has illuminated the experience of women, but there has been a strange and unsettling silence when it comes to the experience of men. In part, it is for men to analyse their own experience, but this can only be done if we break with the invisibility we have to ourselves. For so long identified with the impartial voice of reason, we have in part concealed our power through universalizing ourselves out of a personal existence. It is embarrassing and self-indulgent, or so we tell ourselves, to share our experience, especially when we can hide in the quieter waters of theory. But only if experience and theory are brought into relation with each other, as feminism has discovered, can our understanding develop in a vital and living way. At issue are not only new forms of theory, but crucially different ways of living fuller and more meaningful lives as men.

Chapter Two

REASON

THE ENLIGHTENMENT, REASON AND MASCULINITY

If we are to grasp the development of our dominant images of masculinity and the ways these are worked through in our lives, it is crucial to try to locate these historically. At the core of this process is the emergent identification of masculinity with a particular conception of reason. Ever since the Enlightenment, men have sought to silence the voices of others in the name of reason. Men have taken control of the public world and sought to define the very meaning of humanity in terms of the possession of reason. The experiences of women, children and animals have been closely identified as lacking reason, and being closer to nature. Women were forced to subordinate themselves to men to anchor themselves in the new world of reason and science. The 'Age of Reason' in the seventeenth century brought about a fundamental reorganization of sexual relations of power, as witch trials in Europe and North America were used to institutionalize a relationship between reason, science, progress and masculinity.[1]

These identifications became the cornerstones of what we have inherited as the 'modern world', and the brutality and violence needed to bring this new world into being was thus rendered invisible. The very notion of civilization came to be identified with reason, and any questioning of the place of reason in our lives was tantamount to a challenge to the basic values of civilization.[2]

In recognizing the crucial and shaping character of these identifications, we set the basis for a reformulation of the context in which sexual politics can be grasped. What is at issue here is a historical transformation in world view which involved a transformation, though in no sense a supersession, of sexual relations of power and subordination. This latter transformation, however, is a moment in the first: the identification of masculinity, progress and reason extends in its significance beyond relations between men and women, to set the terms of reference for the ways we also think about animals, nature and children. It extends into the formulation of our conceptions of authority and legitimacy. To take this as a historical and theoretical issue is to see that sexual politics is not treated adequately as an isolated and discrete realm of concern, but is crucially implicated in, and has implications for, the complex totality of relations of power and subordination. This allows both for the development of a critique of a version of sexual politics as a static confrontation between men and women, and for a critique of a particular kind of left-wing orthodoxy which would dismiss sexual politics as merely ideological, and define its practices as separatist.

This belief in reason and progress has structured our philosophical traditions since Descartes. It has defined the very terms of 'modern philosophy' and legitimated reason as the only source of valid knowledge.[3] What is more, it has constituted reason as an autonomous and independent faculty. Reason has been defined in opposition to nature and so to our emotions, feelings, needs and desires. We have to look away from ourselves to discover the objective and impersonal workings of reason. This parallels the way we have to negate our individual experience, needs and desires to conform to the impersonal laws of the capitalist market. It was the Enlightenment that provided a moral legitimacy for the development of capitalism.

Men have achieved enormous power in the public world, and they have been able to develop it as a mirror of themselves. They have been able to set the terms upon which others could be admitted. Often, men presented themselves as 'rational' and 'reasonable', so defining others as lacking these essential qualities which define our very humanity. This conception of reason organized the way imperialist relations between Europe and Africa and Asia were legitimated, so that Europeans could present themselves as bringing advances of reason and science to a world supposedly void of reason and civilization. In large

15

part, the relations between social classes and sexes were organized in similar terms.

A language of reason, science, progress and civilization had been appropriated as the exclusive possession of men. Women could share in this world, but only if they were ready to subordinate their individual needs to serving the needs of men.[4] If they knew a different experience, they had to develop it privately, since it could be given no permanent space in the public realm. Often this meant that women, ethnic groups, gay men and women who could not identify themselves completely with this masculine world of reason, objectivity and progress, felt they must be somehow defective or lacking, or learnt to question its claims as defining the one and only possible reality.[5]

If people still learnt to trust in their feelings, emotions, intuitions and fantasies, they knew they could find no way to legitimate these as genuine sources of knowledge and understanding. They became used to being derided and ridiculed. Sometimes, however, they sustained a certain trust in their different capacities, at least between themselves. This is part of a hidden and marginalized culture which feminism, ethnic groups and the gay movement have worked to rediscover and sustain, as they have sought to discover themselves in their own histories.

We have to look with the greatest care at this Enlightenment tradition, understanding how it has also produced the death clouds of Hiroshima and the ovens of Auschwitz. The societies which produced these barbarisms were continuing a vision of science and progress, that in significant ways we have been brought up to share. These are crimes of a culture that has still to learn to reflect carefully upon itself, rather than project these atrocities upon people it may choose to see as mad or less than human. It is the rationality and planning with which these acts were performed that is part of what makes them most disturbing.[6] Simone Weil was one of the few who attempted to grasp the development of fascism in these terms. She helps to challenge the ahistorical self-conception of a liberal rationalistic culture which would see itself as the polar opposite of fascism. She looks searchingly, in *The Need for Roots*, at the notions of science, power and glory that Hitler learnt to respect and make his own as he was growing up. His visions were in part little different from the hopes and aspirations nourished by the Roman conceptions of power and greatness admired as ideals within a Western culture that has gone on to place us all at the edge of a nuclear holocaust.[7]

This is not to declare ourselves against reason, but to look at the traditions of reason we have inherited and the power they have had to marginalize and denigrate significant aspects of our experience. This has been part of the hope which feminism has held for our times, when it has been ready to question a narrow rationalist tradition and moralistic politics. In its appreciation of consciousness-raising lies a different morality and politics, one which promises to validate the fullness of a person's individual experience.

The very identification of masculinity with reason has tended to blind men to their masculinity as something that has been socially and historically sustained. We are so used to identifying our interests with the universal interests of others that we have often blinded ourselves to the tensions and contradictions in our experience. The problems inherent in this propensity to prioritize the universal have permeated our most radical traditions. Marx's work was often so concerned to see the proletariat as carrying a universal vision that would bring the emancipation of humanity in general, that it also reproduced a traditional rationalist dream of universality.[8] We end up speaking for others before we have really learnt to speak for ourselves. This has become part of a contemporary crisis of masculinity, as the very masculinist conceptions of science, progress, medicine and psychology made in the image of the Enlightenment identification of reason, morality and masculinity are being challenged both in theory an in practice.[9]

Nevertheless, it remains a powerful inspiration in Marx's work to place our understanding within ongoing practical activities and relationships within a capitalist society. We are no longer the observers we may have been in Descartes' and the rationalist tradition which has remained a powerful picture in both phenomenology and structuralism. We are making our lives in our everyday activities. It is no longer simply an issue of the intellectual categories in terms of which we order our experience and the social world. We grow up into an identity and consciousness within particular relationships in our families, within class and gender relationships of power and subordination.

We cannot escape ourselves as we attempt to grasp the social world intellectually. Rather, as the experience of consciousness-raising can show, we deepen our understanding of the workings of relations of power as we gain a deeper grasp of our own experience and relationships.

REASON, DESIRE AND MASCULINITY

For heterosexual men, the particularity of our experience has remained invisible. We have tended to identify and judge ourselves by the ideals and standards of the larger society. But it is only because we continually do such damage to ourselves that we are able to make ourselves in the dominant images of masculinity. We can still experience a strong tension between the ways we experience ourselves and the images we are supposed to live up to, even if we lack a language which can illuminate this. We have learnt to pride ourselves in our struggles against our own desires and natures to be able to identify our sense of self with our reason. If successful, this denial can mean that we no longer have a sense of self which exists separately from our sense of male identity. We are so anxious as boys to prove that we are *not* girls – that is, that we are not emotional, not weak and not governed by our feelings – that we come to identify our sense of self directly with our sense of male identity.

This is part of a deep cultural inheritance that has rendered invisible the splits and fragmentations that have been built into our masculine experience. We lose any sense of the possibilities that have been closed to us as we identify our masculinity with our reason. This becomes so much part of our common sense that we do not realize the denial of our emotional selves, desires and bodily experience that this has demanded. Rather, a rationalist tradition which has made morality an issue of reason so closely identifying it with masculinity, has tended to legitimate this self-denial, making us feel self-righteous in the sacrifices we make of ourselves. We learn to identify our sense of self so strongly with our individual achievements and successes in the public world of work that we do not realize the damage this may do to our capacities for open and loving relationships with others. But the connections we might otherwise have developed to our somatic experience and emotional selves have become so attenuated that we can no longer experience them as a basis for grounding our experience.

This has given credence to a rationalist tradition which, in its recent structuralist and post-structuralist forms, has wanted to argue that experience itself is constituted, along with our sense of individuality, through our language or discourse. We are witnessing a deep critique of pervasive assumptions of the Western intellectual tradition that is sensitive, especially in the post-structuralist writings of Derrida and Foucault, to the historical generation of notions of reason we otherwise take so much for granted. This was part of the power of Foucault's early work, *Madness and Civilization*, though it fails to trace the connection of masculinity to particular notions of reason.[10] This connection, however, has become a critical issue if we are to escape from a culturally pervasive intellectualism and formalism to acknowledge the validity of emotions and feelings, as well as our somatic experience, as sources of knowledge and understanding. Too often within a rationalist tradition these are treated as mental events, as intellectual categories which help organize our sense of a social world that remains strangely independent. Foucault's work, for all its insights, fails to integrate them in any significant way, through his dissolution of the category of experience itself.

This block upon developing any adequate or meaningful conception of emotional life only shows how vital it is, both practically and theoretically, to make central the issue of masculinity and its relation to reason. This can show that the very ability to mould our experience so that it fits in with our rational ideals is itself a sign of how weak and attenuated our relationship to ourselves as men has become. This is part of the problem, not an aspect of a solution. What is more, it can help question the appeal of a moralistic and ideological politics, which can be seen as resting on a tragic and painful realization, so that we can no longer make any appeal to an individual or shared experience.

It is important to stress that when we talk about redefining a fragmented masculinity, we are not thinking of creating a different vision or ideal that men should aspire to. It is this very way of organizing our masculine experience to fit it into external images and ideals that is part of what needs to be questioned.

But we take this to be so much part of our common sense as men that we have to interrupt and question it at different points of our experience. We have to show how we turn our emotional relationships into an exercise of rational decision-making, so constantly transforming the nature and character of our experience. This moves us out of touch with our emotions and feelings which can have no place in our rational deliberations. This is a way we sustain a self-control that is connected to our inherited conceptions of masculinity.

It is as if we only exist in our decisions, constantly judging and validating ourselves according to the correctness of the decisions we have made. Our life becomes a series of discrete decisions and plans. This is the way we feel good about ourselves, unable to give significance and importance to our relationships, emotions and desires. We become so used to discounting our feelings and desires in order to do the 'right' thing, that we are barely aware of how this estranges us from ourselves.[11]

Since this sustains our sense of superiority over women who do not plan their lives in this way, it is difficult to imagine that the very source of our dignity as men can actually be undermining, even hurting and damaging, parts of ourselves. A Kantian tradition, through focusing on the rightness of action by reference to an externalized moral law, has sustained and legitimated this common sense of masculinity, so rendering our behaviour beyond criticism. A structuralist and post-structuralist tradition that ridicules any talk of a 'sense of self', assuming that this is simply the creation of a particular discourse, also helps to make these issues invisible. We end up treating them as the problems of individual men, since our inherited theoretical traditions seem powerless to illuminate the issues at stake.

Often men will not experience it as any problem that they have so little relationship and contact with different parts of themselves. This language seems empty and rhetorical, since it seems hard to connect with. But feminism has made this an issue in relationships, making demands on us as men to give more emotionally in our relationships and take on emotional and domestic responsibilities. This is different from men accepting that these are their own problems, not simply the problems for women struggling to live more equal and independent lives. It is even harder for us, as men, to develop a historical under-

20

standing of ourselves and to realize that the very moral and philosophical traditions which have sustained our sense of identity and power have also weakened and undermined us.

This is something it is difficult for feminism to appreciate, though it has often drawn attention to the differences between men in private and public. It is as if we can only find our strength and identity in the public realm, but often exist as weak, indecisive and child-like in our private relationships. This itself is a symptom of the weak relationship men have with themselves, especially with what psychoanalysis has usefully illuminated as our relationship with the child within us. It is as if the very social processes through which we have 'become men' have separated us and estranged us from the children we were.[12] This cuts us off from our roots in our own individual and personal histories. Freud crucially understood that it is only if we can rebuild this relationship to ourselves that we can gain a securer sense of individual identity. At least this is the way that psychoanalysis has found of identifying and working with these issues, without having to question their deeper cultural and historical formation.

If we live in a 'man's world', it is not a world that has been built upon the needs and nourishment of men. Rather, it is a social world of power and subordination in which men have been forced to compete if they are to benefit from their inherited masculinity.[13] It is a world which has readily identified success in a capitalist world with individual happiness and fulfilment. As men, it has rendered us strangely invisible to ourselves, as it has assumed to make history in our image. Often this has been built upon an identification of fulfilment with self-denial, which was an integral part of a Protestant appropriation of Christianity, and a Kantian tradition in our moral theory. In exploring the cultural roots of our masculinity, we are not simply meeting the challenge of feminism, but we are learning to define what we need and want for ourselves, individually and collectively, in a world in which we dare to value and appreciate, without the fear of being punished. This means learning how we have become the men that we are. In our time this personal exploration of masculinity, however painful and embarrassing, has become a crucial task.

21

Chapter Three

SEXUALITY

What is the relationship between sexual knowledge, power and shame? How is it that sex is something that boys are owed and girls are obliged to be reticent about? How is it that sexual relations have become another occasion for men to prove themselves? Thinking about these issues can help us understand why men can never rest easy with their masculine identity. It can also help us grasp how deeply threatened men were by the early developments of feminism. The language of male sexuality that we have inherited is a language of will, performance and conquest. We need to grasp these connections historically. To do so, we need to understand how our sexualities have been formed within these images and relations. Our inherited traditions have left us with an ambivalent, confused and distorted relationship to our sexuality. This is something that we need to explore personally, if the vital connections and relations are not to be left invisible. We come in our personal lives to identify our reason and our capacity for morality against our sexuality, so that our sexuality is experienced as a realm of our lives we cannot learn from.

Our liberal culture can encourage us to think of our sexuality and our sexual relationships as private and individual matters, whilst a Judaeo-Christian inheritance often feeds our silence on sexuality, through forging a connection between desire, sex, sin and shame. These traditions do not help us to see the importance of exploring our sexual experience as a collective or socially-grounded experience. Sexuality can seem both radically private and too dangerous to talk about. This can make it difficult to develop a language and a mode of understanding

22

within which we can recognize both that our sexualities are forged within oppressive historical relationships, and that our own living-through of their consequences in our day-to-day experience is significant. In thinking through these connections here, I have tried to share my own experience, which has involved shifting through personal and theoretical voices in order to retain a sense of the significance both of these levels, and of their relationship to each other.

POWER, IDENTITY AND SEXUALITY

Even if a man has never made love to a woman, there is enormous pressure to pretend that he has. Sex is the way we prove our masculinity; it is the moment at which we can feel safe from the challenges of others. So our sexual relations become an arena in which we have to prove ourselves. Little wonder that there is little time to enjoy the experience. As boys, this was like adventuring in strange territory where our major concern was with bringing back tales that we could tell the other boys. Even though times have changed since I grew up in the fifties, the deeper structures of masculinity often seem almost untouched.

As boys, we learn to discount the experience of girls from a very early age. They are 'silly' or 'soppy' in their relationships with each other. This is why it can be difficult to handle our attraction for girls who we might otherwise so easily disdain. We often used to keep our softer feelings to ourselves. I remember being able to discover aspects of myself that remained invisible in my relations with other boys, but it was difficult to value these discoveries or really to make these qualities my own, since it was clear that what mattered was the competitive world of school and youth club. I want to explore this process of forsaking qualities in ourselves as men, tracing it back to our early experiences of gender identity, but also looking to the difficulties it creates in our being able to sustain close and loving relationships with our partners.[1]

As a teenager I seemed able to involve myself in close and exciting relationships with girls. We knew that we would always stop short of making love with each other, so the boundary was clear. I think this boundary made me feel safe: I knew what was going on. I did not feel the same way at all when I went off to university – I felt completely out of depth. I felt completely incapable of having equal sexual relationships, and I only seemed able to manage furtive relationships with women whom I did not feel intellectually threatened by. It was as if this was the way I managed to maintain power and control in the relationships, so that I could afford to risk myself sexually. I know that the sense of shame I felt blocked out a fuller appreciation of these relationships, which were in many ways warm and supportive in an otherwise hostile and competitive university.

At another level, it seemed as if I got enormously anxious once sexual boundaries were removed. I could not really handle the fears and anxieties that seemed to emerge for me. I did not have any way of grasping their primary source in my early relationships to my mother and father. All this was to come later. At the time I lived in a quiet desperation. I chose to put all my energies into my academic work: this seemed to be a way that I could prove myself. Luckily, this had also been a way of feeling good about myself when I was at school.

In the late 1960s it came as an enormous relief when the student movement eventually questioned notions of romantic love and the special quality of sexual relationships.[2] This helped reinstate friendships with women which did not have to be sexual. It also weakened the cultural assumption that our emotions and feelings are externally produced, so that we 'fall in love' without having any control over the process. But it was also tied to the prevailing tradition, seeing emotions and feelings as intellectual constructions we had falsely taken as our own. It was still as if our emotions and feelings were no part of ourselves or our identities. Within a Kantian moral inheritance, which has been so formative in the common sense of liberalism, they can be no part of our freedom or identities, but work to determine our behaviour from the outside. It is only through struggling against the influence of these externally determining emotions and feelings that we can hope to exercise the only true freedom we have which is essentially inner. Our freedom comes from the use of our rational faculties. This also defines our liberal morality and is the core of our humanity. It also becomes the basis of our experience of masculine superiority over women who are identified with emotions, feelings and desires. Within this framework, falling in love is a sign of our lack of freedom. It reflects an understandable weakness.

The sixties sustained much more of this traditional inheritance than was ever admitted. There is an important continuity which has not been generally acknowledged. It sought to use will and determination to create a new libertarian morality, and was not open to exploring the contradictions of people's emotional lives. But it did restore the importance of friendships in its critique of exclusive sexual relations. It encouraged people to be more open to the sexual aspects of their different relationships and to imagine their sexual contact flowing from and deepening friendships. At the same time, this failed to give consideration to the strength of our pasts and the ways our sexual identities had been formed within our families, so that it often reproduced simplistic psychological understandings and optimistic ideas of personal change.

People felt they could make their own futures and make their lives fit an ideal they had worked out for themselves. This is paradoxically part of the strangely masculine vision that was also embodied within the Kantian tradition.[3] It made us think we could make ourselves from scratch, and that our inner natures were just as malleable as external nature. Nature was to be reproduced in man's image. So we can talk about an implicit structure of domination that is common to external nature and to nature as an externalized part of self.

This was the dominating image of the scientific revolutions of the seventeenth century. It was no accident that Bacon saw himself as developing a new masculinist philosophy.[4] As men were to take control of nature, measuring their 'progress' through the domination of nature – through bringing nature to her knees – so too were they to reassert their control of women. This was the period of the brutal witch-burnings all over Europe and America. There is no exaggeration when we say that the 'modern world' is a man's world. This is not to say that men have always felt comfortable and easy in it. But we have been expected to pay a price for our power to make this world and to judge others as wanting, according to its standards.

The cultural stress on friendship in the 1960s, which was later to be an important notion of feminism and the refusal of women to negate their friendships with other women because of their relationships with men, has opened a potent strand of critique. For one thing it challenged the possessive individualism, the idea that our relationship to ourselves is essentially possessive, so that we possess this self in the way that we possess any other commodity, that was the social and political inheritance we draw from the seventeenth century.[5] This had become an important part of both the Protestant ethic and the spirit of capitalism. So feminism helped question notions of individual ambition and success that are such an unquestioned part of masculine identity. As men we had to take seriously the notion that we are brought up to treat women and children as possessions, even if we think of our relationships in much more egalitarian terms. We had to face how threatened we felt when women with whom we had relationships demanded to live more independent lives and refused to say what they were doing, or who with. This was no longer our business, if it had ever properly been. We had to realize how our own dependency on women had largely been hidden from us because before they had always been available to us.[6] This often meant realizing how few close relationships we had with other men. Many men have no friendships of their own at all; we have never learnt to value them. We had always been told that our happiness would come with our individual success and achievement.

What was more, this conception was supported in the notion that morality is fundamentally an individual affair in which we are individually proving ourselves to our maker. We could really only claim moral credit for actions we had performed individually. If we did things with others, this would only take credit away from ourselves. Little surprise that we grow up suspicious even of the offer of help from others, thinking that they must be pulling a fast one or putting us down in some subtle way. This is something that men seem to feel acutely, though little has been done to explain the cultural and psychodynamic sources of this situation.[7] Often as men, we do not want to admit our loneliness, even to ourselves: we keep it in check by keeping busy. It is as if we never have time to stop, or fear making this kind of time and space for ourselves.

If the exploration of relationships has been a central strength of feminist work, it has also had to question the moralism and psychological blindness of the 1960s. We have had to rediscover the difference that sexual contact can make to our relationships, and to recognize that we can have different kinds of friendships.

Often this has meant a withdrawal from collective living situations and non-monogamous relationships. This shift has been experienced by many as a withdrawal and defeat, and has made it difficult to explore the return to couple relationships that was quite a general feature on the Left from about the mid 70s. I do not think this should simply be understood negatively, as I think important lessons are also to be learnt from an increasing involvement of people in therapy. Often I think this is part of an ongoing struggle in people's lives, to enrich and deepen experience as they challenge the values and relations of the capitalist society they live in.[8] Sometimes this is simply a forsaking of the aspirations and ideals once shared. But we have to be careful before we make judgements. The history of the Left has been full of a 'holier than thou' feeling, which grows almost inevitably out of the ethic of self-denial that the Left has so often absorbed intact.

Issues of power and identity have emerged centrally, both theoretically and practically, since the mid 70s. I know this from my own experience of intense political involvement in socialist politics in the mid 70s in East London. I hope to share how it proved much harder to sustain a sense of individual wants and needs as we unwittingly learnt to subordinate ourselves to the 'needs of the struggle'. We had worked out a political analysis of the East London area in which we lived, to discover what were the most important struggles to be involved in. We went where we were most needed. Somehow we had automatically learnt to discount our own needs and desires, even though at a verbal level these remained central to our sense of our political lives.[9]

It was as if we were subordinating ourselves to the demands of 'political work' in exactly similar ways as we had grown up as men to put our work and individual achievement above everything else. We now worked collectively, but the underlying structure remained very much the same. But it was also true in sexual relationships, in which men and women in different ways seemed pulled apart by the conflicting demands of the different relationships. Our individuality was more precarious than our inherited socialist traditions allowed. It was as if we were simply responding to what others wanted of us. but had lost a deeper sense of what we wanted and needed for ourselves.[10] In our shared critique of 'bourgeois individualism' we had failed to

27

realize just how precarious was our sense of individuality. We had to go back to the beginning to rethink connections between identity, politics and masculinity.

BEGINNINGS: 1940s

I do not think that we ever talked openly in the family about sexuality, when I was growing up. We made jokes about it when we watched TV, but that was about the limit of it. Sexuality had little public recognition in the adult world of the family. As four brothers growing up together in an immigrant Jewish family which had fled the Continent because of Hitler, we had to discover everything for ourselves. We wanted to be accepted in a world that was strangely different from the world of the family. But we did not really help each other.

Sexual knowledge came to be a source of power in our relations with each other. I remember with shame stories we told our younger twin brothers in their insistent questioning about how babies are conceived. Half in jest, half in protection of our own ignorance, we talked about the role of the big toe in sexual relations. I do not think they fully believed us, but this could only have added to the mystification and painful silence about any honest and truthful talk about sex. I do not think they ever forgave us for doing this to them. They learnt to keep their hesitations and questions to themselves.

This only reflected my own uncertainties: I was always trying to get it straight about the placing and function of the different holes that women were said to have. This was the source of endless dreams, as if my unconscious life could reveal a truth that was denied to me. For many years I reached different interpretations of this secret knowledge. I could not trust information that was given to me, since I had believed so many different things at different times. Sexuality became shrouded in mystery. Part of me was left feeling that the whole thing was just beyond me. I had better stick to firmer ground.

I grew up feeling that sexuality was something to be ashamed about. Sexuality existed as an unspoken presence. There was warmth and affection in the family but this had nothing to do with sexuality. My mother had grown up in the Vienna of the 1920s, and she carried some of the sexual moralism that Freud had helped to question. I remember going to the library when I was twelve and searching for books on psychology, looking for some kind of language for my emotions and feelings. I had to work this out for myself. I needed the authority of the written word to tell me that it was quite normal to have sexual feelings, and that this was nothing to be ashamed about. I already carried enough shame about being Jewish and about growing up without a father, that there was more than an edge of desperation in my searching.

I learnt not to expect help from my family, where the unspoken assumption seemed to be that it would be far easier if people weren't sexual beings at all. From an early age their concern was with indoctrinating us with the need to marry 'a nice Jewish girl' and making sure we did not get anyone 'into trouble' in the meantime. This was asserted with a brutal directness, saying that non-Jews would always turn on you in a moment of anger, calling you a 'filthy Jew'. This was reinforced with references to Hitler's concentration camps, which were a constant nightmare, never far from our minds, always threatening to overwhelm us. But again there was little attempt to share this painful historical experience, only an attempt to silence us with it and force submission.

In a similar way it was assumed that we would not really be able to understand about sex. I think this made us withdraw, knowing at some implicit level an unspoken connection in that the adults had not come to terms with the pain of the holocaust or with their own sexualities. Possibly the connections were closer than we knew, since their generation had had their own sexual developments interrupted with the rise of Hitler in Germany and Austria. We learnt not to ask too many questions. We were to be protected as children from a knowledge that could hurt us. In the long run, I think that this has only made it harder for us.

A TEENAGER IN LOVE: 1950s

I had little to prepare me for the intensity and passion of my relationships with girls when I was a teenager. I fell in love so deeply and intensely that I knew that life could never be the same again. We found a space of our own at the local synagogue club, Danescroft, that was opposite my family's house. We were a group of teenagers that grew up with each other, though we were to take very different paths in adult life. There was a strong bond and affection between us all, though at another level there was always intense competition. We created our own teenage world with its own sexual rules. This was almost exclusively Jewish and almost exclusively heterosexual. It was also mainly middle class.

This was a time of discovery and excitement. There was considerable caring and commitment in individual relationships, but relationships were not guaranteed to last, however intensely they began. There was considerable pain when relationships ended, or when people felt rejected. As boys we held considerable power, though the rules were negotiated with the girls. They had their own solidarities: they set the limits to sexual activities, knowing that boys can never be trusted and would always be seeking to stretch the permitted boundaries of touch and contact. This was in no sense an equal situation, since the girls had their reputations at stake – it was very much a matter of so far, but no further.[11]

As boys, we grew up feeling that sex was something that we were somehow 'owed'. You felt tricked, if not indignant, if someone refused to neck with you when you were going steady. It was no secret to us that girls enjoyed necking as much as we did, but they were expected to be more reticent in the way they talked about it publicly. As boys we felt sex to be something that we needed that somehow we had a right to it. But again there was a difference between the public talk of boys, where we were always asking 'how far did you get?', and the caring and sensitivity that was often part of the tentativeness and shyness of these teenage relationships. We felt forced to present a different image to the public. We felt forced to show off to each other, since our position on the competitive pecking order was established according to who we were off with and how far we went. Our very sense of masculine identity was at stake.

This was where I learnt that you could never rest easy with your masculine identity, but you always had to be ready to prove it. This built enormous unspoken tension and anxiety into my developing masculine identity, and made it impossible to acknowledge any kind of sexual feelings we might have had for other boys in the group. We were so concerned to prove our fragile male identities that these feelings had to be firmly repressed; we could only joke about them. There was an extra edge to all this, as we felt forced to prove our identities in a gentile world, in which we felt that we were already starting with some kind of handicap. Often this meant forsaking the warmth and emotionality that some of us knew in our families, since this had no place in the public world of masculinity. We had to prove that we were other than we really were. The rules of male identity already existed, and we did our best to adjust to them. Though I was barely conscious of coming from an 'immigrant' family, I know that this made me anxious to please others, anxious to show that I was like everyone else. I felt a deep need to adjust to a world that was not of my own making. I did not know how to value what was mine. I felt forced to forsake certain values, to be accepted in a masculine world that I could never feel fully comfortable in or at home with.

Relationships in our 'crowd' did not protect us from the intense pain of rejection. As boys we were expected to take the initiatives in our relations: I well remember the fear and anxiety of asking girls to dance, even though I knew I was a good dancer. I was haunted by a terrible fear of rejection. I remember the intensity of loss I felt when a girl I was going steady with decided to go off with someone else. I thought that I would never recover, especially since she was going off with a close friend. I could not forgive them. I could not pretend that I did not care, or that the relationship never really mattered to me. These were the familiar male strategies. We learnt not to show our vulnerability or our pain, though this was often impossible.

So it seemed that it was the girls who held enormous power, since they could always reject our initiatives. It was harder to see the power we maintained in these relationships as boys. I am not sure why I felt such a deep fear of rejection. I was smaller than most other boys, and did not feel able to assert myself physically. Strength is the easiest way to confirm your masculinity.

It was also because I was seeking to be accepted by others, feeling that I was somehow unacceptable myself, that I was so vulnerable to rejection. It was in the non-Jewish world of school that I had learnt that being acceptable as a man somehow meant renouncing myself as Jewish. It was as if there was something

31

essentially puny and soft in being Jewish. This left me with a very unsure sense of myself. I learnt to identify with my intellect, thinking that this was always a way of proving myself, though this could so easily throw doubts on claims to masculinity.[12]

It was also because I recognized a need for the warmth and acceptance I had often found in my teenage relationships, that I put so much of myself into them and felt so vulnerable to rejection. I felt I needed this support to sustain myself in the harder, more competitive world of school. I was dimly aware that I was trying hard to become someone I was not. My achievements at school hid this deeper process. It was only when I left this comfortable social world for university that I felt out of my depth completely. Sexual relationships became too threatening. But this was the 1960s, and the world was changing.

QUESTIONING: 1960s

The 1960s saw a shift in sexual attitudes, and the initiation of a public discussion around sexuality. People learnt to talk more openly about sexual relationships outside the context of marriage. Sex was to be made more available: it was to become more like other commodities which could be exchanged on the market. This was often the consequence of the heralded liberalization in sexual attitudes. A younger generation saw morality as restrictive and as an inhibition to sexual freedom. Virginity was no longer fashionable. If this was more open, it was also a more threatening sexual world than I had experienced as a teenager.

The rules were no longer so clear, and I no longer had the security of a group I could trust. I felt out of my depth at university, ready to withdraw from the sexual realm: I was terrified. This was a period in which men talked about not wanting to restrict our freedom and independence. Women were expected to make themselves more available, and could so easily be put down if they refused. Fearful of rejection by fellow students, I found some comfort in what was considered the lower end of the sexual hierarchy at Oxford. I had a number of relationships with nurses, but often I was left despising them and myself. I rarely appreciated the warmth and understanding I discovered. There was something furtive about these relationships that remained private and unacknowledged; often it left me feeling ashamed of myself. This only added to the feeling that, despite the freedom, sexuality remained almost sinful.

As a man I was brought up to feel responsible, and often this meant assuming responsibilities which were not my own. This was a way of denying the freedom women had to enter relationships: it was patronizing, but I could not see it. At another level I failed to take responsibility for relationships I was in, insisting they remain private affairs. This was made easier, given the general view of relationships as unnecessary entanglements which were to be avoided in the pursuit of sexual freedom. Often this freedom was on the backs of women. It helped create the frustrations and anger out of which the women's movement was to develop.[13]

It became clear that the sexual freedom of the 1960s had turned sex into a commodity, separated from ongoing involvements in relationships. This helped hide and make invisible the difficulties we often have as men to be emotionally open and responsive in relationships: this could no longer be asked of us, we lived in safer ground. We simply had to prove our potency through the number of sexual encounters we had: sex had become a quantitative experience. It was a way of proving oneself to other men, but also of silencing our own fears and doubts about the quality of our sexual experience. This could no longer be questioned.

Traditional sexual morality was also challenged on the Left, and issues about sexuality and politics rediscovered. Sexual relationships were seen as reflecting the relationships of the larger capitalist culture. Relationships were seen as almost inherently 'possessive' and 'exclusive', in a way which fostered feelings of jealousy. There was a developing sense that these feelings themselves were not 'natural', but were socially constructed and were somehow wrong or inadmissible. If people learnt to relate to each other in different ways, then it was thought these feelings would inevitably wither, and might disappear completely.[14]

Bourgeois social theory had wrongly assumed that these feelings were inherent in human nature. Prevailing social and economic theory tended to assume the desires and wants of individuals, and explained the present structure of capitalist relations as growing from this firm basis. This encouraged a rediscovery of Marx's insight that bourgeois theory tended to assume an ahistorical conception of human nature. This can help explain the connection between a renewal of interest in Marxism and a growing concern with sexual politics. There was a widespread challenge to the notion of what is 'natural', in the construction of a new ethic and expectations in sexual relationships.[15] This helped prepare the theoretical ground for the women's movement's critique of the subordination and oppression of women which had been legitimated in the idea that it is 'natural' for women to concern themselves with domesticity and childcare.

The 1960s were a period, partly, of protest against the felt 'unreality' of life within consumer capitalism. It is hard to recognize this in the harsher days of the 1980s. There was a strong feeling that prevailing modes of knowledge trapped people into an artificial and unreal existence, that failed to make genuine contact with lived experience. This was part of the attraction of Situationist ideas, initially developed in France, of 'society as a spectacle' which made it impossible for people fully to participate as anything but 'observers' of their own experience. People were seeking a different quality of experience and were prepared to risk themselves for this new kind of knowledge.[16]

There was a widespread sense that people had to experience something for themselves before they could genuinely know it; so if there was a distrust of abstract theorizing, there was also a strong desire to learn. This created its own form of historical and theoretical blindness as people imagined they were treading a path that others had never trodden before. But there was also a new honesty and openness in relationships, even if it meant people were hard on themselves, as they hopefully assumed they could transform their relationships through acts of will.

In thinking that we could banish feelings and emotions we had intellectually criticized, we were unknowingly reproducing some of the deeper assumptions of bourgeois culture about personal change. Rather than challenging the basic structure of feelings and thought, people were simply turning it on its head. A deeper challenge was to come from the women's movement's critique of these ideas of sexual freedom. As the hopes were high, so the disappointment and despair went deep.

WILL, MORALITY AND SEXUALITY: 1970s

There was barely any moral theory that grew out of the sexual politics of the 1960s, let alone any clear understanding of sexual morality, which was simply identified with Victorian values of sexual restriction. At some level, the structure of moral theory remained unchallenged as people assumed that they· could change the ways they relate to others through acts of individual will. If jealousy and possessiveness were taken to be 'wrong', then this meant eradicating these feelings within ourselves. This went along with an implicit idea that if we managed to relate to others in different ways, these feelings would automatically come to have less of a hold upon our behaviour.

But this was within a more general cultural context in which our feelings are readily transposed into thoughts, since within a rationalist bourgeois culture that can hardly be dealt with as feelings. We talk about love and affection more easily than we can show it in our relations with others. So we learn to talk about our feelings, being only dimly aware of our difficulties as men in having our feelings and sharing them with others. This was a period of strong ideas and convictions, even if these were often ideas about how we ought to feel towards others. In this period it had become even more important to maintain a strong control over our emotional lives, since we did not want them to threaten this new conception we were developing of ourselves. So it was very much through sustaining the power of will to control our behaviour that we could make sure that we had the 'appropriate' feelings.

So for instance, because we felt intellectually that it was somehow wrong to be 'jealous', even if we could not help ourselves feeling jealous if someone we loved showed an interest in another person, we had to learn to deal with these feelings in ourselves. There was a strong resistance to any idea that jealousy might be a 'natural feeling.' This idea has continued in a more theoretical form in the post-structuralist idea that our feelings are socially constructed and that therefore we should be able to 'deconstruct' them. In the early 1970s there was strong opposition to any talk of the 'natural', because of its use to enforce the subordination of women and marginalize the experience of gay people. This questioning had led to important historical work, but it threatened to generate its own form of historical and cultural relativism. In its own way it has tended to undermine some of the deeper sources of socialist thinking and feeling. If it makes us more aware of the varieties of people's sexual experience and desires, it can weaken our sense of what we share as human beings. This is too easily dismissed as 'humanist'. I cannot help feeling that the very terms of this influential discussion need to be reworked.[17]

The idea that our emotions and feelings are socially and historically constructed gives us no handle with which to work with ourselves. It makes it hard to recognize that acknowledging feelings of jealousy and possessiveness might help us start dealing with these feelings in ourselves. Even if we think that acknowledging these feelings to our partners might serve as pressure upon them, this can make them realize what is at risk in the relationship. This can be an important step for men, since often we do not say how much we love and need others, thinking that this can be taken for granted.

I know that this has often been a way of withholding myself within a relationship. It is a way of maintaining power. I remember how hard it was for me to learn to say to someone that I loved them. It was as if I had been brought up to treat my love as some kind of valuable commodity that had to be dispensed with carefully. Acknowledging our love for others gives them a certain kind of power over us which, as men, we are often wary about. Equally, there are times when we might need to keep our jealous feelings to ourselves, learning to deal with them with our friends, since we might otherwise so easily use them to bind a woman who wants to free herself from dealing with our emotional demands.

I am not suggesting any simple solution to these issues, or implying that jealous and possessive feelings are not to be carefully investigated and changed. I am saying that the framework within which these issues were addressed tended to reinforce, rather than question, some underlying moral features within the culture. People were led to feel the 'wrongness' of these feelings, and encouraged to think that if they accepted the intellectual logic, then they could work to eradicate these feelings within themselves.

This is part of the Kantian moral inheritance which works to identify morality with masculinity, as it insists that our emotions and feelings are not in any sense sources of genuine knowledge. It is only our independent faculty of reason that can give us knowledge about the world. So Kant builds into the very organization of our moral consciousness a fragmentation between reason as a source of moral knowledge, and our emotions, feelings, wants and desires. These are understood together as 'inclinations' which are often experienced as 'interferences' in our being able to do what our reason dictates as morally right. We learn automatically to discount our 'inclinations' and, as men, to identify our very masculinity with our reason.[18]

This becomes not only deeply embedded in our sense of masculine identity, but it also establishes the basis for masculine superiority, since women are so easily identified with the sway of emotions and feelings. Within a Kantian tradition it is only reason that is reliable and constant. It is only reason that can be trusted to offer genuine moral knowledge. So as men, we not only learn to discount our emotions and feelings in deciding what we should do, but we become threatened as they can potentially challenge our very sense of masculine identity. It also means that, as men, we learn not to trust women.

In many ways the moral notions that spread in the 1960s tended to reproduce this deeper structure of moralism. People were hard on themselves as they did their best to live out this new moral code. This has broader implications, since it followed historical conceptions of socialist morality which think in terms of a replacement of bourgeois individualist and possessive values by socialist values of collectivity and communalism. We can witness in both the Russian and Chinese Revolutions a strong emphasis upon the notions of duty and subordination to the revolution and the goals of the larger society. But it is this morality of self-denial which has its very foundation in Kantian moral theory, which was never simply egoistic or self-interested. It always involved a tradition of people being ready to deny their bodily needs and desires to focus their energies upon ends and goals they established for themselves through the independent workings of reason.

It is this notion of the 'rightness' of these moral rules and the blindness it fosters to a consideration of our emotions, feelings and desires which is moralistic. Rather than challenge this deeper inheritance, the libertarian morality of the 1960s tended to reproduce its deeper structure. People were seeking different moral goals and had different expectations of themselves, but tended to invoke a similar conception of how people can change. It is this deeper tradition that elements of feminism have been able to challenge, especially when it was more patient with the contradictions in women's attempts to change, and when it is seeking to reveal and explore these contradictions, rather than to deny them.

With the emergence of sexual politics, we see a new emphasis upon the contradictions in our emotions and feelings. This brought a shift in an earlier libertarian view that put emphasis upon 'acting correctly towards others' which encouraged people to keep their feelings to themselves. People did not want to acknowledge all the 'incorrect' and difficult feelings of jealousy and possessiveness that seemed to stand in the way of developing more equal relationships. Recognizing these feelings could only make people feel worse about themselves, or so it seemed, as it drew attention to how far people were from their new moral ideal. People were less aware that they were living out deeper strands within an inherited moral culture. I remember a conversation in which a friend acknowledged that she had learnt from an early age not to get angry. She thought that if people really knew what she felt, they would not want to have anything to do with her. She did her best to control her emotions and feelings so she could behave more equally towards others. She had learnt to use her will. But underlying all this was a deeper feeling of unworthiness, a sense we inherit from Luther and the Reformation.[19]

This inheritance carries the idea that human nature is more or less rotten. We cannot trust it, nor can we expect good to come from it. We have to look beyond ourselves and our human nature for our notions of justice and morality. We have to learn to mould ourselves to fit these conceptions that we can only receive through our rationality. It is no accident that it is in the same period that we discover our humanity as defined in our reason while our natures – and our emotions, which in this structure are associated with nature – are to be despised as what we share with the animal world.

All this has a deep, if unspoken, influence upon our inherited

However, a radical feminist analysis can make us aware again of the issue of context or framework within which an issue can be dealt with. In the 1960s people learnt that the issue of jealousy or possessiveness was not simply something that could be dealt with within the context of the monogamous couple. The traditional assumption that argued that any sexual or relationship problem had its roots within the dynamics of the relationship, and so could also be dealt with within the context of that relationship, took a knocking. This was only to create unreal and unworkable expectations within a couple. We had to learn about the context or framework in which an issue could best be thought about and understood, and to recognize that institutionalized masculine power contributed to that context.

But if issues emerging within a relationship sometimes need to be understood within the larger context of the sexual relations of power between men and women in the larger society, so they also need to be grounded in family histories which partners bring into their relationship, though they can often remain unaware of their continuing influence. This is difficult to do, especially if people in couple relationships experience talking to others, let alone drawing upon the support of others, as some kind of betrayal to the relationship – as a breaking of confidence and privacy.

Even though the early days of sexual politics tended crudely to dismiss all needs for privacy as if they were expressions of property relations, it did help to recognize how difficult it was to expect all issues to be resolvable within the context of the couple. It opened up the possibility that others outside an ongoing relationship could bring insight and understanding that could be difficult if people were fighting things out in a couple. It helped to redefine people's expectations and helped people to value their friendships.

People could no longer so easily assume that all their needs should somehow be satisfied within their primary relationship. If this was an important challenge to a romantic conception of love, it could also take some strain off relationships, as people learnt to think more broadly about the quality of their relationships with different people. One of the permanent gains of this difficult period was a re-evaluation of the nature and character of friendship.[22]

This was further developed within the women's movement as women refused to forsake their friendships with other women and men once they entered a more permanent relationship. If they acknowledged a primacy of their sexual relationship, they refused to think this meant the subordination of other relationships. If people made arrangements to meet friends, these would no longer be dropped or changed because a man was asserting a claim to go out. As men we had to learn to accept this, though it also made us aware of the thinness of many of our own emotional relationships with other men. For most men it is still common only to draw emotional support from women. It has been difficult to learn to draw emotional support from each other.

The notion that 'the personal is political' was not an attempt to deny the significance and importance of personal relationships. Rather it is an attempt to draw our attention to the issue of power within our personal relationships, as well as being a challenge to the liberal idea that saw it as a matter of individual choice and attitude whether we treat others as equals.[23] Liberalism assumes that we have a freedom to relate to others in any way we choose, at least in our personal relationships. It encourages us to think that we can minimize the influence of class, sexual and ethnic relations of power and subordination. It partly does this through creating a firm demarcation between our personal relations which grow out of individual decisions and choices, and the larger social relationships of power and subordination.

Sexual politics questioned the reality of this freedom in its attempt to show the way our personal relationships are continually affected by what it means to be a man and woman in the larger society. This does not mean we have to conform to traditional modes of relating, but it does mean acknowledging the reality and depths to which we have been affected by our upbringing. It also means being aware of the power of the larger relationships in society. So, for instance, it is difficult to think about having a more equal relationship between men and women unless there is also a redistribution of housework and childcare. This is not simply a matter of learning to give our partners equal respect, or taking up a more equal attitude towards them, though this will be part of the process.

It has been in the context of consciousness-raising that the meaning of the tricky idea that the personal is political has come into its own. This was part of the process of the redefinition of individualism as women and men came to appreciate that what they had always been taught to consider as a unique and private experience, say of insecurity or lack of confidence, was something that was shared by others. In this sense gender was learnt as a social and historical relation. It is in this deeper sense that consciousness-raising is a dialectical process, since it helps grasp the formation of our individuality and masculinity as an ongoing social and historical process, even if it is a history that we have remained too long unaware of. Consciousness-raising can be a process through which men can learn to recover their sexuality as a source of knowledge and pleasure; but part of this process is also coming to understand the dynamics of our own experience through which our sexuality has become tied at such a deep level into our need to control both other people and particular facets of ourselves.

Chapter Four

CONTROL

We need to explore how the Enlightenment has left us with a vision of self-control as a form of domination over our emotions, feelings and desires. Rather than open the way for a different form of relationship with these aspects of our experience, we learn to silence them so that they can be no guide to values and relations. Our emotions, feelings and desires are not the parts of ourselves that are seen to guarantee our human dignity. We can see this inheritance in Kant's writings, which, whilst crucially challenging the idea of the market as the source of all value, spares human dignity and respect by locating these in a` radical polarity with emotion and desire. At the same time Kant defined our dignity as radically individual as he shifted issues of power and subordination within relationships into a space beyond moral critique. I want to argue that we can fruitfully, and indeed, need to build a relationship to ourselves which incorporates a grasp of the ways in which both our attempts to negate our emotionality, and our existence within relations of power and subordination, feed into our sense of identity as men and structure our experience.

The historical reproduction of control as domination has worked to remove men from an ongoing contact with our emotional and somatic lives. Learning to treat the body as a machine has established a division between male sexuality and emotionality. Often it is the fear of losing control that accounts for the instrumental character of men's actions as well as the power of theories which marginalize emotional life. So it is that men also often need to control relationships, feeling that they have a power to grant equality to others if their claims are considered rational. The body continues to be despised within an intellectualist culture, so that notions of sexual freedom have often been drafted upon a deeper masculine structure of self-hate and self-disgust. The universal character of reason gave men a seeming right to speak for all others, but often they did not have the language to speak for themselves.

PUBLIC AND PRIVATE

Since the Reformation, masculinity has been identified with notions of 'self-control'. It was in this period that our modern conception of masculinity was formed. Max Weber helps us to grasp this relationship between Protestantism and the spirit of capitalism, though he does not talk openly about conceptions of masculinity. But his work can usefully be read as the history of a particular conception of masculinity which has been forged within capitalist culture. He helps us think about what often remains a silence in Marx's writings surrounding the relationship between identity and capitalism: certainly, Marx's writings have tended to echo, rather than challenge, the basic identifications of bourgeois society between masculinity and reason, with a control over our inner natures mirroring a control over external nature. Marxism has too often identified with the public world of politics as the arena in which reason should show itself. The conceptions of human emancipation which Marxism has developed have often been too exclusively tied in with the organization of labour in the public world.[1]

Though Marx developed a deep critique of bourgeois equality in the market economy, showing how this mystifies class relationships of power and subordination that grow out of the control of the means of production, he says little, in his later writings about how these relations of power and dependency help organize the sphere of personal and private relationships. If anything, he saw this sphere as mirroring the relationships of the public world. But this was unwittingly to reproduce the rationalist identification of the emotional and sexual with the private. This remained an area of individual choice and particular interests.

It was the damaging notion that the public had to do with the universal, especially when tied to the fate of the proletariat as a universal class, that meant any concern with the private, personal, emotional and sexual was seen as more or less 'self-interested', partial and so unconcerned with the emancipation of humanity in general.[2] But then, possibly it is the idea of 'humanity in general' that needs to be rethought. This is centrally connected with masculinity because it is masculinity which has been identified historically with a universal rationality and so with speaking for all.

The Enlightenment established the identification of masculinity with reason. In fact the new sciences of the seventeenth century saw themselves as a new masculinist philosophy. So a rationalist philosophy saw itself as essentially masculine, and was an integral part of establishing a new pattern of sexual relationships of power. The brutality of the witch burnings was an essential part of this.[3] But it was with the development of capitalism that rationality came increasingly to be identified with the market economy, since the market was recognized as the source of all values. This was something Kant centrally questioned in his moral theory as he tried to show that human beings are beyond a price. But the kind of humanism of equal respect he developed could only confirm morality as an autonomous and independent arena of personal relations. The social world of power and subordination was moved into a space beyond moral critique.

Unfortunately, Kant's identification of morality with reason confirmed the subordination of our emotional and somatic selves, which were lumped together as 'inclinations' that could interfere with the clear workings of our reason. Kant made the body invisible as he identified morality with impartiality and impersonality. This helped produce a fear of the personal as an integral part of our inherited moral traditions which has characterized our inherited masculinity ever since. The personal was derogated as the 'subjective', and so lacking morality. Desires and feelings were experienced as threats to the self-control people had to sustain as moral beings. It was only as rational beings that we could claim to be moral beings. This was the only basis upon which we could claim equality with others.

Within a Christian tradition, human nature came to be fundamentally fragmented. Luther and Calvin made clear that we could not trust our instinctual feelings and emotions. Rather we had to obliterate their influence upon us if we were to be able to listen to the voice of reason. Our senses could not be trusted as sources of moral insight or knowledge. This was part of a beastly nature that we had to learn to put aside. Justice had a completely independent source. This was a deeply ambiguous tradition, since at the same time it fostered an individual and unmediated relationship to God. But it was a denuded and submissive conception of individuality.[4]

This has had a deep influence upon our inherited sense of interiority, or inner life. At one level it is an area of constant struggle and temptation as we are learning to control desires and feelings that would otherwise influence our behaviour. But it can also be an empty space within which we hope to hear the voice of conscience which has its source in another realm. Since it has been masculinity which has been so exclusively identified with reason, it can hardly be surprising that men find it harder to build contact with our dream and fantasy life. Our lives can seem one-dimensional, lacking in depth.

As men, we can discover ourselves to be more focused upon our activities than our relationships, finding it easier to apply universal rules and principles in our behaviour than to respond in an individually caring way to the needs of others.[5] It is as if we have been made to pay for the power we have in the social world, by a blindness and insensitivity in our personal relationships. From an early age we learn to dismiss what girls are involved with. We grow up with a very different sense of what is important. We can find it hard to give significance and put our time and attention into relationships. Since we have often learnt to be independent and self-sufficient ourselves through suppressing our own neediness, it is hard to credit the needs that others express. It is in forsaking our own needs that we prove we have the self-control that makes our masculinity secure.

What is significant here is the way sexuality connects to our sense of masculinity and remains at some deep structure in the culture identified with the animal or the 'beastly'. Our sense of our lives can be so fragmented that sexual feelings can easily be identified as 'weakness', as giving in to temptation. Even Freud carries this deeper masculinist tradition in his writings on civilization and sexual repression. It is as if our tasks as men are 'higher', so that if sexuality is to be recognized as a 'natural need', it is only through its suppression and control that we can set 'our minds to work' on higher tasks that are more worthwhile because they are more enduring.[6] It is in this tradition that women become 'the other'.

We are both attracted and desiring, but at another level we can sense betrayal as we compromise the true meaning of our masculine lives. Misogyny has deep cultural roots. This is the reason we can so easily despise women we have sexual relations with. Because the very existence of our sexual feelings proves our own unworthiness, we can despise any woman who wants to have sexual relations with us. We can withdraw from them as soon as we have had sexual contact. This used to be a very familiar feeling for me, as I felt unable to stay the night in the same bed with a woman I had made love with. I felt a sense of unease, even disgust, after orgasm. I found it hard to touch in an easy and tender way. It was as if I felt I had to withdraw from contact completely. This was a somatic experience that remained in tension with the easy views about sexuality that were around in the 1960s. But it was harder to acknowledge these feelings, even to myself.

I did not want to know the disgust I felt for sex and for a woman's body. This only seemed to confirm the deeper suspicions of the culture, that we cannot escape our brutish nature. It also confirms our sense that everything we have been able to achieve as men has been through our will and determination, through the constant vigilance and control of ourselves. This has to do not only with our sexuality, but also with our emotions and feelings more generally. In a strange way, the notion we inherit of the body as a machine has made us assume that the quality of our sexual relations and the depth of contact we have with ourselves and others is completely independent of our emotions and feelings. The issues are more complex. As we deny our emotions and feelings, so we undermine the reality and contact in our sexual relationships.

CONTROL AS DOMINATION

The way in which we are brought up to identify our masculinity with self-control is that we learn to exert a form of domination over our emotions, feelings and desires. It is this tradition of control as domination that needs careful investigation. We are encouraged to think that feelings and emotions can have no place in a rational determination of our behaviour. Our reason is supposed to act as an independent and autonomous faculty, setting the ends and goals of our purposive action. This influences our inherited conceptions of human action. We are encouraged to think of reasons as 'causes' of human action. We have to seek a strenuous control of our emotions and feelings which can otherwise threaten our very sense of masculine identity.

But it is because we treat 'control' as a form of domination that we develop very little ongoing relationship with our emotional selves. This is why, as men, we can so easily be overwhelmed by our emotionality when it takes hold. It is often men who are 'swept off their feet' in love, or who suddenly have emotional breakdowns. It is as if our very lack of relationship with our emotional and somatic selves means that when they make an entrance, they can so easily overwhelm us. This shows how brittle is the control we assume to have, and how precarious the strength which so often involves a cutting out from our emotional responses.[7] So we have to be careful to stress that it is an issue of the *form* of control that we learn, as men, to develop. We have to grasp the *historical reproduction* of this form of control, showing the ways it works to *remove us* from an ongoing contact with our emotional and somatic lives.

We have to realize that the instrumental character of much of masculine thought, and the goal-orientated nature of action, are formed within this context. As we learn to develop more contact with our emotional and somatic selves, we can expect our thinking to be less removed and intellectualized. The quality of our experience changes as we connect more deeply with our own lived experience. We might possibly be more aware of when we speak for others. A rationalist tradition can automatically make us suspicious of our individual feelings and desires, encouraging us to assess the interests of a whole situation if we are to think of ourselves as 'rational'. We inherit a strong tradition in which the expression of individual desires, feelings and emotions is deemed 'selfish' and self-indulgent, if not irrational.

When we automatically and unthinkingly identify self-control with the domination of our desires and emotionality, we are almost bound to feel threatened when we are asked in our relationship what we individually feel about a situation or problem. As men we find it easier to give a total assessment of a situation, than to say what we feel about it ourselves. In this way we unwittingly seek to control situations and relationships, while often presenting ourselves as honestly engaged with working through the feelings and issues in our sexual relationships. Often we can feel scared and threatened to acknowledge our fear of intimacy.

Even when we desperately want to talk through issues in our relationships, we can experience ourselves as locked out of our own emotions and feelings. It is so easy to experience this as a personal inadequacy rather than to realize that our sense of an 'inner vacuum' has been an integral part of our masculine identity. Possibly we sense that more contact with our emotional selves might threaten our sense of masculine identity, since it will show us as more vulnerable and more needy than we present ourselves to be. As men we are brought up to be independent and self-sufficient.

In short, this means we are ready to support others, but can feel that we have no needs ourselves. We simply have tasks to be getting on with in the world. Our male identity is externally defined even though we might recognize the need for support and understanding in our private relationships. It is as if this is a refuelling point. But often we do not want to be reminded of the dependency and emotionality we show in this sphere. Possibly we should hardly be surprised if we show ourselves as small boys in our intimate relationships, since our emotional lives have never really developed.[8] We have been taught to despise our emotional selves from an early age. Softness means weakness. It means our masculinity is in question.

I would argue that the sharp demarcation in our moral culture, which was given its clearest secular expression in Kant's ethical theory, between a rationality which is conceived as mental and as a source of our freedom, and our emotions and desires which are treated as externally influencing and determining our behaviour, has shaped our inherited conceptions of masculinity. We fear showing ourselves as vulnerable and dependent human beings, since this seems to 'prove' that we cannot be relied upon as 'real men'. We feel we are letting ourselves down. We feel terrified of losing the only kind of control we know, even though at another level we know we are not in control of ourselves, since we barely know what we feel and desire.

But rather than face the pain and reality of this impoverishment, we will withdraw into ourselves. We will refuse to talk about our feelings, nagged by a terrible desperation of an inner vacuum. We might get angry at a partner who is insisting that we say what we feel is going on. It is easy to feel cornered and just hit back. Even though this feeling of desperation at a sense of an 'inner vacuum' is shared by many men, it is rarely talked about, even less theorized. Our inherited traditions of theoretical work do not help illuminate the problems involved. Often they collude to make us think that it is unimportant to dwell upon these kinds of issues, since they are 'personal'.

Marxist writing has often simply reproduced this tendency. It has been a potential strength of sexual politics to dwell upon moments that people themselves experience as significant to them, so validating their own experience. If Lukàcs developed an important and sustained critique of empiricist method, his work stopped short of providing the basis for the insight that critical categories have to emerge out of people's experience, helping to illuminate and confirm what people can dimly recognize as important to them.[9] This is the insight which the women's movement developed through the practice of consciousness-raising. In this sense Marxism can learn from a phenomenological tradition which refuses externally to impose a sense of what 'should be' important to people. We depend upon recognizing the theoretical and personal significance of men, finding a resonance and echo in sharing their experience with other men to develop a shared sense of value and significance. This is a dialectical process, since it involves an ongoing critical relationship to one's experience. It challenges a conventional empiricist tradition which tempts us into accepting the categories in which our experience initially presents itself.

In a similiar way, psychoanalysis when it is well done does not just impose interpretations on people's experience, but depends upon a developing awareness as people deepen the contact they have with their own individual history and experience.[10] Consciousness-raising is a social and political practice which also has an awareness of the importance of people's 'coming to consciousness', though it seeks to context our developing awareness in a broader social and historical network of relationships. Through its own inner logic it can help people to an awareness of the significance of their early family relationships, though it can also be critical of attempts to grasp our social experience within too narrow a framework of family relationships. I know how it helped me to an awareness of the significance of issues of class and ethnicity. We have to come to knowledge and awareness in our own ways. Through consciousness-raising, knowledge has been connected again to philosophical traditions of self and revelation. It is inevitably critical of a Leninist tradition that presented political knowledge as a commodity that could be handed from revolutionaries to workers.

So for men it could be important to recognize and acknowledge the 'inner vacuum' we feel when we are asked directly about our personal feelings. We withdraw from this request. But we also feel exposed, as it seems to touch a raw nerve that we know others have touched before. Suddenly we can feel out of control and exposed. Since usually we have more than enough to say, we can be left anxious at our inability to share more personally. Our identification of our masculinity with self-control has hurt our capacity to share our individual emotions and feelings. It is as if we have to depend upon women to interpret our own experience for us, though we would resist acknowledging this as a form of dependency.

The very universality of our reason has somehow worked to impersonalize our experience. It has made us strangers to our emotional lives. This also makes us more fearful of intimacy, since this seems to herald a loss of control. It can make it harder to enter into a close relationship, since we find it so difficult to share our experience even though we are dimly aware that this could bring depth to our relationship. This can lock us into a terrible circle of isolation and loneliness. We can feel more alone in our relationship as we are aware of our difficulties in sharing more of ourselves. We have to face the fact that often we give very little of ourselves to our partners.

INDIVIDUALISM

Where there is a strong identification of bourgeois morality with individualism, people can feel that in getting away from individualism they are somehow escaping the grip of bourgeois morality. At best, this could only contain a partial truth. It was important in the early days of sexual politics for people to recognize how certain forms of possessive and competitive behaviour deemed to flow from – or to be organized by – the dominant institutions in society. There was a growing awareness that the forms of sexual relations we had grown up to assume, did not simply flow from individual choices but also reflected and sustained the dominant social relations of the larger society.[11]

This was to challenge the pervasive distinction between 'public' and 'private' life, which was so deeply structured into our liberal moral culture. This tended to assume that public life could be a realm of unfreedom and constraint, since it was influenced by the relationships of the larger society, but that private life was essentially an area of freedom reflecting individual choices and decisions. People freely chose their private relationships, which could therefore only express the choices and desires of the individuals involved. Within liberalism the private sphere was therefore assumed to be beyond social criticism.

But it was this aspect of liberal common sense that divided social life into the 'public' and the 'private' that was implicitly challenged in the emerging social movements in the 1960s and 1970s. Sexual politics was to emerge as a new area of investigation and conflict. In another way this distinction was also challenged at the level of parliamentary politics, in the many scandals in the mid 60s that focused on issues of sexual morality and which forced a public questioning of sexuality and morality.[12]

So in the early 1970s it was becoming clearer to many people that the individualism, competitiveness and possessiveness that seemed to characterize our most intimate and private relations could not be completely separated from the larger structures of power in society. But this was also to challenge a significant silence in Marxist theory which also seemed to leave 'private life' to its own devices. Marxism had either worked to dismiss private life completely, or had too easily assumed that issues within intimate and sexual relations would be automatically resolved with a more equal distribution of social goods.

53

Marxism had failed to theorize the significance of private relations, and had unwittingly remained tied to a utilitarian moral theory and a distributive conception of justice.[13] It tended to assume that the hurt and injustice people could do to each other within their personal or private lives was bound to be of only secondary significance. Certainly traditional Marxist theory was left on the sidelines of libertarian politics in the early 1970s, ready to predict that all attempts at alternative communal forms of living would inevitably end in disappointment unless the underlying structure of capitalist social relations were transformed.

If many people were to learn to adopt a more orthodox position in the move towards theory that took place in the mid 70s, this was a way of coping with the hurt and confusion after this experimentation. People often turned their backs on their experience, because it seemed too painful to learn from it. Withdrawal was widespread. Unfortunately this meant that lessons were rarely learnt from this important period of social and sexual experimentation.[14]

If anything, the general identification of individualism with competitiveness had been too totalistic. It left no space for the exploration of different forms of individuality. In the end it was to prove a block to theoretical and practical change. It was left to the emerging women's movement to set new terms, as it learnt from the methods of the Black Power movement about the importance of validating and confirming the individual experience of women. The Black Power movement had recognized the importance of people learning to believe in themselves, learning to validate their own experience. The importance of the notion that 'Black is beautiful' was not simply a reappropriation of language and a challenge to traditional identifications of blackness with badness, but a way of encouraging black people to be proud of themselves, their history and culture. This was therefore also a challenge to traditional notions of morality and individualism which were essentially dualistic in their claims. In learning to identify with one's own history and culture one became more of an individual, not less of one.[15]

This was the theoretical and practical importance of the institution of consciousness-raising that helped people grasp how much of what they had always been brought up to accept as their individual and private experience was in fact shared by others. This was something the women's movement learnt to value as they challenged the treatment of women in both the student and Black Power movements. Individual experience and collective experience were no longer seen as antithetical. This was the discovery of a historical dialectic in practice as women learnt to think about themselves in different terms. As women learnt to value an idea of 'sisterhood', they recognized both an individual identity, asserted in the claim to be treated as a person in their own right, not simply in relation to others, and a new collective identification.[16]

The women's movement had found a way of challenging a deep tradition of possessive individualism, while discovering through consciousness-raising that one's individuality could be enhanced, rather than diminished, through learning to identify with a shared collectivity. But these new terms of political discussion were slow to challenge some of the deeper terms of socialist theory which remain caught in simplistic distinctions between 'individualistic' and 'collective'. This is partly because the issues of masculinity and male sexuality are consistently hedged. Possibly this is because men have so much to lose, but I think also because of a deep masculine fear of the personal and the intimate. Men's incapacity to grasp this sense of individuality is reflected through the problems of developing more equal relationships.

CONTROL, EQUALITY AND CHANGE

Liberalism had brought people up to feel that equality was an issue of individual choice and will. If people were ready to change their attitudes towards each other, then they could have more equal relationships. This made it an issue of will and determination, and very much left it up to men to change their attitudes towards women. It left men feeling that they had a power to grant equality to others if they thought that the claim was rational. Freedom and equality remained a masculine gift.

So for instance, a man might encourage his wife to get a job, as long as it did not threaten the organization of the family. This inevitably placed the division of household and childcare duties beyond discussion. These were clearly seen as a woman's responsibility, and equality was to be constructed on this basis. So it was still a situation in which the control of men over women and children, rather than being threatened, was in fact reinforced. Sexual politics made control central. It became clear that, as men, we are brought up feeling a very deep need to control the relationships we are in. We want things done in our way. We fear losing control. This is equally true in our sexualities, in which there remains a deep connection between our inherited masculinity and the issue of control.

But liberalism also sees social life as divided into different spheres which are all assumed to be more or less autonomous of each other. This places sexuality in a sphere of its own, as if we exist almost as different people once the bedroom door has been closed. This encourages a deep mystification about our sexual relationships, as if they can escape the tensions, anxieties and pressures of our everyday life. It is in this sense that sexuality has been given a privileged position, a space in which our true natures are shown. Foucault's *A History of Sexuality* notices this, but fails to appreciate that this is one of the things that both Freud and Reich set out to challenge. Rather than thinking that it is in our sexual relations that our 'true self' is at last revealed, they want to show how our difficulties in our sexual relations grow out of the difficulties we have in making close and intimate relationships in the rest of our lives.

Rather than demarcating sexual relations, they want to recover their connection with other patterns in our relationships. In doing this, psychoanalysis is challenging the kind of 'freedom' which liberalism assumes us to have. We are not free to make our relationships as we want them to be, unless we are also prepared to acknowledge and work through the influence of our early parental relationships. We can only create freedom from our histories if we are prepared fully to acknowledge them. In this deeper sense, psychoanalysis remains an intensely historical theory. It makes us aware that the present is filled with resonances of the past. It brings us back to a sense of our own individual histories and development, however difficult and painful they were, and so questions the lack of historical sense of liberalism.[17]

People often come to psychoanalysis in their late twenties and early thirties, often at a moment of crisis when they feel they can no longer escape themselves. Freud was right about the lengths to which people go to avoid any deeper contact with themselves: knowledge is not something people often crave, especially when it is about themselves. This is why in some ways psychoanalysis has become more acceptable to many now that it can be presented as an intellectual theory. Often it can unwittingly be a way of learning to use an elaborated language about oneself, so as to keep one's own feelings from welling up. It can become a technology of self-control, a way of keeping things together in relationships that could so easily crumble. This is probably related to ways it creates a separate and autonomous realm of the 'mental', which can supposedly be dealt with in its own terms. Freud's work did not start like this, but it gradually became so. Reich's work remained more subversive, when it was not trapped in a crude scientism, because it stressed the importance of emotional release and challenged the intellectualization of feelings. Reich always saw himself as developing the insights of Freud's early work.[18]

Feminism challenged the idea of liberal equality as an issue of attitude. Equality could not be divorced from the everyday organization of domestic tasks and childcare. It insisted that it was not simply an issue of winning access to a male world and allowing women to compete on equal terms in this world. This was the difference between an equal rights movement and a movement for women's liberation. But we have tended to ignore the significance of this difference for men and masculinity.

There was a challenge not only to the values and relationships of a male world, but also to the forms of masculine sexuality that women had often been forced to submit to in silence. The question of equality had rarely been raised in the context of sexual relationships, especially in situations where the very existence of women's sexuality had historically been denied. It was barely acknowledged that women can enjoy and find pleasure in sexuality, and that they have their own independent sexual needs. This can still be a very threatening idea for men.

In this situation, equality involves more than attitudes. It can involve developing a different sexual practice, in which the pace and rhythms of sexual expression have to be considered. But again this is not something under our conscious control. I know for myself the anxieties and fears this can bring to the surface. Often, heterosexual masculine sexuality pushes things to an orgasm, finding it hard to dwell and take time. Male sexuality is often organized around a goal of orgasm, and conforms to the purposive character of masculine conceptions of human action.

There is also a deeper historical conditioning that affects the issues of equality when it touches sexuality. We inherit a Protestant tradition which has seen sex as basically evil. Like our other natural inclinations, it is seen as inevitably threatening to any kind of moral or civilized behaviour. There is a close identification of the sexual with the bestial, so that giving in to our sexual feelings is compromising our sense of ourselves as rational and 'civilized' men. It should be hardly surprising that sex is to be hurried, as if dwelling with the contact and intimacy is a self-indulgence that is bound to be dangerous. Rather it can be difficult to acknowledge that traditional masculine sexuality has anything to do with vulnerability, intimacy and contact. It becomes the same kind of goal-oriented activity as the rest of our behaviour.

Even if it is harder to remain aware of these negative feelings about the body and bodily experiences in a secularized and permissive society, the tensions and anxieties are never far from the surface, even if many men choose to control them through humour and drink. We are misleading ourselves if we think a challenge to organized religion has drastically affected the deeper structure of these sentiments. The body continues to be despised within an intellectualist culture. This takes different forms, and within structuralism the categorical distinction between nature and culture has dismissed any reference to natural feeling and desire as a form of essentialism. We just have to remember the ways Reich has been derided and systematically misunderstood.[19] If anything, these attitudes can be harder to detect and challenge within ourselves, since they are barely articulated outside of a religious language. There is enormous confusion around issues of sex and sexuality, because ideas of greater sexual freedom and liberation have often been drafted upon a deeper structure of self-hate and self-disgust, which can remain largely hidden and unidentified. This gives people unreal expectations of themselves, especially within a culture that makes us feel that if we cannot reach the high ideals we set for ourselves, we only have ourselves to blame. This has a particular significance for men who are brought up to aspire to ideals, and then feel down-hearted and defeated when we fail to live up to them, or when the experience does not live up to the expectations we have set.

Traditional conceptions of masculinity have been challenged by feminism but these have barely been replaced by new models. It is hardly surprising that the political Right has been able to build upon this confusion through a reassertion of traditional male authority within the family and within relationships. It is because men are brought up to identify masculinity with asserting control in relationships that the demands for sexual equality have been so threatening. It is difficult for us as men not to experience sex as some kind of work we have to maintain control of. It is threatening to realize we do not know how to give pleasure to ourselves, let alone give pleasure to our sexual partners. Then there is the fear which can grow out of the expectation that we should somehow be able to satisfy our partners. We can be anxious enough about our own potency, let alone worrying about the pleasure of others. But then this can so easily become another feature of men taking on a controlling responsibility which is not necessarily our own. This is the way we maintain control. Our rationality ties us to doing what is best for all. We can find it hard to give up this responsibility, because this means giving up control.

We can also find it hard to acknowledge that the difficulties in our sexual relationship reflect issues in our ongoing relationships. A liberal moral psychology tends to construe sex as a unique peak experience in a life made up of other discrete experiences and sensations. This is part of the empiricist tradition we unknowingly inherit. So it becomes difficult to identify a 'politics of experience' that does not express this empiricist conception of experience. But this is what sexual politics has been endeavouring to develop.

Not only does sexual politics make us far more aware of contradictions in our experience, but it forces us to think about the relationship of consciousness to experience, especially where people talk about a 'change in consciousness'. This helps place our sexual relationships within the context of our ongoing relationships, rather than isolate and glorify them. So we should barely be surprised that many people have found a fruitful relationship between consciousness-raising and some form of psychoanalytic consciousness, since both can help root people in their own individual historical and social experience. This provides a moderating cultural influence to a liberalism which can encourage a kind of rootlessness in its suggestion that a person's position in the larger society simply depends upon individual talents and abilities, as well as in its idea that people can make their own identities.

MEN, FEMINISM AND EMOTIONS

The 1960s was a rootless period, in which individuals were concerned to question established traditions. But feminism showed that this new freedom and permissiveness was often at the expense of women. Feminism sought new conceptions of freedom and equality, which more deeply challenged inherited liberal notions. It helped women to a shared sense of womanhood as they sought to discover a new feminist identity. Abstract liberal notions of equality were challenged as they tended to make gender identification an incidental and contingent feature of personal identity. Liberalism has sought to assert that people can be equal as human beings, regardless of the inequalities of social life. A new language of confidence, adequacy and personhood had supplanted, in feminist theory and practice, the liberal idea that capacities and abilities are more or less randomly distributed between individuals.

Women recognized their need for the support and solidarity of other women in dealing with the difficulties of learning self-confidence and assurance. Women insisted on challenging the organization of meetings and the relations of power. They refused to accept that if they had the ability or talent, they had an equal chance to make it in a male world. Women sought to have their own values recognized in the larger institutions of society, refusing to take for granted the masculine terms of discussion. As men we were no longer granted the right to speak for all. Women were learning to root themselves in their own gender experience, learning how much they shared with other women. They refused to stay silent, but insisted on determining their own terms.

But when women demanded that men learn to talk for themselves, they often met a withdrawn and morose silence. It was as if we as men had learnt to talk for others, but had never learnt to find our own individual voices. As women were challenging notions of liberal equality, they wanted to work out more equal relationships with men. They learnt to appreciate consciousness-raising as a way of discovering what they needed and wanted as individual women, recognizing how this had always been defined for them. On this new, though tenuous, ground, it seemed possible to negotiate a more equal relationship. But this was deeply threatening for us as men, especially when we already felt we treated others as equals. Equality was no longer a matter of attitude, but of the reorganization of domestic work and childcare. This meant learning to cook, clean and care, as well as assuming more responsibility for ourselves. We could no longer rely upon women to serve our emotional and physical needs.

Often it was hard to hear these demands. We were frequently reminded of the pain and suffering we had caused our partners, and of the ways we had taken them for granted. We were drawn back into reworking a history we would have preferred to leave alone. Secure in our rationalist convictions that there is little point in working through a history that cannot be changed, it was hard to appreciate how central this reworking was for women who were discovering their individual identities. We were forced to realize the pain that our insensitivity and power had created. It had been an important element of our power that we had never really needed to notice, since we could always minimize its significance in the order of things; but times were changing.

There was also the painful realization of the difficulties we have as men, caught up in the contradictions of our masculinity, to share our individual feelings and emotions. We had learnt how to depend upon our relationships with women for emotional support, but this was very different from negotiating as equals with our partners. It was as if we had got used to women interpreting our needs, desires and feelings for us in this emotional realm, so that we never had to find words and a language of desire and needs for ourselves. This was a way we could have our emotional needs met without really having to show our vulnerability and need.

Women, though, were now beginning to refuse to do this

emotional work for us, and were demanding that we do at least some of it for ourselves. This meant, at the very least, saying what we felt about the relationship and being prepared to negotiate our emotional needs as equals. This was very threatening. Men discovered that it was often easier to withdraw or get angry, than to own up to the difficulties we have with this emotional exercise. We wanted to show we were willing, without recognizing that we could only work towards a more equal relationship if we were prepared to give up some of our control. As men we often had to stop 'explaining' the situations and experiences of others, and learn to work from a more honest and direct expression of our own individual needs and emotions. This often proved almost impossible. Not only had we learnt as middle-class men to intellectualize our experience, but it could bring enormous fear and uncertainty to the surface if we tried to share our feelings more directly. This threatened to challenge the control we were doing our best to sustain over the rest of our lives.

Increasingly, men began to realize that we did not have an emotional language in which to share ourselves without feeling immediately exposed and vulnerable. Somehow this had been a capacity we seemed automatically to have forsaken in the identification of our masculinity with reason. We had often inherited such a deep and unspoken investment in seeing ourselves as 'rational beings', able to determine and control our lives according to ends we set, that we could erupt and get speechlessly angry, even violent, in sustaining this image of ourselves. Often it meant that relationships came to painful and difficult ends.

As men we learnt it was harder to change than we thought. It was no longer simply a matter of will and determination. It was painful to realize that there was often nothing that we could do to make the situation better and repair a relationship once the pain of years of subordination and lack of recognition had come to the surface. As men we are brought up to assume that there is always something we can do to change a situation, to make things better. But this logic does not necessarily work in a relationship. Often we have had to learn to leave partners clear time and space to work things out for themselves without our interference or suggestions. As men, often the hardest thing to learn is to do nothing.

Our sense of masculinity within a Western cultural tradition has such a deep connection to activity, to a sense that we can make our world through action, that it is hard to accept that we cannot always change a person's feelings towards us. Often this makes men bitter, since it can so easily seem as if women are being unforgiving. Our remorse and our pleas for forgiveness seem to make no difference. Since, as men, we are aware of how hard it has been to acknowledge this, we often expect to be gratefully received. When we are told that it makes no difference, that the time has passed when it might have been possible to rebuild a relationship, a violent bitterness erupts as we are brought to face our powerlessness. We can feel betrayed by some nameless cultural inheritance as we are forced to realize we cannot make our relationships in the same instrumental image as we have learnt to build our masculine lives around.

As men it is difficult not to be 'control freaks'. This is the history we inherit, though our forms of control are often subtle. We learn to exert our control in very different ways. Not surprisingly, we never feel easy when this is pointed out to us. I have been challenged about this numerous times. I know how sharing a certain level of feelings can be a way of concealing deeper anxieties and fears, and so of working to control a relationship. This is often more transparent in our sexual relations.

Often we insist upon taking an initiative and setting the pace of sexual relations. I know how hard it has been for me to slow myself down, to be more passive. This seems to be both thrilling and threatening at the same time. I also know how hard it is to talk about our sexual relationships, being clearer about what we like and what gives us individual pleasure while staying in full contact with the experience. It seems easier to think that sex has to be a silent and bodily experience in which language finds no place. But this is crucially because of men's relationship to language and the ways we have learnt to use our language to set a safe distance from our felt experience.

We learn to use language to sustain our self-control. This can mean that our masculine language is deeply instrumental, just as our conception of masculinity has been historically connected to notions of self-control. We do not use language to express ourselves, to reveal our feelings and emotions to ourselves and others.[20] This can so easily be threatening to the control we are doing our best to preserve. This means that our language is formed within an image of instrumental action in which the control we learn to exercise over our desires and needs, emotions and feelings, is not a control developed through contact with this area of our experience, but is a control which is more akin to suppression and domination. We seek to silence our inner lives, our emotions and feelings, so they can no longer interfere with the ends we have set through our reason. This vision is sanctioned in our inherited Kantian ethical traditions.

We assert our masculinities and define our sense of male identity by learning to control our inner natures just as much as we learn to control the social world around us. It is in this context that we have a deeper fear of contact both with ourselves but also in our intimate relationships with others. We do not want others to remind us of the costs of our instrumental lives, since we are so geared to identifying our sense of identity with the individual success and achievements we make. So sexual relationships become an area in which our achievement is mirrored. We do not seek contact, rather we are often silently terrified of it. We can keep moving so as to avoid it. Our sexual 'conquests' make us think that there is nothing lacking in our lives. But it is just this deep lack of contact with ourselves and our difficulties in caring for others that has been revealed. Feminism has exposed a raw nerve of masculinity.

But it is only in rediscovering a hidden history of masculinity that we can begin to question what we so easily take for granted. We have to recognize that there are different forms of self-control and that the connection between masculinity and self-control has formed not only our sense of self, but also the quality of our sexual and personal relationships with men, women and children. It is these crucial connections which have been so hard to illuminate within our inherited rationalist traditions.

DESIRE AND CONTROL

Modern forms of masculinity carry the deep influence of the Protestant ethic and capitalist work relations. Sometimes we can experience ourselves as trapped into a ceaseless activity. We fear giving more time and space to ourselves. We have little ongoing relationship with our somatic processes. The body is to be used as an instrument to serve our ends, rather than to be listened to. Often we experience little ongoing connection with our emotions and feelings. At some level we remain strangers to ourselves. We just do not know ourselves. This partly explains both the difficulties of developing a larger movement concerned with the redefinitions of masculinity and the attraction of therapy for those who have been drawn into this process.

We have to face the difficulties that men have had in changing ourselves in the face of inherited traditions and practices of personal change. This is only partially explained through the fact that men have power in the organization of the larger society, so we supposedly have everything to lose through changing, and little to gain. We also have to face the fact that as men seem to change, different forms of control seem to reassert themselves. If is as if enormous fear seems to surface, since we have been brought up to identify our sense of masculine self with particular forms of control as domination over our emotional lives and desires.

Somehow this goes along with a tendency for many men touched by the challenges of feminism to disown their masculinity in deep feelings of guilt. As men we can be struck and overwhelmed by the sufferings we have caused women and the pain our masculinity has caused the planet. This has encouraged some men into a deeper form of the self-rejection that is even more deeply tied in with our Protestant inheritance. It is partly because of an inherited sense that our natures are rotten and evil that we have had to seek consolation and a possible redemption in constant activity. This is a deeper source for the common experience many men share of being driven constantly to prove ourselves. This can make our contact with other men threatening, since we constantly fear being put down. This is one reason it is common for men to renounce their relationships with other men, and declare that they have always been closer to women anyway. This becomes another way in which we refuse to take responsibility for our own masculinity. Somehow we have to learn to distinguish the suffering and oppression women are constantly enduring within patriarchal relations of power and our individual responsibility within our own relationships.

This is not to deny that we bear some kind of general

responsibility, but it is to bring the issue of individual responsibility into much clearer focus than we usually do on the Left. We should question the tendency to think that if we constantly deny our individual needs and demands in relationships, we cannot be held responsible for anything. Often this only produces a form of hidden passivity which can make us even more demanding in insisting relationships are organized on our terms.

In brief, we have to begin by taking more responsibility for our own experience. This means learning of the different ways we can nourish and support ourselves, so that we are not constantly dependent on our partners. This promises to create a different kind of balance in relationships. But it also means learning to acknowledge our anger, resentments, hostility, fear and demands, rather than hide them. It means learning to control, but not to suppress, our emotions and feelings through giving them more expression, though not expecting they will thereby be met. It means a deep challenge to the idea of self-control as meaning a rigorous domination of the self. But this also means a challenge to the ways our masculine identity is forged in relation to our reason.

Since the seventeenth century we have inherited notions of control as essentially external. It was through the workings of our will and reason that our natures were to be controlled, and we were to be able to enjoy the freedom we know as human beings. It is our reason that makes us distinctly human and separates us off from our animal natures. So, as I have shown, our emotions, feelings and desires can be no part of our identities. This rationalist inheritance has deeply formed our notions of masculinity and the endemic superiority that men are brought up to feel in relation to women who are conceived as closer to nature. Crucially, then, this is not simply a matter that can be shelved as having to do with attitudes towards women that can be shifted, but concerns the very formation of masculine identity.

The way our reason is defined in contrast to our emotions and feelings is what denies them as genuine sources of knowledge. There is no space within which to consider the rationality of our emotions and feelings, learning where they are appropriate to situations and where they seem to carry a power and weight that

66

comes from somewhere else. It was Freud who first helped us think about this more systematically, although he gradually succumbed to thinking of emotions and feelings as forms of thoughts. They are characteristically thought of as 'mental-states' within modern philosophy.

But it is the idea that control is essentially external that has proved such a hidden influence. It meant that in the 1960s sexuality was often conceived of as an alternative morality that could be imposed as an act of will. The conception we inherit of socialist morality replacing capitalist morality as an alternative set of principles to be upheld through acts of will, leaves the relationship of morality to desire untouched. If anything, this should show the significance of sexual politics when it is grounded in the quality of everyday experience.

It was the strength of the Growth Movement and the early breaks with traditional psychoanalysis under the influence of Fritz Perls' questioning of Freudian analysis, to help many people become aware of the different ways we avoid the 'here and now', the present reality of our experience.[21] In this context it became important to repossess the first person pronoun and to learn to express emotions and feelings directly, rather than constantly to use the form 'one usually ... ', which can so easily be a means of avoidance. For many people in the 1970s the growth movement was a context to continue a search for a more honest and direct experience. It was a context that seemed to challenge the moralism of socialist politics and allowed resentments to emerge which had been held in check as many people were struggling to live up to the new standards of libertarian morality. Put more positively, it was a context in which the contradictions of our experience could be more openly explored, where, for instance, we could admit both our desires for independence and needs for dependency.

But it was also a context that many of the Left derided as self-indulgent, refusing to learn what it had to offer and ready to condemn it outright for its individualism and political blindness. It was in the context of Red Therapy and the Growth Movement that some of us learnt how some of these notions could usefully be appropriated and their implicit individualism challenged.[22] At the very least it helped acknowledge the distance that existed between the ways people wanted to be and the reality of what they felt and needed. If this had always been part of a psycho-analytic project, the traditional relationships of power and suspicions of direct emotional expression and bodily contact made it hard to appreciate. Rather than simply repressing these contradictions through acts of will we made them central topics of investigation. For a time we learnt to suspend the 'shoulds' and 'oughts' that are such an endemic feature of masculine experience. This helped bring us into closer contact with different levels of our experience.

But again this is not something that can be intellectually demonstrated. As with consciousness-raising, these notions assume their significance and meaning in the context of a shared experience. This helped develop more of an ongoing relationship to our emotions and desires which we learnt to know, however difficult and uncomfortable they were, rather than simply repress them. The notion of 'self-control' came to have a different meaning. It became a control that was growing out of an ongoing relationship with needs and desires that had seemed too enormous and overwhelming, partly because they had never been expressed and openly shared. As we learnt to know our rage, fear, anger and disgust, our pleasure also came to have a different character and meaning.

This kind of exploration is rarely appreciated as a cultural investigation of our inherited masculinity. The Left insists on seeing it as an individual and private affair, refusing to acknowledge its historical and social significance. Often it is derided as a form of self-indulgence, especially since it challenges, as forms of traditional psychoanalysis often fail to, some of the critical assumptions of a rationalist intellectual culture. We insist on locking it into a 'private realm' even though this very distinction between the 'private' and 'public' has been questioned within sexual politics. Issues of authority and control have become central to the workings of modern capitalism. Psychology has become a centrally contested terrain.

Sexual politics should not be left on the same periphery, as it was in Reich's day, but should be central to our analysis of modern capitalism. An exploration of the contradictions of male sexuality could be central since this touches on the issues of work, success and achievement. But this involves a critique of the analysis of male sexuality in terms of conforming to externally defined male roles, as if it were simply an issue of extending the acceptable range of behaviours open to men. Not only does this analysis in terms of social roles avoid critical issues of social relations of power, but it leaves intact dominant notions of self-control and masculine identity. This has been the weakness of the sociological accounts of masculinity.

Learning to acknowledge more of our needs and desires may bring us into deeper relationship with ourselves but it threatens our sense of self-control. This depends upon our being self-sufficient and so without needs. In sharing our needs we inevitably share more of our weakness and vulnerability. We also deepen our relationships with our partners as we show more of ourselves. This does not mean our sexuality is not socially and historically constructed, but it does involve an ongoing articulation of our sense of self and identity.

Often the notion of the social construction of sexuality has reproduced this very externality. I think Foucault's *A History of Sexuality* has not helped as much as it could have, since it has clouded the issues through presenting us with false alternatives.[23] It has sought to banish the notion of repression through irrevocably connecting it to a notion of pre-given sexuality. Certainly it was part of Reich's work to show that repression could not simply be lifted as an act of will, however he was misinterpreted in the 1960s. He was aware of the defences we have against our feelings, but learnt to respect them as ways we had learnt to cope with a fundamentally hostile world. If we need to be warned about sloppy uses of the notion of repression, we also need to learn its appropriateness to account for the relationship of masculine identity and self-control.

In our twenties it is easy to blame our partners for the frustrations and unhappiness we experience in our relationships. We assume that we are with the wrong partner and we begin our search again. As boys we have never learnt to look at ourselves: we learn to blame the world first. It is always a matter of who to blame for a relationship going wrong. It is often only later when we discover certain patterns reproducing in our relationships that we begin to lose heart. It is often in our early thirties that we look towards some kind of analytical grasp of the histories we bring with us into relationships. Our relationships with parents come to have a renewed significance, often coming into their own as we make these relationships anew when we have our own children and then become grandparents.

But the Left has maintained a strange quality of agelessness, which is another aspect of its inherited tradition of universalism, making it insensitive to the different needs people have at different times in our lives. It is as if we become useless to its purposes when we can no longer function as ageless militants. But feminism has brought a new challenge, as it has discovered the significance of the particularity of our experience. This is something that we as men have been slow to discover for ourselves, often wanting to forsake our masculinity, rather than define it.

As we learn to accept the history of our own desires, we discover the pain with which we have been forced, or have chosen, to forsake aspects of ourselves. Our tenderness and gentleness have been negated, but so also has our anger and rage when this has been identified with our mothers, whom we have sought to distance ourselves from. In an important sense we have been estranged from ourselves as we have learnt to exert a control as domination over our emotional lives and desires. It was through control that we first learnt to exert our egos and assumed a masculine identity in the social world. The relationship between morality and desire in male sexuality has been identified as an issue of control. If this has given us the strength to know what we want to do in the world it has often made us unsure and hesitant in our individual emotional needs and desires. We want and expect our partners to be there for us, but we rarely offer them access to our emotional lives.

As we learn to acknowledge more of our desires and needs without judging them, we will build more of an ongoing relationship with our inner lives. But as we touch the depths of our neediness and dependence, we need to acknowledge that it can be unreasonable to expect our partners to carry this burden for us. We have to learn new forms of support, sometimes through developing new kinds of relationships with other men. This is a subtle and difficult process of exploration through which we learn the inadequacy of the notion of repression as a description of the relationship we have assumed between morality and desire.

But this will also bring into question our work relationships and friendships as we learn to think about what we give and receive in the different areas of our lives, rather than simply accepting them as arenas in which we prove ourselves individually. This can be a frightening process as we learn to take much more individual responsibility for ourselves and our relationships. This can mean facing our passivity in our personal and sexual relationships, and learning to take initiative and responsibility for the care of others as well as ourselves.

The issues concerning the relationship of morality and desire will no longer appear as a matter of deciding upon how we are to treat others. We will need to develop a basis for learning that only if we learn how to value and respect ourselves, which also involves valuing our emotions and feelings, can we have more equal and loving relationships with others. This is a critical issue for male sexuality, but also for conceptions of personal and social transformation and so for socialism. I want to go back to share some of my own steps in learning both the theoretical and practical significance of these issues.

Chapter Five

CHANGE

We need to explore our conceptions of personal and political change. As men, we learn to assume that we can change as an act of will and determination. We intellectualize our experience more easily than we share it with others. Our language becomes a weapon that is forged for self-assertion so that it can make it harder for us to form close and intimate relationships. Therapy can help us face some of these issues and the ways we would discount our emotions and feelings as sources of knowledge and self-understanding. It can teach us different paths to change, as it questions the forms of self-rejection and self-denial that are so much part of the prevailing identification of masculinity with reason.

Therapy also helps us challenge the notion that emotions and feelings are essentially 'irrational', and so opens up different ways of relating to the self. It can help us recognize the tension between the 'inner' and the 'outer' which Protestant culture has done so much to sustain. As feminism helps us to rethink the relationship between the 'personal' and the 'political', so therapy can help us rework the relationship between morality and our emotional lives. The conception we inherit of socialist morality as an alternative set of principles to be upheld through acts of will, leaves the relationship of morality to desire untouched.

POLITICS AND THERAPY

How can we change? What kind of changes can we expect to make in our lives? These questions seem to echo an earlier period of affluence. They seem drained of meaning as we become terrified of the risks of a nuclear war. But they can also gain a new urgency, as if being brought face to face with our own destruction forces us to think anew about the quality and meaning of our lives. It can make us more aware of the quality of our experience in the present, less ready to make sacrifices for an indefinite future.

I came to puberty with the bomb. The Aldermaston marches in the late 1950s gave me a sense of solidarity and hope: we wanted to grow up into a world that had been made safe, and believed that if enough people gave testimony, then the future could be ours. The bomb had cast a shadow over a whole generation that had been born out of the ashes of the Second World War: it wrought havoc with our sense of an assured future, undermining the values of a society which needed people to work hard and dedicate themselves to individual achievement and success.

In the late 1960s, politics and morality seemed to merge again, as the student movement was forged in the moral commitment against the American war in Vietnam, and the sordid collusion of Wilson's government in American war aims confirmed many people's disillusionment with parliamentary politics. A broad cultural movement questioned the values and relationships that many of us were brought up to accept in the families and schooling of the post-war period; a generation rejected the forms of life we had inherited and the kind of compromises with conventional society that our parents had made. We wanted to extend our experience of life, to show that we could bring a different kind of life into existence, through relating to each other more equally. Our ideas had to be tested and confirmed through our experience: it was the beginning of a politics of experience.

The categories of Marxist theory, however, especially as they have been influenced by the writings of Althusser,[1] have made it difficult to reflect seriously upon that movement. Conceptions of 'personal experience' have too easily been derided, as if they inevitably carry empiricist meanings. Insights and understandings that we hard fought for have been too neatly categorized as relating to a pre-existing notion of 'subjectivity' or to a concern with 'a theory of the subject'. Of course, it would be naive to try to reassert the politics and experience of the 'generation of '68', as if all the pain, disillusionment and despair that followed it are not to be given equal weight. But we have to be ready to acknowledge that the theory and practice of the student and Black movements in the sixties, and the women's, gay and men's movements in the seventies, offer us insights and understandings that deeply challenge prevailing Marxist theory. To do this would inevitably be to question the numerous attempts to find a space for sexual politics within pre-existing structuralist theories.

I want here to share a particular experience of relating therapy to politics. It was partly because of a crisis in our political assumptions, and the difficulties we encountered in living out our politics in East London in the mid 1970s, that a group of us felt the need to do therapy. It was partly because some of us were critical of experiences they had already had in traditional Freudian psychotherapy and others of the individualistic assumptions of the Growth Movement, that we also felt the need to develop different forms of therapy. Our experience and ideas were a reflection upon the ongoing discussion about the relationship between Marxism and psychotherapy, though often only implicitly. Our deeper involvement in therapy also affected our politics, our sense of the ways in which people can struggle against the conditions of capitalist exploitation and oppression. For Marxist politics has often developed on the basis of a very crude psychological understanding of utilitarian material interest, tending to assume that personal and sexual relationships will automatically change with the socialization of the means of production. If Althusser has helped challenge such economic determinism, the very autonomy which he grants to ideology, culture and politics can make it difficult for people to understand the importance of believing in the validity of their own experience and transforming a sense of self-confidence and identity as they take more power in their lives.

CHANGING OURSELVES

In fact, the movements of the late sixties sometimes reproduced the deeper assumptions of the very moral culture they were challenging, and the anti-intellectualism that was current made this easier to do. It was generally believed that people could change through acts of will and strength of character. Within libertarian politics, there was a developing recognition that it was wrong to be possessive or jealous in our relationships with others, for these feelings indicated the hold which capitalist morality held over us. If we denied these feelings, we could begin to change ourselves, to cease to treat others as objects. We would be less concerned to establish our identities in competitive ways, and could begin to bring into existence a more socialist morality. If the personal relations of capitalist society were increasingly identified as property relations, we would learn to behave more equally in our relations with others. In this way we challenged liberal notions which would reserve a split between public and private life: the personal became political, as we realized how even relations of love and affection easily became relations of power and possession.

As socialists we were to live according to different principles. But this produced its own forms of moralism, which existed in uneasy tension with the counter-culture's ambiguous recognition of desire. Relationships were criticized for their exclusiveness and possessiveness. The very notion of privacy became suspect, and for a time there was a feeling that the distinction between the private and the public could be forsaken. There was to be an emphasis upon the sharing of experience: people could learn much more from each other if we could only escape from the hierarchy and competitiveness which were such pervasive features of society. Now it is difficult to restore the power and insight which these ideas carried; for they created enormous hopes. They promised to give us more control over our lives, and held out a new dream of self-determination and human equality. Many of these hopes were dashed.

In 1970 I lived in a commune in Somerville, Massachusetts, during a year of enormous experimentation. There was a genuine desire to live our politics, and a suspicion of a socialist tradition that focused our energies into challenging state power and assumed that personal relationships would automatically change when the state owned the means of production. These feelings were given clearer definition in the idea of the emerging women's movement, that there could be no revolution without women's liberation. But the women's movement also challenged the ideas of freedom and equality that had been current in the student and anti-war movements: the prevailing notions of sexual liberation meant that women were supposed to make themselves available to men for fear of being thought 'narrow-minded' or 'prudish'. Women were now demanding freedom and independence on their own terms, and I remember how scared and uneasy this made me feel. For as men we were forced to consider the lived reality of women's oppression, and this punctured liberal conceptions of equality. Even though we might have thought that we related to women as equals, we were forced to recognize the different ways in which we men maintained power and control in relationships. We expected women to give priority to their relationships with us, and were threatened when they asserted the importance of their relationships with other women. Women were challenging the prevailing socialist distinction between 'individualism' and 'collectivism', which too readily assumed that individualism has to mean the essentially bourgeois notion of possessive individualism.[2] This had been used to legitimate the subordination of women. Women were learning the positive power of individualism as a critical notion which was compatible with a collective sense of sisterhood when asserted in the demand to be treated as an independent person in one's own right. Women no longer accepted an existence solely in relation to men.

In our commune we had weekly meetings at which we attempted to talk openly and honestly about our relations with each other; sometimes the men and women would also meet separately. This was integral to our sense of living our politics. This helped me understand how much of what I had been brought up to consider as my individual experience, largely controlled by my individual qualities and abilities, was shared by other men. Althusser touches on this idea in his critique of humanism, though he traps himself in a false duality in wanting to dispense with all notions of individualism as irredeemably bourgeois. The practice of sexual politics, through challenging this dualism, can allow us to escape this dilemma, though it has rarely been theorized. My sense of my individuality certainly changed as I developed a fuller sense of what I shared with other men, and how my expectations for myself had been formed within a particular culture of masculinity. But as my understanding was socialized, it only ceased to be individualistic in a very specific sense, and no longer implicitly anchored in notions of possessive individualism. This led me to understand, for instance, how I automatically invalidated the experience of women I was relating to. I was forced to recognize how 'not being sure about my feelings' could work as a form of control, as could a tendency to make myself indispensable (or so I thought) through being able to understand interpersonal dynamics in a relationship. There are different ways in which we can maintain the power to patronize and condescend in our relationships, especially if our control is being threatened: our anger and violence, even if it remains beneath the surface, becomes another.

The practice of consciousness-raising brought into existence a different conception of how people could change, and challenged the earlier moralism of libertarian politics (as it brought into existence a different relationship of knowledge to experience). This had implications for the ways we organized our house-meetings, since we had already recognized the limits of a political morality built around an act of will, partly because one person had suffered a stricter moralistic regime in an earlier communal experience. This had been organized around rationalistic Maoist conceptions of criticism and self-criticism, emphasizing conceptions of duty and self-denial. Members had to prove their dedication and seriousness, and it was considered wrong to have attachments to individuals, since this showed people were not relating equally. Individual feelings and desires were seen as essentially self-seeking and self-indulgent. Paradoxically, however, this tended to reproduce some of the deepest strains in bourgeois culture's identification of morality with reason and duty: people unwittingly shared Kant's suspicion[3] of feelings, desires and emotions as forces which would only lead us astray from goals we had set ourselves, from our political seriousness. There was a residing suspicion of bodily feelings and pleasure. In a muted form this remains a strong strand in socialist politics.

In our house meetings we wanted people to feel able to participate equally, and this involved trust and confidence. We wanted to avoid moralism and judgements. Some found it very hard to share their thoughts and feelings: it was a new and threatening situation, an intimacy we associate with a more private sexual relationship. As with consciousness-raising, there was a sense of the importance of acknowledging and expressing directly our feelings for each other, however unwelcome these might be, so as to work something out with someone, to clear the blocks in a relationship. Of course there was also an ideology working itself out, in the confident hope that if people were not getting on, or resented each other, the problem could be 'worked through' if they were ready to talk honestly with each other. Others were not simply present as witnesses, but to offer their own experience and insight, while avoiding a tone of recrimination and accusation. We learned the importance of how things are said, of the different levels within ourselves from which we can speak. We can touch each other through speech, though we can also use it as a way of distancing and controlling our experience, of maintaining a certain distance from others, as much as we can use speech to establish closeness and contact with others. But again this is not something people can decide as an act of will, and our experience in the commune tended to show the limits of the meeting situation and the importance of developing a fuller relationship to our personal histories which often reasserted themselves. As we clarified our sense of the kinds of support we could realistically give each other, I was led to think more seriously about the significance of therapy and psychoanalysis, since in our late twenties relationships which we thought we had settled with (say with our parents or siblings) seemed to gain a renewed importance when we tried to understand the patterns which seemed persistent in our relationships. The experience of different relationships can show us that it is not simply a question of individual personalities, but that we seem to reproduce particular situations and patterns within our relationships. This is not to minimize the importance of honest encounter and the quality it brings into relationships: there remains a complicated relationship between consciousness-raising and the different forms of therapy. We can learn from both, as we can learn from the complicated dialectic that can be set up between them.

What did I learn from the experience in Somerville? That solidarity can take time and patience to develop. It is not something that can simply be assumed or appealed to. I learned that I needed the support of others who wanted to live differently, if we were to relate differently to each other: this made it easier to challenge the hierarchy, competitiveness and individual acquisitiveness so deeply rooted in modern capitalist society. For a brief moment, the deep questioning of all aspects of social life from food distribution, collective childcare, to alternative forms of health care, seemed to promise a sense of what Gramsci thought of as a counter-hegemonic culture.[4] We learned the importance of developing a community which could sustain us morally and spiritually, and so to temper our sense of what could be achieved through individual will and resolve alone. It also meant more fully acknowledging the need I had of others. This was not easy to admit: like other men I had been brought up to be self-sufficient and independent, and acknowledging need had become identified with weakness. In my twenties I could barely accept need even in my closest loving relationships; later, when talk of love was challenged as inherently exclusive and possessive, I could comfortably avoid the issue. It took time for me to realize that I could recognize my need for a group of others more easily than within my individual relationships. I was more scared of intimacy. I was brought up to withhold my love, to treat it as some kind of precious commodity which I had to keep safely in reserve. In a strange way I had learned to feel easier and more protected in a group situation. In a group I could achieve a certain degree of power and status for myself. I also learned something about the difficulties of individuality. For all the talk of individualism in middle-class culture, it is often our very individuality which we have been forced to forsake. In the commune we had to work to create an atmosphere in which people felt capable of sharing themselves, and it was hard not to feel judged and tested whenever we opened our mouths. Schooling has left a deep scar in most of us, and our words and language have been moulded in the image of individual achievement. Often we are so used to having the 'appropriate' responses in situations that we have lost a sense of our own thoughts and feelings. At school we learn to do the things we are good at. We cannot afford the ridicule and abuse that awaits failure, and we assume that this individual achievement will inevitably bring happiness. We implicitly learn to judge ourselves through external standards: we think we should be happy because we have done well at school; or a woman feels she should be happy because she has got a husband and family — what every woman is supposed to want. There must be something wrong with us if we do not feel this way. In fact, those are processes of self-estrangement, and an analysis of the workings of educational institutions was an integral part of the libertarian critique of the early 1970s.[5]

Consciousness-raising challenges the individualism of bourgeois society, by helping us to understand how much of our experience is shared. It shifts our sense of individual responsibility for whatever misery and unhappiness we experience. As a practice developed within the women's movement, it has also proved useful for men, but it can be particularly strange and unsettling for men, as we are not brought up to value our emotional and personal experience. It is easy to leave emotional work to women we are sexually involved with, for masculinity has been so closely identified with rationality in bourgeois culture that we are encouraged to split ourselves from our emotions and feelings as if they were sources of unreason. We instinctively protect the purity of our reason, by growing up assuming a superiority of 'masculine' reason over 'feminine' emotion.

Foucault helps us to understand this process historically in *Madness and Civilization*.[6] Foucault's account carries a particular significance for masculinity, since it can help to explain the dominance of reason in modern Western culture and the subordination of a femininity which is identified with nature, with emotions and feelings, with desire. In holding on to our rationality, which was identified with our intellectuality, we have defined the only legitimate source of knowledge. In holding tight to reason as the source of civilization, we distanced and separated ourselves from our 'animal natures', which could no longer be a source of understanding or knowledge. This is as much a reference to a social and historical process as an ongoing way of being for men. In this way we can use Foucault's work to learn that the modern identification of masculinity with a denuded and disembodied conception of reason was established although Foucault is unable to develop his insight in this direction. Kant gave this conception of reason its clearest definition within his moral theory,[7] and it created a framework from which socialist moral theory was rarely to escape.

Men are brought up to intellectualize experience. Our language becomes a weapon that is forged for self-assertion. We prove our masculinity through defending ourselves physically and verbally, though this is mediated in different ways through our class experience. Our speech within a middle-class experience often has little connection to our embodied experience, as we get so used to using it to conceal our feelings and vulnerability so that we can make out in the public realm of work. This latter became an issue in many men's groups. People discovered that they did not know how to use language to open up contact with others. Sometimes some men dominated the group, doing their best to sustain it as an intellectual discussion in which they could feel safe and secure. It is sad to realize that we have used language to protect ourselves against being put down by others for so many years, that we no longer know how to express ourselves directly and honestly. We create a distinction between talking about emotions and expressing them. To say this is not to deny the centrality of expressing our emotions through speech, but it is to recognize that we cannot simply 'decide' to do it as an issue of will. Men find this especially painful to acknowledge, since we have been brought up to feel that our will and determination will bring us everything that we need and want for ourselves. I think this helps to explain the openness in the mid 1970s of some men interested in men's consciousness-raising to the more expressive forms of therapy like gestalt, encounter and bioenergetics.

I had spent years being interested in therapy intellectually, without doing any myself. I had got fed up with being so understanding of other people's problems. This was often the way I had got close to people, though it rarely left me with satisfying relationships, and was a way of protecting myself against my fear of rejection. I was trapping myself into a miserable position of being 'a nice guy you want as a friend but you don't want to sleep with'. It was misery and desperation that led me to seek therapy for myself; but it was difficult to reconcile with my desire to live more of my politics. I had come back to England needing a different kind of political experience, and joined a group of people hoping to move to East London to involve ourselves in community and factory politics. We were impatient with the abstract critiques of interventionism[8] that seemed to limit the politics of the libertarian Left. We consciously identified with the practice of the Liverpool Big Flame group,[9] and involved ourselves intensively in the political struggles in East London. Fired by working-class resistance to the Heath Government, we became militants. But we did not want to forsake our sexual politics. It was harder to acknowledge the importance of individual therapy and our learning from the growth movement in these initial years. It was left within the private realm, at least for a while.

STRUGGLING IN EVERY AREA OF OUR LIVES

Our commitment to sexual politics gradually became more attenuated and more rhetorical as we involved ourselves in community and factory politics in East London. It continued to inform our theoretical understanding, but it was hard to sustain for ourselves as we settled into the intense routines of political work. Again this was a process were were barely aware of. I was teaching while active in the Fords group, a Big Flame group of activists and workers which was doing agitational work at the Dagenham plant. For the most part we listened and learned from the ongoing struggles over working life there, and did our best to produce leaflets written with workers anxious to provide information about what was going on in different parts of the plant. We helped people to their own voice, and did our best not to speak for them. We were learning about a new generation of working-class struggle that seemed to challenge prevailing traditions of political activity.[10] Most of the workers thought we must be students, or at least pretty crazy to get up so early in the morning to be at the gates, when we could have stayed in bed. It is true it was not easy, and often we were tired and exhausted, especially since some of us were holding down other jobs too. But these were exciting times, when we were more than rewarded by the level of activity in the plant.

At another level, however, it was very difficult to sustain a sense of self, or our own needs and wants when we were daily aware of the crushing reality of assembly-line production and class struggle. Our individual concerns seemed to pale into insignificance, and I am sure this is why people who engage in this kind of political work are inevitably pushed towards a form of workerism. In this we reproduce some of the deeper features of bourgeois moral culture: just as we were brought up to identify ourselves with work and individual achievement and to subordinate our own desires, needs and wants to them, so politics became 'political work' which demanded even more rigorous subordination. The very activism that the Protestant ethic seems to encourage came to dominate, as I felt more and more incapable of using any time and space I had for myself. I did not know what to do with myself, and was only happy when I was active, felt driven and did not know how to stop. There always seemed important things to do, and this undermined any sense of whatever individual limits we might have had. We thought we should be able to meet whatever demand presented itself. What is more, the very critique of the hierarchy of skills that we shared meant that we felt we should be able to learn everything, to be as familiar with the printing process as with plumbing and house repairs. Because we resisted the idea that people might just have different skills and talents, people did gain confidence and skill, but it also meant that people with particular expertise tended to hold back, not wanting to use their knowledge as a source of power and control. People were under constant pressure to acquire the same level of skill by means of will and determination, but we became aware of these issues only gradually, and they recurred in Red Therapy.

It is difficult now to reproduce the feelings of this period up to 1976. Similar notions of militancy still dominate in the Left. There was also enormous experimentation in sexual relationships, especially to do with the critique of monogamy. We tended to feel that if we were open and honest with each other, we should be able to work through problems in relationships. But we also retained a strong sense of moralism, which encouraged us to suppress feelings of jealousy and hurt because we did not want to curtail people's newly discovered freedom. By doing our best to control feelings we felt 'unacceptable' – and I suppose our very activism helped keep some of them in check – we were reproducing a different version of the self-denial that dominates bourgeois moral culture. Red Therapy grew out of these contradictions in our experience, as we became dimly aware that the practice of our politics was undermining a sense of our own needs. Even though we wanted our political activity to reflect our personal struggles for a more human life, political life was coming to have an oppressive reality of its own. Need and desperation brought us to therapy, for we needed a different kind of space in which to work out what was happening to us. We realized that we could no longer control all the levels of feelings within us: we were at a point of crisis.

At the same time, we were gradually distancing ourselves from Big Flame, in which it was barely acceptable to discuss men's sexual politics seriously, let alone therapy. Therapy was dismissed in the usual way as a form of self-indulgence, and although at some level the dismissal was connected with the discussions around Leninism and organization that were taking place at the time,[11] the connection was impossible to articulate. Therapy was just something that some people in the East London group did, but it could be no part of the politics of the organization. At the time this did not worry us.

Red Therapy originally got together out of a public meeting in London in 1973 about the relationship between therapy and politics, and where discontent at the individualistic assumptions implicit in the Growth Movement was expressed. A group of us wanted to separate the techniques that had emerged from the work of Reich, Perls, Lowen, Schutz, Kellerman and others[12] from those assumptions. We did not believe that people were totally responsible for the situation they found themselves in. At the same time we recognized that the generalized critique of individual responsibility on the Left was often misplaced, and we felt therapy could be used to explore the different ways we can avoid responsibility as individuals. Growth Movement therapies had all developed in critical relationship to the institutionalization of traditional Freudian analysis, and at the time we were less interested in exploring these interconnections than in learning how we could use the techniques for ourselves. We had learned about the value of therapy for ourselves, so we were impatient with critiques that were not prepared to appropriate what could be positively learned. We recognized that techniques are never neutral, though we did less work upon the philosophical assumptions these different approaches carry. What drew us originally was the critique of the orthodox relationship between 'therapist' and 'patient' and hence the possibility of developing a less hierarchical and more democratic form of therapy. We appreciated the importance of bodily expression and the need to demystify the traditional therapeutic relationship, while finding alternative ways of dealing with transference and projection. Initially we wanted to develop a form of self-help therapy that was not blind to the workings of class and sexual relations of power, and so we felt free to transform techniques as need be within a renewed framework.

Red Therapy went through different stages. It began as a mixed group and later it separated into a women's group and a men's group. Some of the history and methods of working have been written up in Sheila Ernst and Lucy Goodison's *In Our Own Hands – A Book of Self-Help Therapy*. I want to discuss some of the political and moral assumptions we made and the ways these were gradually transformed.

WORKING ON OURSELVES

In the early days we worked at therapy with the same kind of intensity that characterized our political work, tending to think of it in terms of release and expression. We would encourage each other to 'get in touch with our feelings', and because we were so used to holding in our feelings and rationalizing our experience, this was not easy. We are so used to measuring our feelings, making sure of their fairness and justice, that we resist acknowledging them, even to ourselves. It takes time to learn that our feelings do not have to be rational, that it is not simply a matter of proving we are right. Gradually we realize that we harbour all kinds of resentments towards others which we very rarely express because we do not want to hurt them. It is easy to think that, if others knew the reality of our feelings, they would inevitably reject us and we would be left with even fewer friends than before.

Bourgeois culture, and our Protestant inheritance, teach us to hide our natures, to think of them as wicked. This is why we do our best to distance ourselves from our feelings and desires, lest they threaten the relationships we have set up with others. This is part of why it can be so hard to acknowledge the resentments we feel for others: it is hard not to feel that this would reveal what brutes we really are. It is partly because we have so little ongoing relationship with these resentments that we so easily feel overwhelmed as soon as we contact them. It takes time to accept that they are an integral part of our relations with others.

85

Through expressing them we can more easily give our relations with others more substance. We can also be plagued by feelings of 'unreality' in our relations without knowing how to identify what we can do about them, and therapy can help us to understand the importance of acknowledging these feelings without then judging ourselves for having them. But again, this is not something we can just decide to do: we often need the support of a group in which others are also entering into a better relationship with those aspects of themselves.

Certain forms of expressive therapy can be seen as a development of earlier libertarian conceptions of honesty in relationships. You can reach a point where it is difficult to express yourself honestly. Sometimes this is because other feelings get triggered which do not have their source in the present. This is something communal house-meetings often find difficult to handle. Bringing our feelings into the open does not always clear them or help us feel better about each other. It is easy to sink one's resentments, living out our images of ourselves, say as a non-sexist person. So people would deny their sexist feelings, living up to some ideal they had established for themselves. Often in collective experience we do not want to know the resentment, fear, anger and disgust because these challenge the images we have of ourselves. In my Somerville experience we had little sense of a process through which we could go to contact these difficult and unwelcome feelings. We assumed we would be trapped by them, having little understanding of how you could work on your feelings as an aspect of working on yourself. This was the importance of therapy which could theoretically and practically explore these processes. It was no longer enough for us to develop an understanding of our feelings. We needed to learn ways of working with them and so bring us into fuller and deeper contact with ourselves.

Red Therapy became the place where we 'worked on our feelings'. This threatened to be a segmented activity, especially as not everyone in the political group shared a sense of its importance. Sometimes we would wait for the therapy sessions to deal with tensions developing between us. We tended to think of it as a place where we could get in touch with our suppressed feelings we had not allowed ourselves to acknowledge, let alone express. In exploring them, we can often discover new aspects of ourselves, as well as recognize the personal and social processes through which we have forsaken the full range of our emotions. We tended to see emotions not simply as mental events, but also as bodily experience. We need a recognition that emotions and feelings have a suppressed personal and social history, that it takes time and energy to connect to feelings. Wilhelm Reich recognized how emotions are often held in the ways we hold our muscles, so that bodily movement can be an important aspect of a therapeutic process. So, for instance, if a woman is getting in touch with the anger she feels for her husband's thesis, we might focus upon establishing a situation which could help her express this, possibly dramatically through going through the motions of ripping up his thesis. This might be a way of getting inside and exploring these feelings, since it helps provide some kind of structure for them. This can be an overwhelmingly powerful experience for a woman who has rarely let herself touch these sources of her anger and frustration. Being able to express some of this anger, rather than simply talking about it, becomes a way of getting in touch with sources of strength, because it can shift the understanding of a whole period of life. The very expression of emotions becomes difficult when male superiority is partly built upon the suppression of emotionality, and this is why therapy can be so subversive, especially if we have been brought up to assume that rationality is to be automatically defined in opposition to emotion and desire. Emotions are related to beings who cannot think and therefore cannot work things out 'rationally'.

This is one of the powerful mechanisms through which the capitalist social order is presented to us as a 'normal' and 'rational' one. We learn to suppress our emotions as 'unreasonable', 'inappropriate' and 'irrational'. So as children we could be told 'Your dad has to go out and earn money so there is no point – it's just silly – wishing that he could spend more time playing with you.' In a similar way, Susan can be made to feel that David's thesis is so important to the future well-being of the whole family that she is being 'irrational' in wanting him to do more housework and childcare, if she feels angry or upset at him. She risks being put down as an 'emotional and irrational woman', if she cannot see that the whole future of the family rests on his getting on in his career. If she is also working outside the home she might also feel bitter that she has to get up early to work every day and also get up at night whenever the children wake because she 'understands them better'. She supports the family on the basis of a belief in 'equality' because it is generally said that she 'wouldn't just want to be a housewife'. Therefore she feels trapped. Whenever she gets upset or feels desperate at having to get up at 7 in the morning, travel 1½ hours to work and get home at 6.45 in the evening to start cooking dinner, she is told 'This is what you wanted ... you always wanted to work and have a life of your own.' In this situation it becomes difficult for her to say: 'I can't complain, since it isn't his fault that I could only get a job on the other side of town.' Or else: 'There's no point in complaining, or getting upset: that doesn't change the situation' or 'It's no good my feeling sorry for myself; I suppose that I got myself in this mess.' As the saying goes, 'there is no point in crying over spilt milk'. These are just some of the ways women learn to rationalize feelings, to assume it is useless to express them since they only open themselves up to ridicule. These processes are firmly embedded in sexual relations of power and subordination, and are an integral aspect of the workings of these relationships.

In Red Therapy we did our best to work with the understandings of feminism. A politically-conscious therapy was not simply a matter of 'getting in touch with your feelings' about a situation, as if they existed in an untouched realm of their own. These feelings were part of a complicated history of marriage and femininity, involving relations of power not only within the family but also within the larger society. If we were to validate the contradictions at the heart of so much experience, we had to recognize, for instance, how the culture places women in a bind making it hard for them to feel they can be both a 'good mother' and have a job outside the home. Ambiguous feelings need to be explored, since it is one thing to resolve a situation intellectually and another to have worked it through emotionally. Setting up a gestalt situation in which Susan has to talk directly to a pillow representing David can help her to acknowledge and explore the different levels of feeling she has. Expressing her anger can help her contact feelings of need or loss which she might never have explored. This does not make it easy to work out her relationship in her life with David, but it can help her to a certain clarity about herself. It is not simply that our energy is being taken up with suppressing these feelings; our full range of emotions and feelings has a much more integral relationship to our identity and individuality than structuralist theories, which are tied to rationalistic conceptions of language, would help us to acknowledge. In regaining anger, we are regaining a part of ourselves. We also become aware of the ways in which our individuality has been crippled and our sense of self distorted.

Therapy is a process. Within Red Therapy it took time to learn that therapy is not simply a matter of releasing feelings which can help people transform their relationship with themselves. Marx never develops this insight. We not only have relationships with others but also with ourselves, and with different parts of ourselves, our emotions, feelings, body, dreams, fantasies, sexuality. Different societies can encourage us to discount these various aspects of our experience and so limit our relationship to ourselves. These are also ways of appropriating our power and making us serve ends which are not our own. For instance, in Susan's situation she is not simply developing insight into her situation, discovering that she was really angry at her husband, although she has never been given a chance to express it. She also learns about the social relationships of power which make it difficult for her to acknowledge her anger, let alone express it. In validating her emotions she is learning to validate her experience of life more generally. Therapy can help her 'own her own anger', giving a fuller, more substantial sense of reality to her life as well as a fuller sense of her own power. In learning to trust our anger we are learning to trust important aspects of ourselves. Rather than being a form of irrationalism, it is a challenge to a conception of rationality which ties it so closely to intellectuality and which would systematically deny our emotions and bodily feelings as important sources of knowledge. Socialist politics has been slow to learn this because of its implicit acceptance of these notions of rationality. This is equally true of Lacanian attempts to interpret psychoanalysis according to this rationalist tradition, in which conceptions of language are substituted for notions of the mind. Those who argue for the social construction of identity would have us accept the belief that individuality is primarily constituted through language.[13]

Rather than help people clarify their feelings of anger and

rage against the ways they are treated, socialist politics has too often reproduced this very denial and subordination of these feelings through its tendency to identify emotion with irrationality and the politics of the Right. Right-wing politics has been able to develop unchallenged, as socialism has become too tied with a narrow intellectualism. And the Left has also been slow to develop a critical discussion of the new forms of therapy, which has allowed a narrow individualism to develop in the Growth Movement. There has been relatively little grasp within the Growth Movement of Reich's attempts to look at the mass sources of repression and neurosis.[14] Consequently Growth Movement therapy can narrow people's understandings by focusing all our feelings into our personal relationships, as if we can only have feelings about other people. For instance, a teacher might feel frustrated and angry at having to teach large classes, and a therapist might well expect this anger to crystallize personally in relation to the headmaster of the school. In a similar way, a secretary who is angry at her boss's treatment of her would probably be encouraged to see this as individual anger for her boss. Sometimes it will be seen as 'her problem with authority', which then traces back to her relationship with her father. Less often will therapy, as it is constituted in the Growth Movement, be able to focus upon a social and structural relationship of power and subordination and allow this to be the object of the anger and frustration. It will then be easy for the secretary to feel that her problem is in taking orders from others, and she must learn to cope with it herself. Relationships are personalized, as though they simply flow out of the individual qualities of the people concerned. This can often reproduce a basic liberal understanding of social relationships. Of course, there is still the issue of how she will learn to cope with a situation she is powerless to transform. But it will make a difference if her feelings of frustration and rebellion are validated, rather than simply seen as 'her problem'. Increasingly, feminist therapy has developed to deal with issues of this kind.[15]

In Red Therapy we did our best to remain aware of the material contradictions within which people live. One example of this would be the position of teachers. We questioned libertarian assumptions, according to which people could avoid collusion in the prevailing relations of power only by creating a life outside the institutions of state power, because they seemed to create their own form of isolationism. At least in theory we recognized the contradictory situation of teachers who wanted to relate to their pupils in more democratic ways. This was not a situation that simply depended on an individual will, but on seeking the support of others who were struggling for the same thing. This can involve getting together with other teachers to consider classroom practice, whilst doing our best to transform those relationships in which we do have some control. If socialist politics acknowledges the importance of developing a politics of education,[16] it has rarely developed a corresponding sensitivity to the emotional strains involved. Too easily it sees socialist education in terms of a reformed curriculum or a correct individual practice, rather than a contradictory transformation of relationships. In Red Therapy we wanted to work out how people could survive these contradictions. To do this we first had to acknowledge that we had feelings of anger, frustration, guilt, responsibility and inadequacy which neither a professional setting nor socialist politics had helped us to explore. Often we prove ourselves 'good teachers' through being able to contain these feelings, too vulnerable and embarrassed to share them with others. We are unaware of the continuing influence they had on our relationships, and learn to put a good face on things.

The early years of the Growth Movement were locked into an ideology of therapy as the immediate release of emotion. The general suspicion of intellectuality was often justified, since our ability to rationalize our experience had become so extensive that it blocked our access to our emotionality. It was as if our very speech had become disconnected from our lived experience. It took time for a renewed conception of reason to find its place within a developing understanding of human experience. But therapy in this period did help us acknowledge feelings and emotions that we were not supposed to have. Because we, and in particular the men, had so little ongoing relationship with our emotions, it was easy to feel that if we really allowed our anger to emerge it would destroy all our relationships. Similarly we could feel that if our hurt and vulnerability were allowed to surface, we would never again be able to recover our strength. It took time also to realize the way in which we can use one feeling to displace or hide another: as men we often get irritated or angry to fend off our hurt and sadness, and it is only when this anger has been expressed that we have access to the other feelings. But this is difficult to do in a society which only admires strength in men, which is why it can be so challenging to discover our weakness and vulnerability as a different kind of strength. Our masculinity has involved the suppression of significant parts of our experience because they are not 'acceptable'. A great deal is at stake for men when we share our vulnerability, when we acknowledge our need for others.

Therapy can give a teacher a context in which to explore the contradictions of teaching. This is not simply to see therapy as a question of release. For men, it might be important to be able to acknowledge that you cannot cope. We might feel anger at the pupils we teach, though be incapable of expressing it in the teaching situation because we feel the injustice of doing so within the relationship of power. Through exploring our feelings, we reached more understanding of the expectations we set upon ourselves. This took us back to our families, to realizing the ways we are automatically living out our fathers' expectations and hopes for us, or continually proving ourselves to images of our parents without even knowing it. This might have been what took us into teaching in the first place. Even so, it is difficult to give a sense of how these feelings are explored in therapy or show how this can change the ways we are with children and other teachers in the school. Therapy could involve acknowledging the attachments we feel for particular children and the loss we feel when they leave, or the resentment we feel for some of them if they have resisted learning anything. These feelings can lead us to explore our relationship with our siblings, or else simply to acknowledge feelings such as anger, loss, resentment and need that we are not supposed to feel, given the notions of objectivity and professionalism that are part of the official liberal ideology of the school. We could also need to vent our anger at the way some children are treated by other teachers, in a way which would lose ourselves our jobs if we were to vent this anger in the school. Not only does this deepen our understanding of the ways we behave, but it can help change the ways we are with others through giving us a closer relationship to our emotions and feelings.

LOSING OURSELVES

Even within the East London Big Flame group during the mid 1970s, it was difficult to give much priority to therapy. In a very real sense we lived for our politics. Our political activity was intensely exciting, but it could not last, because we were giving too much of ourselves. Even the university teaching I spent time and energy on could not be given much recognition in the public arena of discussion. Political activity had come to occupy the centre of our lives, and our different work situations existed only to make it possible. I could accept this since, by now, I had lost a sense of the importance of teaching and learning: it was something I did to earn money. Even if at some level I never fully accepted this self-definition, I was aware of how much more deeply I was learning through active engagement in the Ford's group, even about issues of social and moral theory that I had spent years relating to intellectually. We tended to think that theory would inevitably flow from practice, but we never really had the kind of time and space to draw more theoretical and practical meaning. Our political work continually offered us new imperatives, and so came to dominate other areas of our lives which we could then only pay lip service to. As long as we tended to think of therapy as emotional expression, it helped us deal with the pressures and intensity of this life. But it left little space for therapy as exploration. But therapy has its own inner logic, and it encouraged us to ask different questions of the political work.

The notion of 'discovering your own needs', current in the Growth Movement, carried a particular resonance for us. Even though we were well aware of the individualism this fosters, and of the ways it too easily reproduces capitalist values, it also reminded us of something important which we were near to losing. How is it possible to sustain a sense of your individual needs and wants while you are engaged in 'political work'? Even though we were trying self-consciously to make a better world in which we could enjoy more human relationships, we found that the very intensity of political activity was undermining that sense of personal wants and needs. We were in danger of becoming shadows of ourselves as we reproduced the ideology of work, in our case designed to guarantee our subordination to 'political work' which has always been at the heart of the general self-denial of bourgeois culture. The libertarian political critique of individualism which had fostered a dualistic opposition between 'individualism' and 'collectivism'[17] left no space for any notion of a creative individuality which could remain as a positive critique of possessive individualism. What is more, therapy helped further to question some of the moralistic assumptions of libertarian politics. We were being hurt unknowingly by the very standards we had accepted for ourselves. We learned to acknowledge our feelings of hurt, rejection and jealousy and the deep sources they had within the history of our relationships within the family. These relationships which we had considered long past had continued to have a deep but unacknowledged effect upon us. This was difficult ground. We could not simply banish our histories as we assumed a new identity of 'militants'. So much Leftist analysis leaves us feeling unsure, guilty and ashamed of so much of our middle-class backgrounds that we do our best to kill our own histories. We learned in therapy that our histories are not so easily banished. They demand to be acknowledged, and our feelings worked through, if we are somehow to settle our relationship with our pasts.

Political activism tends to reproduce some of the implicit activism which has been an abiding aspect in the masculinism of bourgeois culture. We are told that we always have to make ourselves busy, if we are not to be accused of being 'lazy good-for-nothings'. Life is an incessant competition in which we have continually to prove ourselves. This is no different in socialist politics. For the most part competition rules. This has an important connection to the work ethic which is given a particular form within political militancy. We can find ourselves with an increasingly thin and attenuated sense of individual self as we come to see politics as a future-oriented goal with barely any connection to our personal and social needs. This reached a crisis point for many of us with the sharp reversal of working-class struggle in 1976. We could not recognize what was happening. In an inexplicable way we had become dependent on continuing struggle to give substance to our own lives.

As the East London Big Flame group was splitting from Big Flame in 1976 over issues of feminism and political organization, so also were we reworking our conception of therapy. We were no longer satisfied with the notions of group therapy we had developed. We had tended to put too much emphasis upon emotional expression and release. We needed more sense of our limits, of what we could expect for ourselves: we had undermined our sense of having any individual limits at all, through the intensity of political activity. Our lives had become over-socialized as we lost any sense of whatever individual needs and wants we might have; our lives had become defined in terms of our political activity. In a strange way we needed to restore more sense of an inner life – we literally needed more space for ourselves. We needed therapies which could help us also contain our energies, which understood that you have to hold feelings to give them a chance to form and deepen. I felt more critical of forms of primal therapy which could leave people feeling emotionally and spiritually empty. We also needed to discover the individualities we brought with us into the group, and this led many of us to become more sympathetic to individual therapy, feeling that we needed the deeper and more sustained exploration of self that group therapy, for all its importance, can find it difficult to give. We were more aware of the processes through which we could lose ourselves. People in non-monogamous sexual relationships would acknowledge that they were losing themselves, in going on meeting the demands not to be jealous and possessive within relationships. We developed more scepticism about how much we could cope with, and there was a growing sense that we had to rediscover firmer roots in ourselves, and that we had to rediscover a different sense of politics. The period coincided with the close of an intense time of class struggle in the early 1970s. We had put so much of ourselves into our political work, that it sometimes felt as if there was little left of us. Other comrades had burned themselves out before, and we did not think we were any different.

The women had already decided they wanted to meet separately in Red Therapy. Difficult issues to do with sexuality and the break-up of relationships within the group had emerged, and they needed a different context to be worked on. In any case, feminism had been the critical factor in our break with the other Big Flame groups, especially as it related to conceptions of political organization. Meeting separately also gave roots to our politics by giving us firmer grounding for our sexual identities.

Because some of us as men were increasingly sceptical of the militancy we had slipped into, if not the kind of political work we were doing, it was important to explore the relationship of these to notions of masculinity. We already had some idea of how our masculinity related to the ease with which we could adopt a 'politics of self-denial' and so could suppress and forsake aspects of ourselves. I wanted to explore these issues theoretically, since they had a relationship to the traditions of socialism we had inherited. It was time for a change.

LEARNING WHAT TO DO WITH THE PIECES

Therapy helped me to understand how often I have given to others the very things that I needed for myself, the love and understanding I found it hard to feel I deserved. It is difficult to grow up within a moral culture so deeply influenced by Protestantism, without being threatened by an underlying sense of personal worthlessness and, as Max Weber understood, it is through constant activity that we can assuage the feelings.[18] Within socialist politics too, we often live out our own version of this ethic in a private and unacknowledged way. We are trapped by the constant need to be active, with little sense of how this is continually reproduced within the moral culture. This is experienced in a particular way by men who are brought up to be self-sufficient, to feel we need very little from others. We become scared of discovering our needs for love and support, lest they overwhelm everything else in our lives. Being aware of how long we have held them in check, and how little ongoing relationship we have been helped to develop with them, we become wary of any contact with them. This connects to how threatened we can feel by the emotionality of women. Too scared of being reminded of something we have lost for ourselves, we can anxiously assume the needed and protected shoulder. So it is often difficult to accept the love and support that others are ready to give us. At some level we continue to feel they are undeserved, or else we can devalue them by assuming that they have to be worthless if they are offered to us; though it is also true that, as men, we often become hopelessly dependent and needy when a woman threatens to leave because she wants something different for herself. All our suppressed dependency needs express

96

themselves at once. This can itself be experienced as over-whelmingly controlling. As men it is often hard to realize that the damage is done and that there is nothing we can do to make the situation better. This is painful to learn.

Why is it so hard to value our feelings, thoughts and emotions? Our moral culture carries a deep unease about bodily experience, seeing our emotions and feelings as aspects of an animal nature which needs to be controlled. Reich was important in challenging the workings of these cultural assumptions within psychoanalysis itself.[19] Sexual politics can challenge these same assumptions through helping us to validate our own individual experience and making us aware of the different processes through which we are invalidated and undermined. Therapy can also help us understand the ways in which we can collude in this process. The strength of competitive institutions, for instance, can make us compare ourselves with others, so that we feel what we do is never good enough. We grow up being very hard on ourselves: we protect ourselves against the judgement of others by putting ourselves down first. Activist politics in particular can make us constantly aware that we are never doing enough: rather than helping us value our efforts, it makes us live plagued by the feelings of how much still needs doing. And unless we learn both ways of coping with these feelings and learning of their sources theoretically, we can be left in a constant state of tension. Not only are we hard upon ourselves, but we can be constantly critical of others for not doing more. We can move out of touch with the everyday realities of other people's lives and the difficulties they have with families and children. We can lose a sense of what we are struggling for, which is a more equal and just form of human relationship.

Doing therapy made us question the assumptions we made about what matters to people in their lives. Therapy can help challenge a narrow economism in political practice, because it recognizes the importance of sexuality within people's lives and the difficulties of sustaining a relationship. Sometimes we could express these insights, as when a woman who was married to a Ford's worker wrote a leaflet, which we put into the Dagenham plant, about the ways in which the organization of the plant, particularly shift work, dominated the family's life, including their sexual relationship. This brought an immediate response.

We could understand this more as we acknowledged how hard it was to cope with our own lives, as we learned to share the contradictions in our own feelings. It meant acknowledging, for instance, how fragmented we felt between our different activities, how much we hated getting up in the morning to go to the factory gates, how hurt we felt as we were left to sleep alone in our multiple relationships. We no longer assumed that our feelings had to be rational to be acceptable to ourselves or others in the group or that they were the whole story. Often it was only through expressing these different feelings that we could get closer to ourselves as individuals. We developed a sense of the importance of acknowledging our feelings, however irrational and unacceptable they might appear politically and morally. Accepting our feelings as they were became an integral part of developing a less moralistic conception of personal change. Usually it is only when we feel morally justified in challenging the ways that, say, our parents treat us, that we are able to express our resentments towards them. We are so used to measuring and qualifying our feelings, and so concerned to be just in our responses, that we can barely acknowledge the depth of resentments we often feel. Reich recognized the importance of contacting this layer of feelings if we are to challenge the falsity and unreality we feel in so many of our relationships with others.[20] If we constantly avoid these feelings, our relationships will inevitably lack depth. Our politics have to learn the significance of our inner lives. We can barely do this if we are trapped into seeing the 'inner' as a mirror reflection of the 'outer'. If such a prevailing conception helps us recognize that we are working through unresolved conflicts in our inner lives, it makes it difficult to accept how working on our inner lives can affect our activities and relationships. Granting an autonomy and independence to our 'inner lives' can avoid a narrow reductionism, but it can also leave us with a fragmented conception of our experience and a conception of psychology which maintains the usual split between thought/emotions and activity/ practice. We have to look away from Lacan's work if we are not to be trapped within a rationalist framework which does not question the abstract notion of individuality we have tended to inherit within socialist traditions that assume the 'pliability' of human nature, that if the mode of production changes, so will the nature of people. This is the notion of 'humanism' that Althusser fails to critique. He produces a Marxist version of a rationalist conception which would want to see individuals as 'only an ensemble of universal traits'. We can look back to Sartre's *Anti-Semite and Jew* for a clearer sense of what is at issue:

> The democrat, like the scientist, fails to see the particular case; to him the individual is only an ensemble of universal traits. It follows that his defence of the Jew saves the latter as a man and annihilates him as a Jew ... he fears that the Jew will acquire a consciousness of the Jewish collectivity – just as he fears that a 'class consciousness' may awaken in the worker. His defence is to persuade individuals that they exist in an isolated state ... [he] wishes to destroy him as a Jew and leave nothing to him, but the man, the abstract and universal subject of the rights of man and the rights of the citizen.
> Thus here may be detected in the most liberal democrat a tinge of anti-Semitism; he is hostile to the Jew to the extent that the latter thinks of himself as a Jew.[21]

Therapy helped me come to terms with my Jewishness. I could not simply avoid my feelings about this, though I still feel uneasy about them. I learned how I had been made to compromise aspects of myself, my history and my culture through needing to be acceptable to others through the social relations of schooling. I encountered these feelings as I was working through feelings about my father. This also forced a reconsideration of basic issues of Marxist theory, which I need to refer to before returning to a more personal voice.

Marx's conception of the proletariat as a 'universal class', carrying the liberation of 'humanity' with its struggles, has made it hard to consider issues of sexuality and ethnicity within Marxism. Marx's ambiguous feelings about his own ethnicity surely had something to do with this. In his conception of the 'universal class' he carries Hegel's legacy rather than questioning it. Althusser continues this in his conception of the proletariat.[22] Marx was rightly critical of the bourgeois character of 'the rights of man' and the 'rights of the citizen' – in the *Communist Manifesto* he says that those who talk of the 'rights of man' must 'confess that by "individual" they mean no other person than the bourgeois, than the middle-class owner of property'[23] – but he never develops the idea. Marx is blind to issues of sexual and racial oppression in the unitary conception he adopts of the 'proletariat', and these are issues we have to tackle for ourselves. The feminism of the early 1970s learned from the Black movement the crucial importance of validating people's experience and valuing a shared culture and history, if notions of 'individuality' are to be reformulated.[24] Learning of the influences of the social relations of masculinity and femininity, of the relations of power and subordination within which we grow up to gain our sense of identity, transforms the sense of individuality we inherit within bourgeois culture. In helping us escape from the false dualities of rationalist traditions, sexual politics can be so helpful. In order to sustain a notion of individuality which fully recognizes our need for more equal and loving relationships with others, we must restore a dialectic between the exploration of individual needs, wants and desires and the critique of prevailing social relations of power and subordination.

We need to learn that the social and historical sources of the division between the 'inner' and the 'outer' lie in the relationship between Protestantism and capitalism. Protestantism fosters a notion of the 'true self' existing invulnerable within our 'inner lives', making it difficult for us to appreciate our need to express ourselves in the activities and relationships we live. Therapy can help this process, in restoring to us a sense of our own histories. I also think it can represent a profound challenge to structuralist accounts of the way in which individuality is constituted through language. It helps question the implicit rationalism within this view and suggests a less moralistic conception of the ways people can change. It can also help us move beyond the view that people will change automatically with a change in the ownership of the means of production. Reich is still important in helping us think about this, even if he was too mechanical in his attempts to bring Marxism and psychoanalysis into closer relationship with each other. I think this will turn out to be a more sufficient criticism than his assumed 'biologism' which, in any case, is important in a renewed discussion of human needs.[25] We need a discussion of human needs which can recognize how deeply they are historically and socially influenced, without then forsaking them in thinking they are completely determined. Simone Weil attempts to do this in her discussion of bodily and spiritual needs,[26] and a critical awareness of therapy can help the process. It can help us become aware of the difficulties of fulfilling our own needs without at the same time challenging the prevailing social relations of power. This is to question the assumptions of the Growth Movement, whilst also learning from its critiques of traditional psychoanalysis in terms of its institutionalization and the relationship of power between analyst and patient it often fosters.

In the mid 1970s I went to the funeral of the father of a close friend. It triggered deep and unresolved feelings for me, partly about my own father's death when I was still young, partly about my feelings of Jewishness that I had never really resolved until the funeral. I had not realized how deeply these influences had formed me and still seemed to be drawing me. My socialism had not left room for me to consider my masculinity, let alone my ethnicity and the ways they might be related to each other. I was involved in a broader struggle and had in any case broken with the kind of suburban life which many of the people I had grown up with had chosen for themselves. I had barely thought about how Jewish tradition could have positively influenced my politics. More often it was an aspect to hide, rather than to feel proud of. Therapy brought me back to consider aspects of my relationship with my parents. I was somewhat shocked to discover how my parents continued to influence the ways I related to people, for instance how my resistance to committing myself in a relationship had to do with the fear of being invaded, which had childhood sources I barely acknowledged.

Though Marxism is a deeply historical theory, it can often discourage a recognition of our personal, sexual and ethnic histories. The only way that I seemed to be able to come to terms with my history was to acknowledge it more deeply. At this point a historically sensitive formulation of psychoanalysis can be crucial. This meant facing and living through and in part experiencing a personal history I had so studiously avoided. I discovered how I had developed such an intensely inner life as a young person because, after my father's death, I had lost any hope of being able to express myself fully in the family. My 'true self' lay hidden. Because of therapy I could now understand from my own experience the tension between the 'inner' and the 'outer' which Protestant culture has done so much to sustain. I had learned to suppress any negative hostile feelings in order to become a 'good boy', knowing that these resentments had to be kept to myself. I could not express the anger I felt at my father's death. I could barely name the feeling, since the culture made this inadmissible. There was the fear, so carefully manufactured within the culture, that if people knew what I was really feeling they would reject me. I was scared of discovering what I felt, since I wanted to be like everyone else. I learned to deal with my private fears and anxieties, doing my best to keep my feelings to myself. At some level I was ashamed of my Jewishness and ashamed of not having a father like the other boys at school. I did my best to be like them. Schooling helped me think that these differences were purely incidental and that my individuality could be secured through the cultivation of individual ability. It left me feeling split between an identity I developed to cope with school and my Jewish family. I learned to forsake integral aspects of my history, culture and identity. Immigrant children are probably still made to feel like this today. It is a subtle process of violation, in which we collude, in order to be accepted. This is something Adorno and Horkheimer eventually came to realize when they saw the Jews' very refusal to be assimilated as a welcome obstacle to the total integration of the 'administered world'.[27]

Shame eats the soul. It pushes you to become other than what you are, and it creates its own ring of constant fear. It is a powerful form of social control, though we barely acknowledge it because it works away in individual psyches. I was ashamed of showing more of myself, and I suppose this is why expressive forms of therapy came to hold such power for me. Working in groups can be a very significant escape from the private and individual confession, important as this is. It brings our emotional and bodily experience into the public and social arena from which it has been so firmly banished since 'the age of reason'. But we still need to create a language which can fully recognize the significance of our emotional and bodily experience, rather than one which subordinates it within a rationalist framework.[28] This would also involve a renewed framework for moral and social theory.

In denying aspects of ourselves, we are denying our power. This has been one of the important lessons of feminism and sexual politics. Women and gays refused to judge themselves by the standards of a patriarchal moral culture which constantly negated and invalidated their individual experience. This has involved a deep and conscious critique of liberalism, which has always wanted to present itself as standing for 'individuality' and 'freedom'. As we become more aware of the workings of our sexual, class and ethnic histories, we become suspicious of notions of 'individual freedom' which present freedom simply as a matter of rational choice between competing goals. Such notions make it difficult for us to deal with the deeper patterns in our relationships, to accept how bound we remain by our earlier childhood relationships. It was always difficult for me, for instance, to express my needs in my family, even to identify and name the sources of my unhappiness. My mother was left to bring up four small boys on her own, when I was barely five years old. A patriarchal society in the early 1950s made her feel this was an impossible task, since we would inevitably be dam-aged and incomplete, and she was anxious to make us feel that we had everything we could want. There was little space in which to mourn our father, since it was threatening to the task she had set. Hence we learned to be responsible before our time. Our childhood ended abruptly and, as boys, we were told by our mother's friends that we had to look after mum, and were now the 'men' in the family. We did not want to give our mother any more to worry about since we were constantly aware of how much she had to cope with anyway. We felt constantly grateful. It is partly because we were anxiously told by her how happy we were that it became difficult to acknowledge our sadness and misery, even to ourselves. Since she was only working so hard 'for us', it was impossible to feel our anger that she was not at home with us more. It seemed a totally unreasonable demand. In learning to 'make our feelings reasonable' or 'rational', we make them lose their clarity and definition. We cope through suppression. We never learn to experience our sense of loss. If we had expressed these feelings we would have been 'ungrateful'. We learned to bury them deep inside. They lost their voice.

If we each have our own histories, we also share them with others. So, for instance, many men share a history of being brought up to be independent and self-sufficient, closely to identify our sense of self with our intellectual rationality. Possibly it is because I experienced these connections so sharply and early, that they carry a particular significance for me. Because we see our experience mirrored in the organization of the larger structures of power, it can be difficult to experience the various ways that this upbringing has left us at odds with ourselves. We have little sense of the tension between our individual bodily sense of time, rhythm and space and the routines of the larger society we grow up to conform to. Our social theory has few ways of opening up such an investigation.

Heterosexual men often have an experience of feeling locked inside themselves, unable to share themselves even with those to whom they feel closest. Often this is a desperate silence, which might explain the attraction of more expressive forms of therapy for men who have got involved in consciousness-raising groups. This gives some kind of experiential background to people's involvement in therapy which already challenges the ways men in particular learn to distance ourselves from our own experience through humour, cynicism and irony, so that we never risk ourselves. We cannot be hurt. We learn to make ourselves invulnerable. We learn not to care too much or too deeply about anything, or else we throw ourselves intensively into activities. Feminism has challenged some of these patterns, and it often challenges men who have become isolated from any meaningful support outside their sexual relationship. Ill-prepared to meet challenges to traditional relationships, men have often reacted with violence and bitterness.[29] The scant attention which Marxism has given to our emotional and inner lives can sometimes encourage masculine insensitivity and blindness.

I do not think we have yet been able to develop the insights of Freud and Reich for the current renewal of socialist politics.[30] Relating psychoanalysis to a structured language of the unconscious tends to isolate its insights from our understanding of social relations of power and subordination. The Frankfurt School, before Lacan, understand how individuality has been fragmented within capitalist societies, so that it can no longer be assumed, but has to be struggled for.[31] Red Therapy and the individual therapy a number of us followed afterwards helped us work with our own fragmentation. Our political activity had left us in pieces. We had to recover a sense of our own needs for space, time and even privacy. We were no longer prepared to prove our political seriousness through forsaking individual needs, and so we needed to develop a critique of moralism and the politics of self-denial. We had critically to re-evaluate our political and moral theory. We had to learn to nourish ourselves and to find a place for the fulfilment of human needs, rather than their denial, in our socialism. I learned how hard it was to ask for what I needed, to change the balance of giving and receiving in a single relationship. We started on different ground trying to be more aware of the quality of our own experience and relationships, learning from the difficulties of changing our own relationships. In its own way this leaves us with a deeper grasp of the power of social relations as we come to terms with our own family and sexual histories, rather than suppress them out of guilt or shame. We learned, for instance, how hard it is to give to others in an honest and direct way, if we have not even learned to give to ourselves.

As we become more consciously aware of our own needs and of the ways in which we might fulfil them, we become less confident in our rationalist dismissal of religion and spirituality. If we want to understand rather than simply dismiss as having 'sold out' their convictions and experience, the vast numbers of people who did not find what they needed in politics in the 1970s, and turned to different forms of spirituality, we also have to see this as an aspect of the difficulties of Marxist theory to grasp modern, radical movements.[32] This can be related to the corresponding difficulties for socialist politics in learning deeply from the challenges of sexual politics and therapy to conceptions of personal and social change. People often looked away from socialist politics because it could no longer articulate what was meaningful and significant to them, and they did not want to forsake the only lives they had. We need to renew our interest in William Blake, Edward Carpenter, Wilhelm Reich and others who suggest a challenge to the ethnocentrism of a socialist politics unwilling to learn from the traditions of the East.[33] In their own ways they recognize issues of the fragmentation in individuality and the unreality and poverty of personal experience which has become so pressing in the 'administered world'. Opening these issues involves developing a critical relationship to Marxist traditions which have been blind to issues of sexuality, ethnicity, even ecology, which led the Frankfurt School initially to recognize the significance of Freud.[34] It involves learning more deeply about the relationship of Christianity and Marxism in Latin America and Poland. It means challenging traditions which identify socialism with state control and nationalization. It also means learning to take the relationship between therapy and politics seriously, even when to do this involves challenging readily inherited political assumptions.

I have tried to share an experience as well as raise more general theoretical issues. This is part of a commitment to learn from the social movements of our time, however difficult it is to voice what we learn within the established moral and political language of our culture.

Chapter Six

IDENTITY

A real challenge to liberal individualism involves not only challenging the image that is offered of the subject as a consumer encouraged to identify with the commodities they own, but also in understanding how precarious individuality actually is. This involves understanding the sources and processes through which we experience ourselves as fragmented or alienated. It has been an abiding strength of feminism to challenge a liberal moral and political theory that insisted that we are all persons equally able to live free and independent lives.

Women came to understand how they had been undermined in relationships of power and subordination. They had lost self-confidence and a sense of the worth of their abilities. They were left with a weakened sense of identity. Similarly, issues of identity became crucial in the sexual politics of gay men and lesbians. People learnt to take pride in themselves and their experience, no longer being prepared to feel shame for their desires and feelings. Many people learnt that failure to attend to our own process, and so in an important sense taking responsibility for your emotional life and relationships, creates a situation in which you are continually looking to someone else to complete your existence.

I want to show that, though men often have a strong sense of identity within the public realm, this is often at the cost of a more personal sense of self. Because there is a strong connection between learning our masculinity and learning to be impersonal, rational and objective, we are often left with a weakened sense of individual identity. Often we are left estranged from our feelings and emotions, learning to read off our feelings from the world around us. This produces a false sense of objectivity, and we become so identified with the goals and ends we set ourselves, especially at work, that we are often blind to our emotional needs. Feminism has crucially grasped the ways women have been rendered invisible within the public realm, but it has been rarely appreciated how men are often left invisible to themselves. This is a reason why, as men, we are constantly projecting our difficulties on to others. It is these processes that need to be explored.

POLITICS AND IDENTITY

Dena Attar in 'An open letter on anti-semitism and racism' published in *Spare Rib*, sustains an original insight of feminism when she says:

> [it] means working hard at trusting each other, at developing our own analysis and avoiding glib over-simplifications. I think it also means going back to the politics of experience in the sense of making sure our rhetoric *means* something to us and isn't just a form of words.[1]

This is an insight we often seem close to losing, especially when it comes to thinking about the relation of different forms of oppression to each other. We can find ourselves trapped into a language of externalized systems when we consider, for example the relationship between 'capitalism' and 'patriarchy'. A more personalized voice is often particularly difficult for men to hear, because we are brought up to have so little trust in ourselves as we learn we can only rely upon the impersonal workings of reason.

Because we develop a sense of self in relation to others in a deep-seated competitive relationship, we lose any sense of what it could mean to trust other men. We are so used to seeing other men as competitors who will not lose any opportunity to put us down, that we do not know how to begin in this process. This also makes a 'politics of experience' difficult for us since we are so used, as men, to using language as an instrument with which to defend ourselves. We put a distance between ourselves and our experience and we rarely use our language to bring us into closer contact with different parts of ourselves. When someone says to us that we have to be sure that 'our rhetoric means something to us and isn't just a form of words', it is difficult to know what this means. So much structuralist and post-structuralist work has made this even harder to grasp, since language is supposedly working to organize whatever sense of 'experience' we have. This can seem to offer us a controlling power over our experience without the risk of vulnerability and honesty, so becomes a tempting solution for many.

Politics has to remain in constant contact with therapy and with the moral conceptions which inform our understanding of how people change. So much socialist politics has been built upon taken-for-granted conceptions of masculinity, that a reworking of masculinity is inevitably a reworking of notions of socialism so often built around ideas of work and self-denial. But as therapy helps us accept more of ourselves, we learn to think again about our personal needs and the ways we negate and discount them.

This is a particularly unsettling idea for a feminism that has often built its vision of men around the idea that women are constantly learning to subordinate themselves to care and look after the spoken and unspoken needs of men. This is part of what makes an exploration of men's emotional and personal needs so crucial, for part of the frustration that so many women feel is that men are so unclear about their needs and so difficult to relate to, especially when they pretend not to have any needs at all. This is so often a way of sustaining their power in the relationship. It can be a constant source of difficulty, especially as men, so radically ignorant of themselves, learn to take this out on their partners in abusing their power in relation to them. This can encourage men into seeking all kinds of substitute gratification, fearful of risking themselves in a more honest exploration of their personal needs and desires.

Again this is not to argue that needs are pre-given, but rather to refuse the structuralist alternatives which say that human needs are *either* given *or else* they are socially constructed. These alternatives have crippled our intelligence. What is clear is that as we shift our relationship to ourselves, so will our conception of needs change. Rather than doing our best to minimize our needs and taking great pride in the sacrifices we make of ourselves, we can begin to think about what we value and care for.

As men, we are so used to discounting our needs to do the tasks we have set ourselves, and so used to drawing our sense of individual identity and happiness from our individual achievements, that it is often hard to recognize the needs of ourselves and others. Men often feel they should not have needs at all, especially since they are brought up within a liberal moral culture to be self-sufficient and independent. This notion of masculinity is the cornerstone of our liberal moral culture, which seems unable to reconcile its language of individual rights with a language of needs. But it remains threatening to explore our needs, because we become aware of how little we give ourselves and how little nourishment we receive.[2]

But often, as men, this talk of needs seems abstract and difficult to relate to. This is partly because it touches something painful when it reminds us about how used we are to not getting our emotional needs met. It also is another reason for finding a structuralist theory tempting, because it denies the significance of this very discussion.[3] It can help us feel that we are not missing anything in our lives after all. But often people also withdraw from a discussion of needs because it seems too legislative. They think, in typical liberal fashion, that the next step will be telling people what they need, even when they do not agree to it themselves.

This is a danger, but one that is not avoided if we insist on simply talking about wants and rights and limiting our talk of needs to such basic things as food and warmth. Often it is our needs we are rediscovering, not simply things we want for ourselves. For instance, is it that as a father I just want to spend more time with my child, or that I need to? This involves a refusal to think of our individual wants simply as individual preferences which somehow are equally indicating individual egoism. At some level a sense of how important it is both for me and my son Daniel to spend more time with each other makes me more dissatisfied with a work situation that does not acknowledge this kind of need, and a society which insists on marginalizing this experience. But it also gives me a different vision of relationships between men and children, and a clearer sense of the kind of society I want to live in.

PRECARIOUS IDENTITIES

In the early 1970s, the Left opposition to individualism was dogmatic and moralistic. This has left deep scars, as people were forced to experience their retreat from collective living as a totally negative withdrawal. I have argued that we need to learn much more about the complexities of this experience if we are also to recognize the ways in which Thatcherism developed on the tide of a reassertion of an individualism that was threatened. This found a resonance in many working-class people.

The critique of individualism was initially partly a challenge to the relationship modern capitalism was building between individuality and consumer goods. This seemed to foster an identification in which individuals could see themselves reflected in their goods. Crudely, we could buy happiness if we bought the right cigarette. But the Left was too anxious in its critique of consumerism to grasp the nature of the changes that had taken place in working-class life since the 1930s. It tended to elaborate a student experience in its rejection of consumer goods, though it also helped set the terms for feminism's rejection of the treatment of women in general as sexual objects.

Sometimes I think it is only going to be through a fuller understanding of the way a dialectic between identity and power works through our experience, that we will come to a theoretical renewal of historical materialism. It is as if a fuller grasp of the nature of feminism and sexual politics can help develop an understanding of historical materialism. Often we are trapped into thinking too externally about the relationship of feminism and Marxism, as if they are complete systems that can somehow be brought into closer relationship with each other.[4] This is the same false path people have followed in bringing Marx and Freud together. It is when we fully realize how we are living in a different social and historical reality, and are searching for notions which are genuinely illuminating of this lived reality, that we will discover a more useful relationship.

The move against collective forms of living in the mid 70s partly grew out of the difficulties individuals had experienced in developing these new forms of living. I lived collectively through an intense period of political activity. I learnt enormously from this period of sharing my life with others: it was what I needed for myself, and at the time I thought it was the way I would always want to live – it was a situation that I felt easy with. In many ways I personally found it harder to deal with the intimacy of a couple relationship. But I tend to think now that it was not fundamentally misconceived to think about a 'correct form of living', but that people need different relationships and living situations at different points in their lives. Crucially this means being in touch with what we need for ourselves individually, and it was just this connection that was difficult to sustain during this intense time of political involvement.[5] This was a questioning that had become quite impossible for us as political activists, because of the ways we had learnt to prioritize the needs of the political struggle. We had been ready to forsake things that used to be important to us, if only because there was still a vision that some kind of revolutionary change was imminent. But at some level it was also frightening to discover the ease with which I had given up my intellectual interests and love of books. I felt this did not have any place in the activist life I was living. In the few empty moments I had for myself I could not read, even if I wanted to. It had become almost a physical impossibility for me.

In this activist time I felt anxious when I had any time to myself. I did not know what to do with it. I knew that I was learning so much from my ongoing political work at Fords, but I did not know how to give myself the time and space to integrate this experience. I think this is something men fall into quite easily. I suppose it was partly that I had learnt to discount my individual needs and desires; I did not know any longer how to give them weight and importance when I was confronted with the daily reality of the Fords plant grinding down people's lives. But I did not experience myself as making any kind of sacrifice since there was nothing else that I would have wanted to do more at the time. In some way that kind of self-denial was little different from what most men are brought up to accept a second-nature within a capitalist society. At some level I was proving myself in the proletarian image of the political activist.

It was partly through the experience of collectivity in the early 1970s that I came to learn the vulnerability of my own individuality. Even though I was effective doing things in the world, there was another sense in which I did not seem able to make quite simple choices for myself. I had always had

112

tendency to be pleasing and adaptive to others. This has deeper sources in my experience in an immigrant family and in the feeling that, being Jewish and not having a father, I had somehow to prove myself to others. I found it hard to establish my own terms. I felt too ashamed and uneasy about parts of myself, though at another level I inherited a deep feeling for justice, that was finding a genuine expression in politics. In some way, this all had to do with the ways I learnt my masculinity. Somehow the sense I had was that I was not acceptable as myself. This combined with a sense that I had to learn externally what it meant to be 'English', as well as learn what it means to be masculine. I had to learn a way of being that I could not experience within my own family. But I could not show my vulnerability to others, since this would have given them a reason to put me down and, in any case, being a man meant being strong and learning not to need others.

I learnt to be quick on my feet. I was not physically strong and able to defend myself, or so I felt. Only later did I learn that I was strong, though I had not learnt to trust this, and that is what matters in your relations with other boys. I learnt to get on by using my wits and intelligence. I was quick and adaptive, I learnt to prove my point through initially accepting the terms offered by others and then subverting them from within.[7] This is still the way I tend to think. I still find it hard to set the terms of discussion or establish the terrain for intellectual work.

I think this helps show how important a proving ground the kind of working-class organizing I was involved in could be for me personally. Even though I went to a school in a working-class area and had some close relationships, a residual fear and suspicion remained. I can still feel this class-feeling reasserting itself if I have strayed back into a middle-class world. People with class power in society can easily ignore the realities of class relations of power and subordination, which so easily become invisible to them. But this also shows the precarious basis of my own individuality. It was only later that I gradually realized how much this had also to do with the way that masculinity is culturally identified with rationality. In learning to be a man I was also somehow weakening my sense of individual identity. This has to do with the impersonality of masculinity. Learning to be a man means learning to be impersonal.

It was painful to learn that as we got involved in non-monogamous relationships, we did not necessarily feel less controlling and possessive as men. In a similar way collective living can be an extremely important context in which to learn to relate more equally and openly with others, but it might conceal difficulties we otherwise would know in our more intimate relationships. Realizing that we are often reacting to our experience in the family can be threatening if we are doing our best to obliterate feelings of jealousy and possessiveness we have experienced growing up in nuclear families. We often want to rid ourselves of our histories as we create new relationships for ourselves. But this itself is a form of liberal voluntarism that ignores the ways our experience has been grounded in emotional relationships in our families. This is no less materialist, even though Marx made this no part of his analysis. Rather it is part of an important dialectic of experience to appreciate that, unless we acknowledge our histories, we will be controlled by them, even if only through reacting negatively to them.

It is part of a Protestant inheritance to think we can eradicate our feelings of jealousy and possessiveness through suppression. As Freud realizes, our repressed feelings return in different forms to haunt us, even though we cannot often recognize them ourselves. It was through a recognition of the difficulties people were having in changing themselves in collectives, and the resentments they were storing, that many people were led to look for a deeper historical understanding of the formation of our emotional lives and gender identities. This partly explains the growing interest in the theory and practice of different forms of psychotherapy. But often this shift has happened privately and uneasily. There has been relatively little discussion of their significance, or of the new models of personal and political change which they foster.[8] People are naturally suspicious of making claims in a period in which everyone is doing their best to survive intact in the hostile world Thatcherism has created.

But for me it was the experience of an activist life that helped me learn about ways I discount my own individual wants and needs. This was partly a form of self-estrangement as I defined myself more externally, finding satisfaction in reaching collective political goals. But this also threatened to make me more superficial and one-dimensional in my experience of myself. I found I had less to give to others in relationships; it was as if I was lacking a certain definition of myself as I had become generally used to doing what was expected of me. Political work is no different from other forms of work in this crucial respect. Somehow masculinity was working to undermine its own limits, as if it was constantly a matter of pushing myself to work harder and harder. The only limits I knew in this period were to be externally given in physical exhaustion. This is yet another aspect of the Protestant work ethic's relationship to modern forms of masculinity.

As men we constantly feel obliged to take on more tasks and responsibilities than we can properly handle. It is not only that it is difficult for us to say no, since this is not an issue in other areas of our lives. Rather, it is difficult to accept that we cannot manage to do something we would want to do. This is not simply a matter of disappointing others, which is a difficulty women have become more aware of, but of letting ourselves down. It is as if we have lost any inner sense of our own limits, as we are constantly struggling to do more. This is often the only way we can feel good about ourselves.

It is as if it is only when we are completely tired and exhausted that we feel able to look to others for love and support. We feel that we deserve the comfort of others, though we are also left in a condition in which it is quite impossible to give anything of ourselves. We silence the demands of our partners as they can see we are beyond the limits of exhaustion, and we expect to be congratulated for our efforts. We can feel bitter and resentful when our partners show resentment and scorn for the condition we have got ourselves in, and we feel an injustice is being done since often we are meeting deadlines and commitments which are not of our own making. This is part of a vicious circle of masculinity.

Often we are too tired and exhausted to make love. Our energies have gone elsewhere, and if we can bring ourselves to have physical contact, it is often grabbing. We are often seeking to relieve ourselves, rather than have intimate contact with our partners. The culture of masculinity makes us feel good in our exhaustion, knowing that we have pushed ourselves way beyond our limits. We can feel speedy and happy, though also, at another level, out of touch with ourselves. In this atmosphere it is hardly surprising that we feel suspicious and uneasy if our partners accuse us of being 'out of touch with ourselves'. This kind of language often makes no sense to us at all. We dismiss it defensively, possibly aware that it could only help illuminate the processes of our experience if we had more of an ongoing relationship with ourselves. But it is just this which traditional notions of masculinity deny us, as we learn to identify ourselves externally, feeling happy in the mirror reflection of our achievements.

We learn that we must be happy, because we have made a success of ourselves. We read off our feelings from the social world around us. We barely get a chance to value a connection to our inner lives, which in traditional empiricist conceptions are themselves simply reflections of an external reality. It is as if we cannot make sense of any ongoing relationship to our inner lives. This makes us insensitive to what our bodies can teach us, since we assume that all knowledge has to come from the external world. We rarely learn to listen to ourselves. The dominant empiricist traditions encourage us to think that all forms of knowledge are essentially knowledge of an external world. It is no accident that this tradition was an integral aspect of the scientific revolutions of the seventeenth century which helped establish the identification of masculine superiority with the possession of reason.

NEEDS AND DEPENDENCY

In the period of sexual experimentation in the 1970s, it became clear to some people that developing more than one sexual relationship was no guarantee that, as men, we were challenging our possessiveness. Rather it brought some men into a period of acute crisis, as they realized they were being pulled apart meeting the competing needs of different relationships. Dividing the week into different portions which were more or less equally distributed did not prevent familiar problems and frustrations emerging in the different relationships. Life became a lot more complicated and fuller, but feelings of rejection were often nearer the surface. Time was carefully measured but often it did not respond to the inner needs of a relationship. Equality was carefully maintained but often our feelings had a different pull. It became threatening to delve too deeply into one's preferences if one was committed to maintaining more or less equal relationships. If later, people came to talk more openly of primary relationships, there was a fear that others could be used to provide relief and support for a relationship which was to be given automatic precedence.

These were difficult and painful days for many. People drew different lessons. I know that it made me feel just how difficult it was to give and receive within a single relationship when I was so out of touch with my own individual needs. I did not any longer know what I wanted for myself, so I did not know what I wanted from a relationship. I grew suspicious of my own motivations. I knew I did not want to be alone or lonely, but that did not seem a basis for a relationship. I seemed to be incapable of making even simple decisions for myself. I had to begin again to learn to make the simplest requests of my partners. In 1976 a period of intense political activity was coming to an end, and I felt exhausted and empty. I had to learn to nourish myself in simple ways before I was really ready to give to others in a relationship. I felt in pieces, and I know that others in our collective felt the same. This was a time for individual discovery as we were all individually asking ourselves what we wanted to do now that the wave of political struggle seemed over. Few of us just wanted to sit it out. Many of us felt the need for some kind of individual therapy.

As men, we grow up with a sense that to acknowledge our individual needs is to acknowledge our weakness. This is one reason that relationships are bound to be precarious. It is difficult to experience our needs for dependency without feeling our masculinity is being threatened. Often we have denied these needs for dependency for so long that we rightly feel they could overwhelm us or bring too much strain into our present relationships.[9] Even though men often resist the idea of therapy as self-indulgent, they rarely realize how they are reinforcing traditional roles in insisting their partners deal with this enormous backlog of dependency. Often this is preferable to the sullen silence, but it can exhaust our partners too. I think it is important for us to learn to take more responsibility for this area of our lives, even if this means admitting we need the help of therapists. I think this is an important step in itself.

But often we resist the idea that we need the help of others. We think that if we have friends to talk to, we should not need to pay someone to listen to us. Often we are too busy. But it is this refusal to give time and space to ourselves that often makes our relationships with others more superficial. If we never learn to deepen the contact with ourselves, how can we hope to share ourselves with others? If we never learn to nourish ourselves through giving ourselves more of what we need, what hope is there of our being able to nourish others in a relationship?

Often we come to our partners out of a sense of need and inadequacy, and we create a barrier between ourselves as a tight couple and the rest of the world. This is a constant danger that eventually weakens both partners in a relationship. The ease with which people come to despise themselves and despise their partners in long-term couple relationships shows that the mechanisms are deep-rooted. Often when you are caught up in this situation it seems impossible to do anything about it. Partners feel increasingly bitter and unforgiving to each other. There seems to be no way in which words can build deeper contact and communication as people are locked into their positions. This seems so hard to avoid.

The traditional view that people are incomplete in themselves, and so need a partner to complete them, has deep social and cultural roots. We often feel we are going through life looking for a partner who can make things right through completing us. If things are going wrong in our present relationship, we are always tempted into thinking we have not yet found the right person. As men this encourages us constantly to look beyond ourselves for the means of our happiness. We never really learn to take control of our emotional lives. Rather we learn to blame others for our misery, and often feel resentful when others seem happy when we are not. Even though feminism has challenged this traditional view for many women, it has generally remained intact for men. We rarely develop an emotional language in which we can identify our growth and development as human beings. We have little sense of working on ourselves emotionally.

Rather, we inherit a false sense of control over our emotional lives, thinking that we can always make things better through acts of will. We culturally learn to cheer ourselves and put a good face on things. But often this means that life barely touches

118

us. We only learn to distance ourselves from our own experience. Often we end up feeling depressed, as we have learnt automatically to suppress the anger and resentments we feel. Not only do we learn to keep our feelings to ourselves, but we often become uneasy and embarrassed when others want to share themselves emotionally with us. Very soon we feel we cannot cope and we do our best to escape the situation. It is as if we cannot help feeling, whatever we want to think intellectually, that emotions themselves are unseemly and should not really be shared. Often the loneliness and needs of others serve only to trigger our own feelings, reminding us of parts of ourselves we have suppressed and do not want to know about. Often we end up suppressing others so that we do not have to deal with ourselves.

From a very early age, we grow up learning to discount our feelings of need and dependency. Freud felt we are forced to do this to separate ourselves from our mothers and learn to claim our masculinity. In this way we learn to identify with the goals and ends we set for ourselves. This is how we learn to fulfill ourselves. But at another level it estranges us from our ongoing emotional lives which could otherwise help us to define ourselves individually, as well as ground us in our relationships. As men we learn to look to the future and identify with the projects we set ourselves, so that in some important sense we come to live in the future. It is difficult to give a genuine importance and value to our relationships, and so in an important sense, to ourselves. At some level we never really learn to take personal experience seriously, as if we can only exist in our achievements and accomplishments. Often this can mean we are passive in our relationships, ready to fit in with the demands of our partners without really knowing what we want ourselves. But often this passivity marks our lack of presence in our personal and sexual relationships. Often we are active in the public sphere of work but passive, even infantile, in the private sphere of relationships. This is partly because as men we have been forced to deny our feelings of need and dependency which have no place in the public sphere. We are watchful, anxious not to betray ourselves through letting others know what we are feeling.

This process becomes so automatic that we barely realize how closed and impenetrable we are. Often it is our partners who have to pick up the pieces for us at home. It is almost as if we exist as different people. Our partners have to bring us back to ourselves, if they are to have any hope of relating to us more personally. But often we remain unsure and withdrawn. We think we are letting our partners have their own way as we agree to arrangements they have made. But often this is really being patronizing, since we are failing to take responsibility for caring. For instance, very few men seem to take the time and consideration to buy presents. Most of us leave it up to our partners, giving ourselves the excuse that they are better at it anyway. But this can be frustrating for them, because they inevitably feel that it is almost as if we do not exist at all in this sphere of life. They do not have anyone to push against, as we are constantly withdrawing and conceding, refusing to engage in the ongoing conflict of relationships. Often we withdraw resentfully when it comes to an emotional conflict. We rarely acknowledge our own difficulties because this would be to admit our vulnerability. We can fear being accused of not being man enough. Often we withdraw, feeling that there is no way through this, hoping that our partners will 'get over it soon'. This is a pattern that seems likely to be repeated in both straight and gay relationships.

IDENTITY AND RELATIONSHIPS

We cannot think of these issues in terms of the limitations of the traditional masculine role. Nor is it enough to say that as heterosexual men we have to learn to take more responsibility for our emotional lives and for our caring relationships with others. The problems are more deeply rooted in the very formation of masculinity both historically and psychologically. We have to grasp the social and historical construction of masculinity in ways that illuminate issues of contemporary masculinity. Too often this kind of analysis places us in a position outside and beyond the touch of the investigation. In this way we often preserve a false sense of objectivity and impartiality, without realizing that it is our masculinity and male identity that is at issue.

It is this implicit theoretical framework that can reinforce the very notions of male superiority we are talking about. For all the insights of post-structuralist analysis, it has failed to make problematic the identification of male identity with rationality

120

that has been such a defining feature of modern culture. It has been forced to reconsider a 'theory of the subject', so reintroducing the very fragmentation we need to question. If Marx was blind to the importance of these issues, at least he constantly recognized the danger of separating our social and historical understanding from an analysis of the capacities and qualities of people.

Walter Benjamin was constantly urging the Frankfurt School to realize how the notion of the autonomous individual, which had been the basis of bourgeois social and economic theory, had been destroyed by changes in capitalist society itself.[10] The autonomous individual with a clear grasp of his or her wants and desires had become a legitimating fiction in this new period of capitalist development. The left was only revealing the poverty of its own theory by insisting on thinking of individualism as essentially 'bourgeois'. It just showed how theory had lost contact with historical reality.

Benjamin was centrally concerned to understand this historical shift in all its complexity, though he remained suspicious of an anthropological history associated with Buber. He helps us realize a point which has emerged centrally with post-structuralist theory, how as individuals we are fragmented, existing almost as separate pieces with little relationship to each other. It is as if we can no longer speak with a unified voice. We have to let the different parts of us find their own voice to make sure we do not create a false sense of harmony. We have to begin by accepting the reality of our condition. This is painful, since we seem to inherit enormous powers of self-delusion.

Even though as men we benefit from the organization of sexual relations of power, we are also hurt by them. But we resist any sense of the ways we are hurt and damaged as a sex, since this itself is a sign of our vulnerability. As men we are so often living out ideals of ourselves – thinking of ourselves as the reincarnation of Marx, Lenin, or Jesus, that we do anything to displace the reality of our own experience. We do our best to separate from those periods of our lives when the bad times got through to us. It always seems easier to blame our partners, or to analyse the larger situations we are in, than to take full responsibility for ourselves. I think this is one reason it has been difficult to explore masculinity in the wake of the feminist challenge.

It has been easier for men to withdraw in guilt and shame, than it has been to own the reality of our own masculine experience. It is as if though women have been rendered invisible in history and the public realm, men have been rendered invisible to themselves. It becomes difficult to think of ourselves as estranged or as emotionally limited, if not crippled, through the processes of our upbringing because the very notion of a 'self' has been banished. Liberal theory has often objectified it, while Marxist theory has treated it with ridicule and disdain. Possibly it is in seeking out the shared assumptions of masculinity that we realize the depths of a feminist critique.

This crucially concerns our experience of male identity. If we never learn to exist for ourselves as men, what do we bring into our relationships? If we lack a depth of contact with ourselves, how can we expect to discover this in others? If we do not know what we need for ourselves, how can we negotiate more equal and loving relationships with others? Unless we have a firmer grasp of the difficulties we face as men, we will be constantly projecting these difficulties on others.

This is part of the material reality of our relationships, though we desperately need a language to illuminate it. Possible we have lost confidence in the idea that people could somehow be liberated in spite of themselves. But this is part of the same masculine rationalist dream that we need to recognize ourselves in. Feminism has taught us that we have to do it for ourselves individually in our own way since we cannot simply take the word of others. Consciousness-raising is intensely individual at the same time as it is socially and historically grounding.

We cannot think of reclaiming our masculinity unless we are prepared to accept the hurt, confusion and guilt that it has left us with. I learnt this for myself out of the despair of the mid 70s. I could not pretend I was different from other men because I had learnt to be 'anti-sexist'. We could not rely upon the world changing, so we had to begin making our relationships better. This was a hard enough task that taught its own humility. It involved returning to look at the ways we had learnt as boys to use language to hide and conceal, rather than to express and share ourselves.

Chapter Seven

LANGUAGE

Because rationality is taken to be a universal quality, it becomes difficult to realize how rationality becomes an important basis for male superiority in social life. One of the women's movement's more powerful insights has been the identification of the ways that power relationships can be consolidated and sustained through men's assumption of a stance of overview of a situation, creating a relationship of communication in which what women have to say is branded with the status of the particular, whilst men offer what they see as an encompassing and objectively-grounded account. To see this is to see that men and women do not have the same relationship to language. In the light of it, it is important to explore men's relationships to language, sensitive to the possibility that men can learn to use language to distance and hold in check their experience. This is an investigation which structuralism leaves little space for, convinced as it is that experience is itself constituted through language. The effect of displacing experience in this way is to close off questions about people's different relationships to language and expression; experience is assimilated into language so that qualitative differences in experience cannot be recognized, let alone grasped in their full significance. Language remains at some level autonomous of experience.

It is a strength of Wittgenstein's later work to challenge a Cartesian rationalism that has underpinned the identification of masculinity with reason that has been so crucial in a post-Enlightenment culture. Wittgenstein is undercutting the claim to superiority we grow up to assume as men over our feelings and emotions. I want to show that rationalist conceptions of

123

language fail to illuminate, how, as men, we can learn to use language instrumentally to conceal ourselves and in so doing form and shape the kind of personal and sexual relationships we can have with others.

LANGUAGE AND MALE IDENTITY

Within a liberal moral culture, the very notion of personal identity has been made problematic. As individuals we take ourselves to be the embodiment of universal qualities though we acknowledge that some people have more of these qualities than others. Some people are more intelligent than others and some can run faster. This is deeply rooted in the rationalist tradition. We witness it in that aspect of Kant's ethical theory that would argue that we are each deserving of respect since we are equally moral beings, or at least have an equal capacity for morality. But Kant was also careful to identify this capacity with our individual powers to reason. This was a possession which was historically since the Enlightenment more closely identified with masculinity. Our very sense of masculinity was consolidated as an experience of superiority over our wants, desires, emotions and feelings. To prove our masculinity, we had to keep our 'inclinations' in check. We had to learn to dominate our inner natures. But this also meant that our masculinity could be upset or challenged. It was not anything we could take for granted, but had to be constantly proved. We still live in the shadow of this conception. We can experience it for ourselves as men in our constant tendency to push ourselves to the edge of exhaustion as if this is the way we can prove ourselves individually and sustain our self-control.

But reason is essentially impersonal. The more our sense of self is identified with reason, the more we are in a process as men of impersonalizing ourselves. At the same time, we have to recognize that historically this was important for the emancipation of classes and ethnic groups who would otherwise have been discriminated against, excluded and humiliated. But at another level this is emancipation at a price, since it is also a pact with the devil as it makes for instance, your blackness, Jewishness or gayness, essentially *incidental* aspects of yourself. We learn to give up these aspects of our history and culture to be treated as equals by others.[1] It is as if we have to pay the price of the painful and difficult work of deconstructing our identities to be treated fairly and equally with others. This means we have to learn to redefine our interests so that we can articulate them in universal terms. In capitalist society this means we want to be richer and more successful than the next person. Our class and ethnic identity become private matters but no part of the 'official identity' we can assume in the larger society.

In this way we become *estranged* from important aspects of our history and culture. We lose an important source of our own power as we are left divided. It should be hardly surprising if those suffering from class, ethnic or gender oppression find it hard to define themselves clearly in the larger society. I have learnt how subtle but powerful is the way that in, discounting my Jewishness, I have discounted an important source of my power and identity.[2] But people often feel uneasy and embarrassed if you bring these 'emotional considerations' into serious intellectual discussion. Rather we are encouraged within a liberal moral culture to think of our class and ethnicity as 'emotional attachments' we will eventually outgrow. It is clear that emotionality has culturally to do with infancy.

This is an integral part of assuming our masculinity in the larger society. I remember feeling that being a 'real man' meant being taller than I was, stronger than I was. Very far from being a residual category, masculinity was something we had to give our lives aspiring towards, never sure that we would ever really make it. It is no accident that the idea of a 'Jewish man' was experienced by me as a kind of contradiction in terms. Jewishness was related to the emotional, and so with the feminine.[3] Growing up, we had to work hard to reassert a notion of Jewish maleness, often forcing ourselves to react against weakness and vulnerability more harshly. This was a potent source of shame.

I am concerned to understand how our inherited conceptions of masculinity connect to processes through which we learn to *displace* important aspects of ourselves. This seems to weaken and impoverish our individuality, but it also makes it harder for Jewish men to define themselves in their own terms, as they are constantly anxious to compete or prove themselves to others. In some way this can make Jewish men adaptable and understanding in their relationships, though at another level leaving them rigid and unforgiving. I know how subtly I work to get my own way, doing well at concealing my tracks. This can mean taking out particular tensions and frustrations on those closest to us, assuming they understand a predicament we have often never explained to them, since we rarely have the language to explain it ourselves. It is of the essence of the situation that we can never make ourselves acceptable to others, since we are constantly on edge that they might discover a different side of ourselves. This is a no-win situation. What is more, we lose our strength in the process.

We betray our cultural integrity as Jewish men, and in a real sense we emasculate ourselves as we are constantly doing our best to prove ourselves in the eyes of others. They inevitably withhold their final approval, since with this they lose their power over us. It is an exhausting and painful process, though one rendered largely invisible through the success and achievement we may have individually achieved. I have had to fight it through myself. I am left haunted by a sense of weakness, since this is no way to discover my own historical and ethnic grounding. But it is a powerful way of sustaining those who have institutional power in the larger society, since the cost of a particularistic identification seems to be minimal, especially if we no longer have a language in which to illuminate the bargain we have struck. Since they set the terms, they are made invulnerable to criticism. This is an important aspect of the centrality notions of equality of opportunity have assumed in legitimating relations of power and subordination in late capitalist society.

Even though this is a predicament that could illuminate the situation of working-class people, women and ethnic minorities, it also reveals something central about contemporary masculinity: the identification of masculinity with rationality undermines the identity of men. The impersonal character of reason makes it hard for us to appropriate a history and culture of masculinity, especially one in opposition to the dominant culture.[4] What is more, it weakens any sense that this could be important to us individually as men. We learn to ground ourselves in our ideas, in our heads. This is the way we protect ourselves. We do our best to capture the claim to be rational and reasonable, which seems to move our own behaviour and experience beyond criticism. It is always others – usually women – who are emotional, if not hysterical. It is always us who have to wait patiently for them to calm down, before we can add the weight of our arguments to the situation. We learn not to lose our self-control, since this is often the basis for our feeling of superiority in the situation. We hold tight.

As men, we are brought up to identify with our 'rationality' as the very core of our masculinity. We learn to appropriate rationality as if it were an exclusively male quality and we deny it to others, especially women. We also deny it to animals and children. The very possession of reason amounts to a claim to superiority, though this can be difficult to realize, since it is also taken to be a universal quality shared by all human beings. This is one of the sources of ambiguity in the liberal tradition of equality. So it becomes difficult to realize how rationality becomes an important basis for male superiority in social life.

Since we identify 'rationality' with knowledge, we systematically deny knowledge to women and children, who are more closely identified with emotions and feelings. Emotions and feelings are systematically denied as genuine sources of knowledge, though they may illuminate how individuals have responded to situations; but often they are indications of weakness and a lack of self-control. They are antithetical to our very sense of masculinity. Even feelings like anger become indications of a lack of control, which men learn to be wary of. This has powerfully influenced the shape and tone of our language and the relationship men grow up to have with language. Even though we are powerfully influenced by traditions, such as romanticism, which show language to be expressive, helping to articulate and form the nature of the self, these visions have been continually marginalized within a scientific culture which, at least since the seventeenth century, has powerfully identified masculinity with dominant forms of scientific knowledge.

The dominant view of language has been a correspondence theory which has seen our words as existing in a one-to-one relationship with objects in the world. For our sentences to have meaning, they have had to correspond to an existing state of affairs in the empirical world. This view found a powerful form in the twentieth century in the writings of the Vienna Circle and the early Wittgenstein, but it articulates a vision that has its source in the scientific revolutions of the seventeenth century. This was the historical period in which our common-sense notions of objectivity and impartiality were formed. From the beginning this was closely tied to a reformulation of masculinity. Lukàcs helps illuminate some of the key antinomies of this period, within *History and Class Consciousness*.

Foucault's early work, entitled *Madness and Civilization*, is also crucial in showing how our notions of reason and objectivity were historically formulated in the sixteenth and seventeenth centuries. He shows the crucial importance of a distinction between reason and unreason in isolating certain forms of behaviour as threatening.[5] We could no longer learn from the insights of madness or treat it as an occasion in otherwise normal lives. This was also the period of the witch trials and the violent and brutal assertion of a new form of masculinity identified with the new sciences. These historical processes have been rendered invisible and their brutality legitimized as we have learnt to think of this as 'The Age of Reason'. This has become an integral part of the identification of reason, science and progress. To question science in this new period was to stand in the way of progress. This legitimized some of the worst forms of oppression and suffering.

Often the tensions in our modern experience have their source in this period. Both capitalist and socialist societies have sought to legitimize themselves in this conception of science. We cannot understand their development unless we are prepared to place them within the historical framework of the Enlightenment. This was something the Frankfurt School only partially managed to achieve in their pioneering study *The Dialectic of Enlightenment*. They tended to assume the identification of progress with the domination of nature, but at least this opened the way for a more ecological critique of Marx and the tradition of Marxism. It was with the new self-identified masculinist sciences of the seventeenth century that the split between reason and emotions, feelings and desires was most clearly institutionalized. This inevitably fragmented our experience as we found our emotions, feelings, dreams and visions denigrated as forms of 'unreason'. This was systematically to negate the experience of women and destroy the sources of any forms of instinctual knowledge. We were to learn systematically to separate the workings of our intellectual reason from our felt experience and embodied natures.

Even though analytical philosophy has done important work in questioning the appropriateness of Cartesian dualism for our understanding of our experience, we continue to live our lives in its hidden grip.[6] We still believe in the autonomy and independence of reason. We deny our bodies as genuine sources of knowledge, and we tend to see them as machines which do the work of carrying our minds around. We marginalize what we could otherwise learn from the knowledge of our hearts, as we continue to think in the dualistic terms of mind and body. This is one reason that Reich has been so despised and misunderstood. He threatens not simply the conceptual terms in which we constitute our identities, but the very organization of our everyday experience as he calls us into a different relationship with ourselves. We find it almost impossible to think clearly of ways we are more open or closed to our experience, even though we can be dimly aware that nothing in our experience seems to touch us.

Reich understood this in terms of the over-bounded character of people who have developed a rigid armouring, but he did not connect this enough to the learning of our masculinity or to the historical identification of reason with masculinity. This helps to estrange us from a deeper understanding of self, as we somehow take up a position beyond our own experience. We lose any sense of *grounding* ourselves in our own embodied experience as we identify our sense of masculinity with being objective and impartial. This involves our discounting our own experience and so denying one of the deepest sources of our identity and knowledge.

Descartes saw the human body as a machine organized according to mechanical laws.[7] The body was to be made a part of the natural world to be investigated using the methods of the new sciences. The person was to be identified with the mind, which was seen as essentially impersonal to the extent that people acted rationally. In its own way this was to give secular expression to a Christian tradition which had often denigrated the body as a source of spiritual knowledge. Our bodies held us to the animal world that we should learn to control and dominate. Our sense of ourselves as 'civilized' depended upon us claiming a superiority to the natural world of animal wants and desires. It was as if we were continually trying to free ourselves from the demands of the body, which would inherently undermine our freedom and autonomy as it determined our behaviour externally. Women were taken to be 'unfree', to the extent that they allowed themselves to be moved by their emotions and feelings. This was the way Rousseau and Kant argued that women could only be free if they agreed to subordinate themselves to men; but men could only guarantee their own freedom if they insisted upon identifying themselves with their rational powers. We had to learn to disdain our emotions, feelings, dependence and desires, lest they were to fundamentally compromise our masculinity.

Not only were men to learn to identify themselves with rationality, but this was to be fundamentally separated from any sense of embodied experience. Even our bodies are no part of our identities as men. We had to investigate them as matter, as part of the empirical world. In a very real sense, as men, we are fundamentally estranged from this world which we can only observe from a distance. It is no accident that issues of perception became central to modern philosophy. We become historically obsessed with the truthfulness of our perceptions of a world that is estranged and distant.[8] We are systematically estranged from a world we can only 'observe'. We conceive of the mind, in Richard Rorty's phrase, as the mirror of the world.

This conception of mind has been crucially significant, not only for the form of modern philosophy, but also for the gender experience of masculinity which is so closely identified with this form of rationality. This reveals a much deeper connection between masculinity and the forms of philosophical thought in which they have implicitly found expression. Within the rationalist tradition, men learn automatically to relate to themselves and their social relations in an instrumental way. Of course this is not specific to men, since women come under this pervasive influence within a masculinist culture. This means they are also constantly encouraged to turn their experience into a test in which they have to prove themselves, even if this is not so closely identified with a sense of women's identity.

For men, our very identification with our reason gives us a vantage point of superiority in relation to women outside and beyond our own lived experience, which we can only appropriate in the most abstract of terms. We are trapped as observers, not only of the natural and social worlds, but also of ourselves.

We are left as observers, rather than as participants, in our own lives. This is part of the pervasive distinction between subjective and objective understandings of the social world within which social theory has so long been trapped. Marx attempts to reinstate a sense of ourselves as sensuous beings who are practically involved in activities and relationships. But unfortunately he does not systematically develop the hints left in the 'Theses on Feuerbach'. These ideas have found echoes in the continual renewals of Marxist theory which have recognized the enduring significance of Hegel for Marx. Richard Rorty has looked in *Philosophy and the Mirror of Nature* for similar breaks with a Cartesian inheritance in the dominant tradition to be found in the writings of Dewey, Heidegger and Wittgenstein.

The abiding strength in the rationalist tradition was to reinstate the active importance of the mind in organizing our experience.[9] The categories of the mind through which we organize our sense of the empirical world was Kant's direct challenge to the empiricist tradition of Hume. Empiricism tended to see the mind as a passive receptor of impressions and ideas coming from the world. But within the empiricist tradition we can also discover a powerful democratic strain which recognizes that each person could test for himself or herself the results of scientific knowledge. People were no longer expected to accept things on faith. People learnt to challenge traditional forms of religious authority as they learnt only to accept the authority of their own sense-experience. This was part of a democratic impulse of the new sciences of the seventeenth century, even if it eventually gave way to a new basis of hierarchical authority built upon the possession of knowledge. More particularly, it has been within a British empiricist tradition that the emphasis upon perception has been most developed.

Analytical philosophy was partly initiated as a challenge to theories of sense perception and sense-experience in the period after 1945. This tradition has had its influence upon empiricist traditions of social science in fragmenting our conception of social knowledge into discrete pieces of data that can be collected. But the rationalist tradition has had a deeper grip upon the development of social theory. Both Weber and Durkheim remained deeply influenced by the Kantian tradition, and most of the phenomenology which has developed within sociology has

131

remained trapped within this intellectualist framework. But both traditions, as Lukàcs realized in his *History and Class Consciousness*, leave people as observers of an external social reality which they cannot change. Our understanding is not something we can develop in our active involvement in relationships and activities. This is an insight that connects Marx to the later Wittgenstein. In their different ways they are both contesting the influence of Descartes. In Wittgenstein this is clearest in one of his latest works, *On Certainty*.[10]

The identification of masculinity with reason has left a strong impulse for men to become observers of their own experience. We struggle for a certain form of impartiality and objectivity in assessing a situation fairly. Consequently the difficulties we often have as men to say what we personally feel and experience in a situation has deep cultural and historical roots. As men we often become more adept at assessing the different interests involved in a situation than saying what we want individually and negotiating with others on this basis. Rather the forms of moral rationalism we inherit tend to make us feel uneasy about asserting our own individual wants and desires. Often we think of this as a form of 'selfishness'.

This also has deep roots in our upbringing in a culture in which we learn automatically to discount our individual emotions and feelings as having no part in our 'true rational self'. This is a process which psychoanalytic theory can sometimes illuminate. As boys we often learn to identify emotions and feelings with our mothers, and with the feminine. This is something we are forced to separate from to prove ourselves as men. We also have to separate from what we identify as the feminine within ourselves. Masculinity is such an uneasy inheritance. We have to be prepared to defend it at any moment, even if this means striking down parts of ourselves.

We would need to investigate these processes in a way that is specific to class and historical moment. It has only been with the development of a more egalitarian ethos between the sexes that a man's word has been questioned as law within the home. Since domestic life has often been automatically organized around men's needs, little has had to be said: men had to talk very little. D.H. Lawrence illuminates this in *Sons and Lovers*, when he shares his growing up in a mining community. John Cleese has talked about the lower middle class of Weston Super Mare, 'where emotions were kept as hidden as possible. Making scenes wasn't allowed. Anger wasn't shown. It was wrong for anyone to assert themselves. You had to work out what everyone else wanted. All change was dangerous. "You haven't changed a bit" was a tremendous compliment.' (The *Guardian*, Monday 2 January, 1984).

Class differences are very significant, as are the forms of control men can exert in relationships. But within a supposedly more egalitarian period, issues of control are still central if we are not to experience our masculinity as threatened. Often we use our reason to define 'what would be best in the situation', and so get others to agree. In this way we often assume to take the interests of others into account without really giving others a chance to identify and *define their own* interests. It is in the name of reason that we often, as middle-class men, silence others at the same time as giving them no chance of getting back at us. Often this remains a potent source of power, as we can in all honesty present ourselves as working out the most 'rational' way of doing things. Our rationality is often a hidden weapon, since it allows us to assimilate and control the interests of others. It also puts us beyond reproach.

It is within the context of an instrumental notion of mas-culinity that we learn our language. Often this is a practical language of action, where we are setting out to prove ourselves to others. Since it is what we think that makes us what we are as men, we find ourselves without any natural connection to our emotions and feelings. These are not experienced as integral aspects of our individuality. Our individuality is defined in relation to our thoughts, and often our emotions and feelings have to be turned into thoughts so that we can deal with them in familiar ways. At best we can learn to talk about emotions and feelings.

In the middle class, men have often grown up to be reticent, even scared, of sharing emotions and feelings, lest they threaten the control which sustains our very sense of masculinity. We can feel apologetic and embarrassed if we are emotional with others. We fear that others will see us as weak and unmasculine. We often prefer to withdraw into a sullen silence, unaware of how controlling this silence can be. Our emotions automatically seem to signal a lack of control. We find it almost impossible to identify our anger, resentment or sadness as a rational response to a situation. Only *in extremis* can we allow ourselves these feelings. Rationality has to do with coolness and control. It seems to have no place in our consideration of our emotional and somatic lives.

LANGUAGE AND EXPERIENCE

Men have often assumed a control of language. Since we automatically assume that language has to do with reason, logic and rationality, we easily treat it as our own. Certainly men have often had power in the larger society to define the reality of others, but we have to be careful not to assume universally that language itself is 'man made', in the sense Dale Spender developed in *Man Made Language*.[11] Women have not simply had to conform to a reality men have created, as long as they have remained within the private and domestic sphere. It has been in the public realm that men have most clearly created the terms on which women could gain access. But we should not forget, as Gramsci was struggling to show in his *Prison Notebooks*, that even here, language is essentially contested.

Gramsci was developing a tradition in which language is embodied in ongoing social relationships in which people are constantly clarifying and redefining a sense of their individual needs, wants and desires. Language does not constitute individuality in the way structuralism has assumed. Gramsci also realized the tension between what we say and what we do, especially where relationships of power and subordination are involved. Oppressed people are constantly trying to make language their own, as they attempt to discover and redefine their experience. This is an ongoing historical process, in which women are not to be conceived as completely passive. Our common sense remains inherently contradictory as it brings together different elements in men's and women's experience.[12]

Again, we are questioning the pervasiveness of a Kantian inheritance which sees language as a set of categories, or a framework, that we place over the social world to make sense of it. At one level, as language users we are already involved in such a system of meaning, but at another level it supposedly remains a more or less arbitrary construction. This is part of the linguistic relativism which exists in both structuralist and phenomenological traditions.[13] This is why it is so important to understand the historical appeal of this form of relativism. This has to do with the same tradition of rationalism and its internal connection to masculinity. This kind of theory promises an overview of a culture or society, in terms of the categories or classifications people invoke to order their experience. So it promises a superiority over others, who in their ignorance do not realize the contingent nature of the social world they have 'constructed' or 'negotiated' for themselves.

But the different forms of the rationalist tradition give no way of situating individual experience socially and historically. The very notion of experience was abandoned as irrevocably tied to an empiricist tradition. Even though phenomenology, in particular, has aspired towards some notion of reflexivity, apart from the early work of Gouldner which was more influenced by the insights of the New Left, this has been an intellectualist exercise. The current was flowing too quickly in other directions to allow this form of personal and intellectual self-consciousness to develop outside the context of feminism and sexual politics. This was politically too threatening, but also too threatening to the impersonal character of masculinity. As Lukàcs realized, people were left in a fundamentally contemplative position towards a social world from which they were estranged. Certainly people had learnt within the rationalism of structuralism to change the world through giving different interpretations of it, but this was different from the historical transformations of Marx and Gramsci.

As long as we continue to see language as a screen or net to be placed against the social world, we remain trapped by the picture Wittgenstein articulated in the *Tractatus*. Unfortunately this is the conception of language informing Spender's work, which otherwise illuminates central issues of the relationship of language to relations of power and subordination. The view Wittgenstein was developing in his later writings is less aware of relations of power, but has a keen awareness of how we learn to talk in the context of learning social activities.

Language is no longer conceived as a single system, though it remains important to acknowledge our capacities to use language.

Wittgenstein remarks that 'Children do not learn that there are books, that there are armchairs, etc., etc., but they learn to fetch books, sit in armchairs, etc.' (*On Certainty*, p.476). We learn language as an integral aspect of learning to do these things. In some crucial sense our language grows out of and extends these activities.

Norman Malcolm in his article, 'Wittgenstein: the relation of language to instinctive behaviour' (*Philosophical Investigations* Vol. 5 No. 1) argues that

> the child who retaliates against the one who crashes into him does not do this because he 'knows' or 'believes' that this caused his fall. He simply does it. It is an instant reaction, like brushing away an insect that is tickling one's skin (p.6).

He goes on to question an empiricist reading

> that the child affirms in his mind the proposition that the other one certainly knocked him down, or that the child has a *perception* or *intuitive awareness* of the causal connection between his being crashed into and his falling down. No. Wittgenstein means that the hitting back at the other child is *instinctive* ... The 'certainty' he is talking about is a certainty in behaviour, not a certainty in propositional thought (p.6.).

As Wittgenstein himself says:

> The primitive form of the language-game is certainty, not uncertainty. For uncertainty could never lead to action. The basic form of the game must be one in which we act.

Wittgenstein was concerned fundamentally to shift our relationship to language and challenge our inherited rationalism, when he remarked in *On Certainty* that 'Language did not emerge from reasoning' (p.475). As a child learns words and sentences, this marks a transition from say, non-linguistic to linguistic expressions of pain. In learning linguistic expressions of pain the child learns 'new pain-behaviour' (*Philosophical Investigations*, p.244). As Malcolm reminds us, Wittgenstein calls these 'first person utterances, Ausserungen, to indicate that they are *immediate expressions* of pain, fear, surprise, desire and so on, and are not the result of thought' (p.3). In this way Wittgenstein is undercutting and subverting our common sense rationalism which has built itself upon a fragmentation in our experience between what is 'natural' or 'instinctive' and what is 'cultural' and 'linguistic'. This is a dualism that finds powerful expression in Descartes and Kant. Against this conception is the vision that our language grows out of our pre-linguistic behaviour and can only be grasped if we ground it in these early experiences. So we can see how deeply was Wittgenstein's challenge to our inherited traditions when he says in *Culture and Value*:

> The origin and the primitive form of language-game is a reaction; only from this can the more complicated forms grow. Language – I want to say – is a refinement; 'in the beginning was the deed' (p.31).

So we can see how deeply misguided it has been to interpret Wittgenstein's notion of a 'language game' as if it were a linguistic phenomenon, so putting his work at the service of a tradition he was seeking to subvert and challenge. It is only in the context of our deeds that we can begin to grasp the meaning of our utterances. As soon as we separate language as a system of meanings, we have losts its vital interconnection with the on-going practices of everyday life. It is as a critique of theories of language as an independent and autonomous system through which we make sense of or organize our social world, that we can possibly think of Wittgenstein as developing a form of 'linguistic materialism'.

Wittgenstein is tacitly subverting the basis upon which we identify masculinity with reason. He is unwittingly and unknow-ingly undercutting the claim to superiority we grow up to assume as men over our feelings and emotions. Rather he can help us understand how we have hurt ourselves through mis-understanding and misconstruing the place of reason in our lives. We have set up a duality where none should exist. We have failed to realize how our thoughts are nurtured from the same ground of actions and deeds as are our emotions and feelings. To the extent that Kant has encouraged us to identify our morality exclusively with our reason, he has limited and injured our sense of ourselves as moral beings and the nature of our relationships with others.

Rationalism has continually undercut our sense of connection with others, forcing us morally to justify whatever care and help one individual might give another. This is related to our inherited notion of masculinity as independence and self-sufficiency. As soon as we act from feelings, we are accused of being 'soft', as if our masculinity is affirmed in our insistence on finding reasons for each of our actions. There is no way to acknowledge our need to be dependent and vulnerable in our relations with others if we are to give these relations depth and substance. As men, we fear this vulnerability which threatens our very sense of masculinity.

Malcolm realizes how Wittgenstein places our relations with others on a different basis, though he resists drawing the implications for our sense of morality and politics. I think it important to quote this part of his article in full since it helpfully shows how rationalist notions are questioned:

> This conception of certain linguistic expressions as replace-ments for unlearned reactions, was seen by Wittgenstein to extend to some of the sentences that we use to refer to other persons. Not only 'I'm in pain' but also 'He's in pain', can take the place of instinctive behaviour. In *Zettel* Wittgenstein ob-serves that 'it is a primitive reaction to tend, to treat, the part that hurts when someone else is in pain, and not merely when oneself is' (Z 540). . . . Wittgenstein asks himself what he means by saying that these reactions are 'primitive'; and he answers:

> 'Surely that this way of behaving is *prelinguistic*: that a language-game is based *on it*, that it is the prototype of a way of thinking and not the result of thinking.' (Z541).

> Wittgenstein is disagreeing with a 'rationalistic' explanation of this behaviour – for example, the explanation that we have a sympathetic reaction to an injured person 'because by analogy with our own case we believe that he too is experiencing pain' (Z 542). The actions of comforting or trying to help, that go with the words 'He's in pain', are no more a product of reasoning from analogy than is the similar behaviour in deer or birds. Wittgenstein goes on to say that

> 'Being sure that someone is in pain, doubting whether he is, and so on, are so many natural, instinctive, kinds of relation-ship towards other human beings, and our language is merely an auxiliary to, and further extension of, this behaviour. Our language-game is an extension of primitive behaviour. (For our *language-game* is behaviour). (Instinct) (Z 545).'

So through our words we find another way of comforting those in grief. We could just as well put our arm on their shoulder. This questions any attempt to privilege our language. But it also challenges crude versions of historical materialism which would seek to relate language as an aspect of ideology to an underlying level of material relationships. When Wittgenstein says that language can replace pre-linguistic behaviour, it is to be understood that it serves as an extension, refinement or elaboration of that behaviour. This is the ground we have to place it back into if we are to recover a sense of its meaning and significance in our lives.

Philosophers have mistakenly interpreted the idea that the meaning of an expression is in its use as meaning words and sentences have to be placed in a larger linguistic context of use. This mistake is common in the appropriation of Wittgenstein's writings in conversational analysis in sociology. This places his writings firmly back in the very 'rationalistic' tradition he was struggling to break with.[14] But it is only when we learn how much of our experience has been shaped within this tradition that we can begin to grasp the difficulties of breaking with it. This also involves breaking with an inherited conception of masculinity.

We limit our understanding of the nature of moral relations in assuming we always need to give reasons to explain why one person should care for another, especially if the person is not a close relation or friend. This assumes egoism is to be identified with self-interest and universally treated as the natural character of our relations with others rather than as encouraged by the social relations of a particular society. Morality begins when we give reasons to extend a sense of fair and equal treatment beyond those for whom we have feelings. It is within an assumed framework of liberal individualism that the moral discussion between egoism and altruism takes place. But Wittgenstein questions the basis upon which this distinction is often drawn. In doing this, not only does he question the priority we give to reason in our moral relations, but he opens up a way for the recognition of our emotions and feelings in the 'natural, instinctive, kinds of relationships towards other human beings'. It is not that our language constitutes our individuality and defines these moral relations, but, as Wittgenstein says, 'our language is merely an auxiliary to, and further extension of, this behaviour'.

This marks a profound challenge to the assumptions of liberal individualism. It is not simply that some people will feel this way towards others and others will not. Rather, what is presented as the 'normal' situation of egoistic self-interest becomes something we need to explain, even if we acknowledge the enormous differences that exist between individuals. Possibly it is at this point that we require a clearer distinction between ends individuals choose for themselves, so indicating the different ways individuals find their happiness, and some sense of shared human needs.

Liberal theory often resists any such distinction, wanting to treat needs as if they are simply an extension of the ends people individually choose for themselves. This reticence may grow out of a healthy suspicion that, before we know it, some people will be claiming to decide the human needs of others. But this only makes it crucially important for people to identify and recognize their needs for themselves. Nor can we ever be sure of the road individuals are going to take. This is an arrogance that has sometimes been shared, in their different ways, by both revolutionaries and psychotherapists.

But what Wittgenstein helps us reinstate is a sense of the core nature of our needs for others. We misconstrue the place of morality in our lives and we misunderstand ourselves if we think we can exist as totally independent and self-sufficient people. It is this very masculine ideal which can damage and hurt men's lives. This is not a matter of placing before ourselves ideals which are unworthy, but of recognizing the harm we do ourselves through attempting to form ourselves in their image. This is not something we can begin to grasp unless we already question the identification of masculinity with reason.

This helps us realize that this is not simply a matter of replacing one ideal of masculinity by another. If we already assume that our emotional, somatic and spiritual lives can have no bearing upon the nature of our moral lives, all this talk of 'hurt' and 'damage' carries little weight. It is simply that we learn tacitly to accept to live up to the ideal of self-sufficiency that we have automatically grown up to accept. As men we grow up to feel good if we do not need anything from others. As I have argued, it is a sign of our strength that we can be supportive for others without needing any support for ourselves. We prove our masculinity through showing we do not need anything from others.

Wittgenstein suggests that if we deny our needs to respond directly towards others we are denying something important in ourselves. This is no longer a contingent issue. This is a direct challenge to Kant's idea that we should gradually weaken our instinctive responses towards others, since not only are they unreliable, but they take away from the moral worth of an action performed purely out of a sense of duty. It is Kant who helps sustain traditional notions of masculinity as he warns us of the help others might offer us since this will lessen the moral worth of our own individual efforts. Even though Kant was centrally concerned to illuminate the nature of human beings as moral beings, his implicit identification of reason, morality and masculinity, especially in his earlier more systematic writings, minimized the importance people can have for each other.[15] Our moral lives are essentially individualistic; we are constantly proving our moral worth as individuals. At some level others are distractions taking us away from our moral tasks, or else occasions to show our moral goodness. Our relationships with others are essentially secondary to our sense of moral identity, even our sexual and personal relationships.

Within a 'rationalist' culture, men learn to use language as a way of asserting themselves individually. We learn to hide our vulnerability since we know it will be interpreted as weakness. Language itself comes to exist as an independent and autonomous system that has been separated from any ongoing sense of our somatic and emotional selves. In this way language is less likely to betray our masculinity as it shows us to be vulnerable and feeling human beings. In bringing us into a different relationship to our language Wittgenstein is also bringing us back to ourselves. But he is also implicitly questioning the way our male identities are constructed out of our achievements, as if the accumulation of wealth and property necessarily reflects back on the quality of self.

As we learn to discount our needs for others, we also learn to grow up as men to discount our history and culture of masculinity. We are more than our reasons and thoughts. We injure ourselves as men, as our culture leaves us with a distorted sense of the importance of reason in our lives. What is more, it even weakens the quality of our thought, as reason constantly becomes formal and abstract as it is systematically separated from emotions and feelings. But we also impoverish ourselves as we learn to deny our history and culture to become equal citizens in civil society. As Mill realized, we become so anxious to prove we are 'normal' like everyone else, that we develop a real fear of anything that would make us different from others. Mill realized in *On Liberty* that even though people heralded individualism within the moral culture of liberalism, the social relations worked to impoverish people's sense of their own individuality.[16]

When we learn to use language as boys, we very quickly learn how to conceal ourselves through language. We learn to 'master' language so that we can control the world around us. We use language as an instrument that will help show us as independent, strong, self-sufficient and masculine. But as we learn to deny and estrange our individual and collective needs and wants so that we can live up to these ideals of ourselves we form and shape the kind of personal and sexual relationships we can have with others. Even though we learn to blame others for our unhappiness and misery in relationships we also know at some unspoken level how our masculinity has been limited and injured as we touch the hurt and pain of realizing how little we seem to feel about anything, even our friends and close relationships. Often we feel trapped and lost since the culture continually tells us we have the world to inherit. We do not know that the price is often knowledge of and relationship to ourselves.

Chapter Eight

STRENGTH

As men, we often learn to identify strength with independence and self-sufficiency. This can often make men withdrawn and inaccessible personally. We learn to dismiss 'personal issues', since morality and politics are defined in exclusively impersonal terms. Often we have had to forsake our relatedness to others to prove our masculinity. So it is that issues of autonomy and independence are set up often in quite different terms for men and women.

Women often grow up learning to care for others, and so to put the interests of others before their own. Often it is difficult to disentangle what they want for themselves and what they need for themselves. So it is that relational identities are constantly threatening to take over. For men, identity often involves an externalized relation to self, in which men learn to measure themselves against individual success and achievement. This is what often makes relationships problematic for men. It can be hard for men to learn to care for others in a way that is sensitive to their emotional needs and desires.

VULNERABILITY

As men, we often learn to lock our hurt and vulnerability deep inside ourselves. We do not really want to know about it ourselves. Sometimes we get angry and irritable at people, to fend off our sadness. This is a much more acceptable way for us to behave since anger is often identified with strength. At other times we talk over our feelings as a way of keeping them in check. Often it is a matter of learning to cope with situations, discovering reasons why we should not feel hurt, for instance because someone has not invited us to their party. We constantly give ourselves reasons to smooth over a situation. We do not want to feel rejected, and we certainly do not want to trigger the well of rejection and loneliness that at another level we carry around inside us. It is as if our emotions and feelings have to be 'reasonable' and 'rational' for us to allow them at all.[1]

We are so tied in with rationalist images of ourselves that they often seem to have a stronger reality than whatever feelings we have. We are so used to discounting certain emotions and feelings that often we do not even recognize them when they happen. John Cleese can remember a moment when: 'I made a really spiteful remark. It was like hearing someone else say it. I thought "That wasn't me. I'm not a spiteful person." I was ashamed, but I had to adjust my image of myself.' (The *Guardian*, 2 January, 1984). This kind of remark can help show the place of certain images in our lives. It is as if we shock ourselves if we get angry, feel resentful or spiteful, while at another level we can know that we have these feelings all the time. But we learn to keep them to ourselves. Often what is so terrifying to our public identity is showing others that we can be spiteful or resentful. Then the game is up: we feel as if we have been caught out.

Often it is not that we do not acknowledge our need for affection to others, but that we do not allow ourselves to experience the need for ourselves; we learn to discipline ourselves. Often it is hard to admit that we need affection especially if this means we are not 'really masculine'. Unless we fully acknowledge this difficulty to ourselves, we will tend to blame others. Often we have denied these needs for so long that we think that we do not continue to hurt because of them. We begin to feel that only weak people need affection, and that we should show our strength and independence to others without showing our vulnerability. But often we reach a point where we cannot express this need even if we feel it. We feel too embarrassed and uneasy with others.

Sometimes, for instance, it is easier to go for a sexual contact rather than ask for care and affection, even though this is not what we really need. We can feel frustrated and silently desperate as we blame others for our experience. We want affection and contact, but we seem incapable of asking for it. Part of this is the fear of rejection, but often this is connected to a fear of threatening our masculine sense of ourselves. It is as if the cost of our traditional masculinity has partly been in an estrangement from our needs for affection, dependency and vulnerability.

Freud has been able to illuminate how masculine identity has been achieved as separation from our mothers, through the workings of the Oedipal phase. We have had to forsake our relatedness to others to prove our masculinity. It is as if our experience of male identity has been formed so that we can only be ourselves as men as long as we remain independent and separate from others.[2] This helps explain some of the difficulties we can have as men in establishing close and loving relationships. As long as we are in control, we can feel secure. But as soon as our partners demand that we give more of ourselves emotionally, and learn to centre more of ourselves in the relationship, we find it difficult.

Through the separation from our mothers, we seem to separate from what we identify as the 'feminine' within ourselves. So we can only be men if we separate ourselves from our needs for affection and dependency. It is only if we fundamentally redefine our masculinity and the homophobia which is so often an aspect of male heterosexuality, that we can discover ways of integrating these aspects of our experience. But this also involves challenging the rationalist tradition that has identified masculinity with reason, weakening any sense of how our masculine identity develops out of our shared sense of experience, culture and history. As heterosexual men we seem to exist without any shared history of masculinity. There has been astonishingly little work done when we contrast it with the work of gay men.[3] In a strange sense we have been brought within a liberal moral culture to exist in future time. We are brought to identify closely with the decisions we need to make for the future. We are constantly looking beyond ourselves, working out how we can live out the ideals we have set for ourselves.

Since we are brought up within a liberal moral culture to stress our independence and separateness from others as men, we can find it difficult to discover and value what we share with other men. We are suspicious, as heterosexual men, of any shared historically-specific experience of masculinity. Rather, our inherited rationalism constantly reasserts itself, most recently in a post-structuralist form, as we prefer to see masculinity as a 'social construction', but one we can personally distance ourselves from as individual men. This is one reason it has been so difficult for heterosexual men to make use of consciousness-raising. Often this gets caught in a tense exercise of intellectualizing experience. We often do not know how to share ourselves more directly. But this also connects to the ways we have been brought up to relate to language.

As boys we learn to protect and hide our vulnerability. We learn to use language to defend ourselves. Philosophers who have recognized the importance of language as a means of expression, as Wittgenstein has done in his later writings, can nevertheless make it hard to explore the ways we also conceal ourselves through language. There are times when it might be quite appropriate to conceal what we know. It is a matter of the difficulties we have in showing our feelings when we would want to. Because Wittgenstein was concerned to challenge an entrenched notion in the philosophy of mind that, for instance, presents our language about pain as if it were the description of a mental state, he was concerned to show our expressions of pain as other forms of pain behaviour. This deeply subverts our inherited empiricist traditions. But as people have tended to misunderstand him as some kind of linguistic behaviourist, they have also failed to recognize the significance of his emphasis upon the rules making up a language-game. His argument against the 'privacy' of our experience has fostered an emphasis upon the public character of language learning. But this only traps us if we are not careful into the very dualities, say between 'private' and 'public', that he wanted to question in his later writings.[4]

The philosophy of language has tended to foster a notion of language as an impersonal and neutral system of rules. Wittgenstein has been assimilated into this tradition of thought that would also assimilate semiology into the same development. This has helped explain the influence of linguistics in recent years. If anything, this should show the depths of an inherited rationalism. Feminism has often wanted to remake itself in this image, rather than challenge its foundations. We lose the crucial insight into the relationship between language and power which

Gramsci asserts so clearly in his *Prison Notebooks* when he talks about a group which has,

> ... for reasons of submission and intellectual subordination, adopted a conception of the world which is not its own but is borrowed from another group; and it affirms this conception verbally and believes itself to be following it ... that is when its conduct is not independent and autonomous, but submissive and subordinate. Hence the reason why philosophy cannot be separated from politics ... (p.327).

It has been the tensions between thought and action which structuralist work has found it impossible to illuminate. Like phenomenology it has tended to get stuck into accepting that if a group is affirming a conception in its language and theory then this is the world it has constructed for itself. Both traditions have wanted to say that notions of 'independence' and 'autonomy' are themselves defined within the context of language since otherwise we would have to be appealing to a point beyond language to evaluate these different claims. This has made these traditions incapable of grasping the issue. This is something Simone Weil seems to have learnt from her reading of Spinoza.[5] Both were led in their own way partly to challenge the inherited rationalist traditions of their times.

POWER AND PROTECTION

But we need yet other terms to discuss men's instrumental relationship to language. We need to distinguish between the power which men as a sex sustain in the larger society, and the struggles of individual men to live up to this ideal of themselves. We have to make sure our language can illuminate how we experience these issues. We have to learn how we have grown up to use language to conceal our fear, dependency and vulnerability. So as small boys, we pride ourselves in learning not to feel scared or not crying when we have had a fall. We learn to make ourselves invulnerable, and place our experience at a safe distance from ourselves. Even though Wittgenstein does not explore these processes, he does leave us with a sense of the damage we are doing to ourselves as we interfere with what would otherwise be natural processes of expression. What is more, we place language at a distance, as we learn to express ourselves in the third person.

We are often concerned as men to live out a strong and independent image of ourselves. After a time we cannot help ourselves, as it becomes almost second nature for us as men to act out our ego feelings of anger and resentment when it would be more appropriate to the situation to act out of our heart feelings of sadness which could bring us more in contact with ourselves. We become familiar with a certain level of anger and irritation as a way of fending off others but also of keeping our softer feelings in control. We become uneasy and scared of letting ourselves experience a deeper level of feeling since this could bring our need and vulnerability closer to the surface of our experience. Rather, we choose to maintain a distance from a deeper contact and relationship with ourselves. We fear anything that would bring us into a fuller contact with ourselves, since this could threaten the images we have created for our masculinity. We are wary of questioning our familiar patterns.

As men we often learn to hold ourselves tight. We learn to maintain control in whatever situation we are in. We will not let things get to us, but choose to stay cool. This also means holding our bodies in a particular way – blowing out our chests and keeping our bums tight. This is what we take to be a masculine notion of strength. We have no sense of bigness in our feelings. It is as if our feelings are held tight in our heads but have no existence in our bodies. We assume that power is a clenched fist rather than an ability to experience a whole range of feelings and emotions. There are very different roots to our personal power. What is more, it is difficult to bring this issue into focus, since we tend automatically to assume it is a matter of putting more value on ideas than upon emotions and feelings. We will think that individuals will want to make different choices about this having already turned this into an intellectual issue of values. But this only shows how difficult it is to bring these issues into proper focus within our prevailing moral traditions of thought and feeling.

Our grasp of our emotional and somatic lives is already hedged in, if we approach them within a rationalist tradition in which personal identity is already conceived in terms of consciousness. It becomes difficult to appreciate that we are dealing with our relational capacities, with our capacities to have more equal and open relationships with others. At another level, this means acknowledging the power of social relations to hurt and harm us, rather than simply to restrict the choices we have available to us, or the goods and satisfactions we can appropriate. This means seeing that men can be injured, even damaged, because of the notions of 'strength' and 'power' we inherit in our culture. This does not simply give us a false and misleading ideal but affects the very processes of development of our capacities as human beings. This is not simply an issue of personal relations but affects the ways we think of morality and politics within a liberal moral culture. It is the very fragmentation of our experience into discrete and autonomous realms that is brought into question through this analysis.

INDEPENDENCE AND DEPENDENCE

Somehow we grow up to identify male identity with separateness. This means that as men we can have a strong sense of ourselves as separate and independent human beings while at another level have a very weak sense of personal self. We develop little ongoing dialogues with ourselves, and so can have little sense of our individual needs and wants. Rather we identify strength with not needing anything from others, as if we can only sustain a sense of our independence if we keep people away altogether.[6] In telling ourselves that we do not need the love and support of others, we gradually make ourselves incapable of receiving these from others. It is as if our emotional exchanges have been transformed into exchanges between goods. This makes little sense of the challenge from our partners that we give so little of ourselves in our personal and sexual relationships, since we readily assume we are working for our partners and families, rather than for ourselves. This is part of how an ethic of self-denial leaves men with so little understanding and relationship to themselves.

Since we grow up to think that we are strong if we can do without the help and support of others, it should be little surprise that our partners are left feeling isolated and alone. Often it is because we think we are doing everything for them, that we do not let them know that we need them, since we often experience this as weakness. Often we are withdrawn and inaccessible though we can also present ourselves as more open than we really are. I know how easily I do this. I assume that others will not know the difference, but of course they do. This is part of the myth of control we think we have over ourselves and the ways we present ourselves to others.

At another level, this just shows how dependent we are, since often we rely upon others to bring us back to ourselves, to interpret our emotional lives for us. But we do not recognize this as a form of dependency at all, which means that our partners get little acknowledgement and credit for the emotional work they are constantly exhausting themselves with. It is as if, as men, we have never really learnt how to have a relationship with someone, even ourselves. But this is rarely seen as more than a personal issue, since we do our best to define morality and politics in exclusively impersonal terms. This is an integral part of the universalism of our inherited moral traditions, but it is also part of our resistance to acknowledging that men and women might grow up with different relationships to themselves, as well as to morality, language and politics. Feminism challenges us too deeply for it not to be resisted, even if this resistance takes the form of attempts at co-option.

But it is difficult to identify the ways our inherited masculinity undermines a sense of personal self. Feminists have argued that men know who they are because they live in a society and culture that is made in their own image. But this can be to mistake the institutional power which heterosexual men undoubtedly have in the larger society to define the reality of others for the lived personal experience of men themselves. The issues of autonomy and independence are no less important for men, but they have to be set in different terms. Women have constantly had to struggle against defining themselves in relation to others. They exist as daughters, wives and mothers, but not for themselves. These relational identities are constantly threatening to take over, leaving women with a feeling that they have no existence and identity in their own right. Gay men and lesbians have had to learn to value and recognize themselves in an identity that the society constantly attempts to denigrate and abuse.[7] Blacks and Jews have constantly had to struggle against accepting the invisibility which a liberal moral culture offers if they are to be acceptable as equal citizens. In these different conditions, people are learning to define their own identity through recovering a shared history and culture.

Often it is a matter of learning to feel pride in what society has denigrated, refusing to accept the terms in which the dominant culture has chosen to define your reality. In each situation it is a matter of discovering particular sources of strength, sometimes revaluing what is judged as weakness, though sometimes acknowledging a shared history of oppression, abuse and humiliation. Through sharing a vulnerability, people have come to a renewed understanding of the sources of personal strength. In sharing themselves with others, they have ceased to feel ashamed and refused to feel guilty for themselves. This marks a profound political transformation of the personal, that had one of its sources in the struggles against the Vietnam war. This is a tradition men often find hard to understand. It has yet to be appreciated theoretically.

IDEALS, WORK AND MALE IDENTITY

For heterosexual men, the issues of independence and autonomy have barely been posed. The sociological analysis of the male role and the importance of sharing domestic tasks in bringing greater sexual equality has hidden some of these issues.[8] Our inherited sense of independence as men exists as a sense of separateness from others. It is built upon an exclusion of our feelings of need and dependency. As therapists have often discovered, our sense of masculinity is externally defined, since it grows out of an idealized relationship with a father with whom we often do not have an ongoing daily personal relationship. In this sense, masculinity exists as an ideal that we are constantly struggling to aspire to. Our gender is not anything we can be relaxed and easy about. It is something we have constantly to prove and assert. This was part of the deeper importance of work in men's lives, since it was through doing a 'man's job' that men could feel secure in their identity. This was a way of putting anxieties at rest, even if it meant working all the time. At least this was a place in which men could feel some security in themselves. Work is more than a source of dignity and pride.[9] It is the very source of masculine identity, so that without work – a common condition in the 1980s – it is as if men cease to exist at all.

It is as if as men we do not have an identity which belongs to ourselves, but an identity which is externally defined and only exists as a reflection of a working situation: so when men lose their jobs, they often lose a sense of themselves. This is not the same for women, who often have a clearer place and identity in relation to the family. But when men do not have a workplace to go to, they are often stuck at home feeling empty and lost. Often they will not even move themselves to put the washing in the machine, since they have never done it, and in any case, it is their wives' job. Working-class women often describe their husbands as being 'under their feet', as if there is no space for them in the home that has become the woman's domain. Since she has often had little else in her life, she is not going to take kindly to a change. She has her own routines to keep, and she does not want her husband to 'get in the way'. Often men become withdrawn and morose, as if the only meaning they had in their lives was as a 'provider', in which role they could feel useful and important.

Often it is because we are so identified with our work and activities, that without them we are lost. It is through our actions that we expect to get our approval and recognition from others, though often activities can also take us away from what is happening inside us. This is a way we continually fend off our sense of our own needs, as if we do not need anything at all for ourselves. Sometimes we get angry at others so as to control an emerging vulnerability and neediness, though often we are barely aware this is happening. But often in relationships we can show a sulky resentment, rather than asking directly for what we want. We do not want to articulate our needs and hurt at having lost a job. Often men keep this sense of rejection to themselves, telling themselves that their partners cannot really understand anyway. Often it is easier to put a brave face on things, letting others think things are really OK, rather than accept and share the intimacy of hurt and rejection.

Men often block off this deeper level of vulnerability which has become estranged from their very sense of masculinity. Since it is this sense of masculinity that is brought into question through not having a job, it can feel all the more important to hold tight and show resilience. This can become desperate because of the way our very identities are tied up with an externally-defined sense of masculinity. This is the only identity that can traditionally belong to us, since from our childhood our sense of self has been built upon a sense of being different from 'soppy girls'. Often we get stuck in this rigid and unyielding sense of ourselves. We resent the attempts of others to get close to us. We reject the understanding they have to offer thinking we can still prove our masculinity by showing we do not need anything from others.

In its own way, this can help reveal the weakness of a post-structuralist tradition that would argue that our individuality is constituted through discourse. The attempts to assimilate the different realms of our experience to notions of discourse serves to hide the tensions that exist between the sense of masculinity we inherit from childhood and the material relations in which we can realize this. In a period when a younger generation of school leavers in the 1980s may have no work to go to, the traditional relationship between masculine identity and work is threatened.[10] Sometimes this seems to mean that young men become tighter and invulnerable. They will neither let anything touch them, nor acknowledge, at least to adults, that at a deeper level they feel unsure and adrift. Often they need time and space to come to terms with themselves and redefine their inherited masculinity. You can see this process happening in aspects of punk culture.

In concealing our vulnerability to ourselves and others, we learn to present a certain image of ourselves. We become strangers to aspects of ourselves. This reflects itself in our relationship to language as we distance and disown parts of ourselves. We refuse to experience parts of ourselves that would bring us into contact with our hurt, need, pain and vulnerability since these each threaten our inherited sense of masculinity. This is perhaps changing for a younger generation of boys who have experienced more open and equal relationships with girls, but often people freeze against this new uncertainty and feel too threatened to share their vulnerability. Often we silence this emerging panic through moving into activities. We defeat the emergence of softer feelings and we close off from any fuller contact with unfamiliar parts of ourselves. We learn to use our language in the process. We learn a language of irony, disdain and cool. Different generations of men have learnt to distance themselves from their ongoing experience. It is as if we learn to exist at one remove from ourselves, as if we show how clever we are if we can observe with irony the details of our own lived experience.

Recent post-structuralist emphasis upon disclosure, useful as it can sometimes be in shaking up our inherited assumptions, has presented itself as materialist in a confusing way. Wanting to claim allegiance to some kind of Marxist theory, it has fallen back into a Kantian epistemology in which it is now language, rather than the categories of the mind, which organizes our experience of the social world. In a similar way to Kant's questioning of the notion of 'things in themselves', people have argued that you cannot appeal to a realm beyond discourse, as if to assess and evaluate the reality which discourse has defined. All we can do is bring another discourse into play which would tactically seek to challenge prevailing definitions. A familiar example from Laclau's work is the treatment of fascism.[11] In Italy, the fascists did not simply create a new terrain of political argument, but did their best to redefine and take over a well-established socialist discourse which already had some appeal for working people. We can no longer think in terms of issues of morality and of 'truth', since these are notions that are defined within a particular discourse, nor can we look to a notion of experience against which discourses can be tried. At some level this reproduces familiar relativist positions which maintain a strong appeal in our culture, even though they leave us powerless to morally condemn fascism. Not only does this remove us individually from the analysis, but it serves to reproduce a similar relationship to the social world that we know from a Cartesian tradition without the same claims to knowledge and certainty. It is this denial of any personal presence that has been such an endemic feature of the relationship between masculinity and rationalism.

Within these traditions it becomes difficult to raise issues about the relationship of language to our experience since, at some level, our experience has been assimilated into our language. I have already shown how this was no part of Wittgenstein's intention. Equally we could show that as we claim more of our experience and learn to relate to different parts of ourselves, so our relationship to our language changes. We gradually learn to bring our language into closer contact with our ongoing experience, articulating what emerges for us as we acknowledge more of the reality of our emotions, feelings and desires, and not what we would want them to be. But this means developing an inner relationship of honesty to ourselves, knowing that this is an ongoing process and that we will only gradually learn to have a fuller and more honest contact with ourselves.

Though we can decide that we want a fuller contact with ourselves because of the felt unreality and poverty of an experience in which nothing seems to matter to us, we cannot simply bring this about as an act of will. But possibly the first step could be to admit to ourselves and then to others if we remain unmoved and untouched by others and feel that something is dead inside us. Even if we decide that we want to change this situation, we also have to realize that it is not a matter of giving reasons to ourselves. If we experience and despair of an unreality and poverty in our experience, this can often begin a process of questioning our inherited rationalism and the relationships we have had with women and men. Even if we give ourselves all the reasons in the world why we should not bother with these issues and should feel happy in our lives we know that it makes no difference. Our experience is finding its own voice. We can no longer rely upon simply maintaining a strong sense of self-control if we have learnt for ourselves how this only seems to weaken and impoverish our experience. Rather than telling ourselves all the time how we would want our lives to be, we have to learn to listen to ourselves and accept more of how things actually are for us. As men we have never really had to learn to take this path.

I have learnt how hard it is to give myself time, even an hour for myself a day. There are always things I am supposed to be doing. A feeling of panic and anxiety emerges at the very thought of spending more time with myself. Either this has to be 'wasting time' or else I can feel that it is not 'deserved', as if we have to deserve whatever rest or happiness we can give ourselves. But this is also odd, because of the very limited sense we seem to develop as men that we have 'selves' we could want to relate to. We only seem to learn that the 'self' is something we have to

155

control tightly, since otherwise it might upset our plans. We have learnt for so long not to show or express too much, since others might put us down or use this against us. At all times we have learnt to show ourselves in control, keeping our shoulders up and our bums held in as if we are saying 'I'm going to be in charge, however much it hurts me'. We do not realize the cost and injury we do to ourselves in holding down our passion, power, energy and strength to appear as the 'reasonable' and 'self-controlled' men we are supposed to be. We never really give ourselves much chance to know ourselves better or develop more contact with ourselves, since as I have argued, this all threatens the 'control' we have been brought up to identify our masculinity with. We feel trapped though we do not know how we are constantly remaking this trap for ourselves.[12]

At some level we seem to become disinterested in ourselves, especially as our lives and relationships seem to become routine. Since we have so little relationship with ourselves, it is easy as men barely to realize that we expect so little and give so little in our relationships with others. Often we seem even to enjoy non-relationships in which we are giving and receiving very little of ourselves, since this at least does not threaten our traditional sense of male identity. As men we are so concerned not to need others, since this is only a sign of our dependency, that our relationships are often unclear and ambiguous. Often it is easier for us to be angry at others for not giving us anything, especially if we are tired and exhausted with over-working, though often we have not asked. Often it is harder to realize that we have not slowed down enough to give anything to ourselves through all this. It is as if we starve ourselves emotionally, and then feel surprised that our lives feel so empty. That this can seem obvious at the same time as it is so very hard to make some of these connections for ourselves, shows the depth of our in-herited traditions of thought and feeling which need to be challenged.

Chapter Nine

INTIMACY

As men we learn to treat emotions and feelings as signs of weakness. This makes it difficult for us to come to terms with our emotional lives and relationships. This can make it hard to identify emotional needs, for as we are less sensitive to ourselves, so it is hard to be responsive to others. This is partly what makes the challenges of feminism threatening to men. As men identify with their independence and self-sufficiency it can be difficult to acknowledge the nature of our dependency within relationships. All too often, men can take their partners for granted. As men learn to identify their own emotional needs, there will be less of a fear of intimacy. As we learn to accept our emotional life as an integral part of our masculine identity, there will be more basis for creating equality in our relationships and developing a different kind of presence in relationships.

FEAR AND WEAKNESS

As boys, we are brought up to distance ourselves from fear. We learn that we have constantly to prove our masculinity, we can never take it for granted. This builds enormous tension into contemporary conceptions of masculinity. Fear is defined as an unacceptable emotion, but in disowning our fear and learning to put a brave face to the world, we learn to despise all forms of weakness. Strength is identified with a stiff upper lip, as we learn systematically to discount any feelings of fear. We learn not to show our feelings to others, since this is an immediate sign of weakness. This is a deep cultural inheritance. A remark in Sue Cartledge's diary that was printed in *Spare Rib* shows the way that women are also deeply affected:

I have always clung to a false idea of strength – the suppress-it-all, stiff-upper-lip, model. But real strength is recognizing your own weakness and allowing others to see it too. I must free myself from the tyranny of the past before it destroys any more of the present and future.

I so desperately want somebody else to be my solution. But I should know by now that it's an impossible dream. Of course, another person can seem to bring great happiness for a while. But unless you can resolve your own problems, they will sink it in the end. And the great happiness you feel comes from *you* – from your own capacity for love and joy which the romance (temporarily) liberates. May 1981 (*Spare Rib*, 136, Nov. 1983).

It can be hard for men to hear that 'real strength is recognizing your own weakness', since this threatens our very sense of masculinity. It is hard enough for us to acknowledge our own fear to ourselves, let alone show it to others. In estranging ourselves from our feelings, we block whatever access we might otherwise develop to our inner lives. We learn to respond externally to others as well as ourselves, doing what we have learnt to be appropriate. Often this means doing things for others. But this produces its own form of insensitivity and blindness, though we remain largely unaware of this.[1]

As men it can be hard to acknowledge the conception of strength we inherit as a 'false idea'. It is even more difficult to appreciate the ways it can destroy the quality of our present experience or the depth of our relationships with others. We fight any such recognition, since it promises to compromise our very sense of masculinity. The dominant traditions of social theory maintain a silence over these issues as they are safely relegated to the private sphere. The Marxist language of social relationships tends to treat these considerations as 'bourgeois individualism', thereby blocking any serious consideration of people's relationships to themselves, though this was an important theme in Marx's early conception of alienation.[2] Not only does this make us insensitive to ourselves, but it blinds us to the hurt we do to others in our relationships. We use our power in relationships to encourage others to deny their feelings of vulnerability and weakness, lest they only get put down by us. This can make it difficult for women to show their hurt to us, but this does not mean it goes away. We can often treat this as an occasion to show our own strength as we offer our shoulders for support. In this way we can keep our own vulnerability in check.

As men we grow up without ever really learning to care for others. We expect women to care for us, but we do not really know how to care for them. We are so concerned with defending our position in the world of work, and with sustaining our sense of individual achievement, that we want our partners to identify themselves with our success. It is this very identification that women have been traditionally brought up to make. They have learnt to put others' interests before their own, and they have learnt to discount their own individual needs and wants.[3] This meant that they learnt to expect very little emotional support from men. But this situation has changed with feminism and women are recognizing how little they get in their emotional relationships with men. I have been constantly challenged for not giving enough of myself in my relationships, though it has taken time to grasp what this means.

Caught up in the competitive world of work, men can experience any kind of demand from their partners as a kind of betrayal. Often men feel – or at least tell themselves – that they are doing all this work not for themselves, but for their wives and children. They experience themselves living at the edge of frustration, and so expect to be esteemed, not challenged in their intimate relationships. We can feel that we are owed the support of our partners so we can compete against other men. This is what makes men react so impulsively and aggressively when they are told they are not giving enough in their relationships. As men we can expect our partners to do the emotional work in supporting us at work, but we resent it if any demands are made on us to respond more openly in our emotional relationships. Sometimes it can be easier to participate more in domestic work and childcare than it can be to change the tone of our emotional and sexual relationships. Often we simply do not understand what is being asked of us. We dismiss the demand as 'emotional' and we silently hope that it will go away.

Because our traditional notions of masculinity place us at such a distance from our own emotional lives, it makes it difficult for us to know our own emotional needs, let alone respond to others. It can make it hard to give the kind of support that is needed. Sometimes it might simply be an acknowledgement of how difficult it has been for someone in the early months of a new baby. I know how hard it was for me to learn to do this, thinking that somehow I was being blamed, that if only I had been willing to do more, things would have been better. It is the idea that it is always a question of doing more that is so tied to our masculine selves.

As men we think we should be able to cope with any situation that life presents us with. We are constantly pushing ourselves beyond our limits, thinking that we thereby make ourselves invulnerable to the criticism of others. In this sense our masculinity has become 'super-human', and we have little sense of our individual limits. We exhaust ourselves taking on much more than we can manage, proving our very sense of masculinity in constantly pushing ourselves against our limits. We barely acknowledge our own tiredness. We work as if we are machines, oblivious of our own bodily needs, and strangely proud of this. Often we so exhaust ourselves at work that we have little left for our emotional and sexual relationships. We are drained and empty. We are oblivious to the economy of our energies. Because we are so exhausted, it is difficult to listen to demands when we get home. The truth is that we have wasted ourselves at work, but we expect to be praised for our exertions, not castigated when we get home.

EMOTIONAL NEEDS

Since we so easily discount our own emotional needs and wants, it can be difficult to respond to the needs and wants of others. As we become more sensitive of ourselves we can become more open to others. We cannot simply decide, as an act of will, to be more sensitive and open to our partners. This is difficult for us to admit since we are brought up to assume that we can do anything that we put our minds to. This brings us face to face with an area of powerlessness, though we do everything before acknowledging it. We refuse to admit that our education into masculinity might have left us emotionally undeveloped. This is something that J. S. Mill had to learn about himself. In his autobiography he talks of the utmost rationality of his upbringing and the way that this education had left him as a child emotionally. This is a predicament we do our best to avoid.[4]

160

We prefer to pretend to be able to cope with emotional situations that we can barely grasp; often we simply do not understand what is involved. We hide an endemic fear of personal emotions and personal conflict behind a wall of rational disdain. We protect ourselves with our own rationality. We fail to acknowledge our own deep hurt, since we can only think of this as weakness. We fear that if we allow our softer feelings to surface, we shall never be able to regain control of ourselves. It is this form of wilful ignorance and fear of the personal that has come to characterize contemporary masculinity. It unifies men who would otherwise conceive the world in very different political terms.

We are no less men because we have learnt to identify our needs to be held and touched. Freud realized that sexuality is also a site for regression, and that many of our infant needs can also find expression. But it is often only in the context of a close and trusting relationship that we can share these parts of ourselves, that we can learn to integrate them as parts of ourselves. So we have to be open to making discoveries about ourselves and so suspend our judgement of what is 'normal' or 'appropriate'. But this knowledge threatens the very form of control as domination of our emotional and sexual lives that we have been brought up to take for granted. This was a control which meant distance from our emotions. The less we knew the better. Our bodies were to be trained and used as machines. If we acknowledged needs, these were simply the mechanical needs of a machine. This had nothing to do with our individualities, which were defined through our reason. But this is a 'tyranny of the past' which has to be carefully deconstructed because it cannot be overthrown unless it is known in all its intimacy and power.

As men we never learn to take responsibility for our emotional and sexual lives. Even though men constantly talk about how important their wives and children are to them, and this idea plays a significant part in organizing their sense of their work lives, it is also difficult to make this a central reality for them. I mean that, as men, we learn to identify our sense of individual self and achievement with our work lives. It is as if our egos are built for the public realm. On the other hand it is a striking fact that if women are living successful work lives, they can often feel dismal failures if their sexual relationship is going wrong. This seems to exist nearer the centre of their experience than ever seems to be the case for men.[5] I think it is a constant struggle for men to treat their emotional and sexual relationships as primary. It seems to come after the demands of work, even when the relationship is approaching an obvious crisis. Somehow this is connected to the difficulties men often have in caring for others.

A fear of intimacy has held men in a terrible isolation and loneliness. Often men have very few close personal relationships: we learn to live in a world of acquaintances. We grow up learning to be self-sufficient and independent, we learn to despise our own needs as a sign of weakness. Often we ask very little from others, though we do expect them to do our emotional work for us. But since we are largely unaware of these needs, we rarely appreciate others for doing this. This becomes another part of invisible female domestic labour. But since we have such little sense of our own needs, it can be difficult for us to appreciate the needs others have. This often makes us crude and insensitive in our caring for others.

This is partly what has made women seem so unintelligible to men. But men have rarely appreciated this as a brutalization of their own natures, or had much sense of how traditional notions of masculinity could be a 'tyranny' which is able to destroy both their present and future relationships. Even our existing theories of ideology fail to do justice to the material significance of our sexual identities, since they tend to treat them as emotional and thereby beneath rational consideration. Where our sexual identities are treated as social and historical constructions, we are left with little sense of their ongoing interrelationship with a developing sense of self. This gives us little sense of conflicts individuals are left with or the ways in which people can change.

Often we fail to acknowledge how dependent we are on our partners, because dependency is automatically interpreted as weakness. This means that we often leave our partners hanging. We fail to realize ourselves the importance of others and we fail to let them know. Sometimes this is connected to a fear of loss and separation. We think that if we let our partners know how much we love and need them, we are somehow compromising our independence. Often men think about this in terms of 'freedom', though it is often connected to a fear of intimacy and commitment. It is as if it is almost second nature for us to withhold ourselves emotionally. We fear our own vulnerability, scared of what it might reveal about ourselves. If we reveal more of ourselves, we prefer it to be in the dark of the night. Often it is only in the context of sexuality that we can allow ourselves to be close and intimate. This is sometimes the only way we know of reaching a little closer to ourselves.

Because it is often the intimacy that we fear, many men turn to pornography, since this seems to offer the excitement without the personal vulnerability.[6] This seems to be a way of feeling sexual without having to feel intimate. Often, as men, we confuse our needs for intimacy with our needs for contact and sexuality. Our sexual needs are given more public recognition and seem to confirm our masculinity, rather than threaten it. For this reason we often go for the sexual contact as a way of fulfilling our needs for dependency, even touch. Somehow these have been made difficult to identify, let alone acknowledge.

Often we end up attempting to fulfill a whole range of separate, even contradictory, needs in our sexual contact. Because we are so unused to making these crucial differentiations for ourselves we often end up feeling dissatisfied. Since we do not have a language in which to identify our emotional and sexual needs, and since the very recognition of needs seems to compromise our masculine control, we seek to satisfy our different needs without really being able to identify them. Our needs are undifferentiated. Often we might simply want to be held and nurtured, but this very passivity seems threatening, so we attempt to satisfy these different needs in the context of our sexual contact. Often we blame our partners for not being ready to interpret our needs for us. But this is simply to shift a responsibility which is ours.

SEXUALITY AND INTIMACY

It is partly because we learn to identify self-control with self-sufficiency that we never learn to identify our different needs. We assume that we have to be constantly active in our sexual encounters. This is why we can feel fear if women take a more active role in sexual relations: we seek to place strict boundaries upon this activity. But it is also because sex becomes orgasm-oriented that we can feel nervous and uneasy if our sexual encounters do not reach towards any such end. We fear making close eye contact and slowing the whole process. I know what deep anxieties this has brought for me. It is so easy to assume that our sexual contact has little to do with the depth and quality of our personal relationship. We prefer to see sex as an autonomous sphere, which has little to do with the closeness and intimacy. The Left has often reproduced this notion, seeing sex as a 'physical need', like drinking a clear glass of water, as Lenin said to Clara Zetkin. This was to treat sex as a commodity, rather than to challenge this bourgeois conception. Unfortunately, it is this undifferentiated conception of human needs that has been made an integral aspect of historical materialism. It fosters a kind of universalism that carries an Enlightenment heritage. So it becomes impossible to recognize that in clarifying our needs, we are also defining our individuality.

If at some level it is important to reassert Freud's notion that we are sexual beings so that, in some sense, we wither if we are completely deprived of sexual contact, it is also important to stress the individuality of our sexual needs. As we change, so do our sexual needs. Defining our sexual needs and learning to articulate them clearly is an integral part of defining our individualities. But these are also needs which are often shaped within the context of a developing relationship with a partner. As we learn to define the kind of touch and contact we like, we also have to realize that our needs will not always be completely met. Sex has to be negotiated and this can mean conflicting demands.[7]

This means being open to discovering what our individual emotional and sexual needs are at the moment, recognizing that they will change later. It is this which gives individuality and character to our emotional and sexual lives. But this also means learning to be vulnerable, and learning to risk ourselves with others. As we formulate our desires and needs, we are learning to reappropriate significant parts of ourselves. But this can mean identifying our needs for dependency and passivity as well as, at different times, our needs to be active and independent. This involves taking an individual responsibility for our sexual lives as we learn to voice our individual needs in a clear and open way. But this is threatening to the kind of control we have grown up to assume. We have to be open to discovering these needs ourselves, which means learning to attune ourselves to the needs of our bodies.

This is no longer simply a matter of using our bodies as instruments to satisfy our sexual needs, but learning to respond to the needs of our own bodies as they emerge. This can be a very anxious process. We would no longer see power as a matter of control, as a matter of getting others to do what we want which is often the core of masculine fantasies about sex. It involves learning to take a different kind of responsibility for our individual sexuality. As we deepen the contact we have with our own bodily experience, we begin to appreciate just how estranged we have been from our emotional and somatic lives. We learn to transform our understandings of strength, power and control. These notions come to have a different meaning and significance, as they are rooted in an ongoing contact with different levels of our experience.

I have sometimes felt that it is wrong to have to articulate and negotiate my sexual needs. I want my partner to be able to respond to me intuitively, and I recognize the ways in which language can so easily get in the way. This expresses a deep masculine fantasy about sexuality. Often it ignores the reality of the situation we are in. It replaces it with a dream that has little to do with the experienced reality of our sexual lives. This connects to the difficulties we often have in recognizing our partners as equal sexual beings, rather than as extensions of ourselves. It is as if we inherit as heterosexual men the deep cultural myth that women are fundamentally there to pleasure us. We feel this, though at another level, we share the culture's fear of pleasure and so the fear of sexual pleasure as undeserved. Often we have to take our pleasures in silence.

RESPONSIBILITY, SEXUALITY AND CONTROL

There is another sense in which we fail to take responsibility for our sexual lives: we grow up to see others as the source of our happiness and pleasure. As Sue Cartledge says in her diary, 'I so desperately want somebody else to be my solution.' We constantly look to others, so that we do not have to take responsibility for ourselves. This is something that liberal individualism

165

has failed to illuminate. It has turned sexuality into a goal or end, and so into a measure of individual achievement and success. Sex becomes an issue of masculine conquest which reflects upon the male ego. Not only does it become difficult to ground sexuality in the issues of ongoing relationships, but it becomes difficult to give it a centrality and importance in our lives. It simply becomes another area in which men are forced to prove ourselves.

But, as I have already said, the familiar socialist critique of 'bourgeois individualism' has blocked the possibility of developing Marx's early insights into the ways in which individuals are estranged from themselves in capitalist social relations. The Marxist emphasis upon production has marginalized a serious discussion of sexuality and sexual relations of power. It fails to encourage us to think seriously about what it means to assume responsibility and control in different areas of our lives.[8] It is nervous about thinking in terms of individual responsibility at all, unless it has to do with the self-denial that is expected of a person who is to be 'seriously' considered as a revolutionary. But if socialists cannot even take responsibility for our own lives and relationships, what are we offering to others? We have been trapped in a particular masculine rationalist myth which offers us overall control of the larger society through the workings of our reason. This is another version of the familiar idea that work has to come first in the Protestant ethic.

Feminism has brought these issues home. It has punctured the pretentiousness of so much rhetoric on the Left. It has forced us back into taking more responsibility for our relationships and childcare. Often this meant a withdrawal from politics, in the late 1970s. But for many people this has meant a reconsideration of the sources of their political involvement, which has been no bad thing. Men were learning that they could analyse the fate of the international capitalist economy, but were speechless when it came to talking through issues in their sexual relationships. If men carried power in the structures of capitalist society, it was becoming clear that this was at a considerable price in terms of their own capacities and desires.

As men, we had learnt to put our work first, because this was where our identity was formed. We expected our partners to accept this, since this was the source of the family's income. This was also the source of our individual power: it was the way in which the demands of women and children could be silenced. But with the questioning of feminism, it became clear that there were areas in our lives in which 'the emperor had no clothes'. We became angry, spiteful and jealous, as we accused women of being irrational.

We did not understand why they were bringing up hurts from the past. We did not want to be faced with our past behaviours, especially when we assumed that this could do no good to anyone and could not be changed. We did not understand the need for the past to be opened and the pain shared if it was to be purged. We could not believe in this as a redemption, since this was not a process we were a part of. We could only think they wanted to hurt and punish us. If we were shocked at the depths of resentment, even hatred, and felt we could not recognize ourselves as the figures of total evil, we could only respond defensively. Often little was learnt as relationships ended.

If we feel hurt and rejected, often the only solution we know is to find another partner who appreciates us. It is because at some level we have never learnt to take responsibility for our emotional lives that we assume that if things go wrong, then it means we have been with the wrong partner. The Protestant ethic has so damaged our sense of the worth of our own natures that we can only look beyond ourselves for the source of our joy and happiness. Even then it can feel as if this is undeserved. As men we are cast into ceaseless work and activities to prove our worth. Often when we are alone or doing nothing, we feel lost. It is as if we only exist in the image of others. This is part of the narcissism that Freud recognized in the male ego. Often this means that men are constantly assertive in the public realm and seem to have a secure and independent sense of themselves, but this sense of strength may have not deep personal roots in the self, but be based on quite brittle foundations.

Feminism has often failed to understand the nature of masculine strength, power and identity. It has presented it too clearly. It has not understood how brittle it often is. Often it cannot have deep roots, because it is built upon the denial of emotional and bodily experience. As men we learn to live out the image we have of ourselves and we cut out any feelings, intuitions or thoughts that do not fit with it. It is because we identify our identity with our reason that we are so capable of doing this and because we grow up to deny our emotions and body as genuine sources of knowledge. But this leaves us with a strength that is confirmed in our activities in the world. Often it means we deny our feelings of loneliness and isolation so as to be able to sustain the notion of strength as self-sufficiency and independence. But often this puts great strain on our emotional relationships as they take the weight of all these unacknowledged needs that do not cease to be important to us because they are not openly acknowledged.

There is a different kind of strength which grows out of a capacity to identify our own needs. This involves learning to identify our own problems and taking responsibility for them ourselves. We no longer see others as the source of our own feelings and emotions, expecting them to make us feel better. There is a traditional vision of relationships in which both partners are seen as incomplete in themselves and they come together to find a completeness. Often this means seeking in others what we have never learnt to give to ourselves; this has deep sources in childhood when as boys we were looked after by other mothers. We never learn to take a very basic responsibility for ourselves. This has to do with cooking and cleaning, but it also has to do with learning to identify and fulfil our own emotional needs – we often expect women to take the emotional initiative in relationships. We want to have our needs met without having to articulate them since the very acknowledgement of our needs compromises the self-sufficiency we have been brought up to identify with.

At another level we are fearful that if we ever contacted our unmet needs, they would be so overwhelming that no one would want to have a relationship with us. We interpret this as weakness. It is difficult to realize that it is just the kind of sharing that others are often demanding of us. It is this which promises to give our relationships greater depth, but it is also difficult for partners when we swing between denying that we have emotional needs at all, to a sense of being totally overwhelmed by our needs. This relates to our own disconnection with this level of our experience. Taking more responsibility for ourselves means expecting to do some of the emotional work for ourselves. This promises to create a sense of balance in a relationship. This means being aware, as Sue Cartledge showed herself to be, that 'the great happiness you feel comes from *you* from your own capacity for love and joy which the romance (temporarily) liberates.'

This means that, as men, we have to learn to meet more of our own needs, learning to give the time and attention to ourselves that we so easily dismiss as 'self-indulgent'. Not only do we need to learn what we are capable of giving to ourselves but we have to take more responsibility for working on our own emotional and sexual issues. The truth is that not only do we take our partners for granted, but that we also take ourselves for granted. We do not know how to give our relationships the kind of priority we say they have for us. But this involves learning to live in the present reality of our relationships rather than putting everything off to a future which never comes. This means exploring what matters to us individually and challenging the notions of masculine success and ambition.

FEAR, DESIRE AND MASCULINITY

When we give attention to our sexual development, we find ourselves questioning Freud's account of a boy's Oedipal resolution. Freud stresses the absolute finality of the boy's resolution of his Oedipus complex. As he says, 'In boys ... the complex is not simply repressed, it is literally smashed to pieces by the shock of threatened castration.' ('Some psychical consequences of the anatomical distinction between the sexes').[9] At least Freud helps us recognize fear at the core of our sexual identities as boys. We are shocked into giving up our sexual desires towards our mothers at the threat of castration by our fathers.

This shows the level of risk that is attached to the welling up of sexual feelings, so we should hardly be surprised if later we have difficulties in integrating them into our ongoing sense of self. Often our sexual feelings are represented as free-floating so that we barely have to take responsibility for them. This inevitably minimizes the risk of our sexual feelings, even if it makes it that much harder for us to own and integrate our sexual experiences.

Within Freud's account we are left feeling the wrongness for our sexual feelings towards our mothers. We are made aware of the threat of our fathers as rivals and we are forced to repress our sexual feelings, even though they are deeply embedded. Fear and repression are at the core of the formation of masculine sexuality in Freud's account. Nancy Chodorow's *The Reproduction of Mothering* helps us understand the weight of this relationship for boys:

> Compared to a girl's love for her father, a boy's Oedipal love for his mother, because it is an extension of the intense mother–infant unity, is more overwhelming and threatening for his ego and sense of (masculine) independence ... This mother–son love threatens her husband and causes him to resent his son. The intensity of the Oedipal mother–son bond (and the father–son rivalry) thus causes its repression in the son. (p. 131)

So Freud shows a deep connection between the formation of male sexuality and the fear of castration. As boys we fear retaliation for our desires. This sharpens our need to repress love for our mothers, or so the story goes. We learn to fear our own sexual feelings, lest we be unable to control them. This is the source of a deep ambivalence which can show itself in the guilt men seem to feel when they become aware of their treatment of women. Often the first challenge of feminism is met by an attempt of men to forsake our very masculinity, as if we are to feel guilty not simply for what we have done to women but for the very fact of being men.

Perhaps this tendency connects to the primal guilt men feel in relation to the love we share for our mothers. Not only are we forced to forsake these feelings out of fear of revenge and castration but we are also bought off the benefits of masculinity into identifying with our father, who would otherwise have crushed us. So if we are to hold with Freud's theory, we get some insight into a possible source of the ambivalent feelings many men seem able to feel towards our masculinity. It is surprising how often you hear men who want to distance themselves from the explorations of men's consciousness-raising groups, saying that it is not an issue for them since they have no difficulties in their relationships to women and that, in any case, they feel closer to women than they do to men.

If we think of the Oedipal fear that as boys we had of our fathers, it is hardly surprising that boys feel such uneasy feelings

towards other boys, though this has to be placed in the cont
of the competitive relations in the larger society. From t
beginning our identification with our father is built upon fe
and anxiety, though this is something we bury for ourselves. As
Chodorow describes the situation:

> A boy gives up his mother in order to avoid punishment, but
> identifies with his father because he can then gain the benefits
> of being the one who gives punishment, of being masculine
> and superior. (p. 113)

This begins to show the depths at which notions of male
superiority are tied in with the development of a masculine
heterosexual identity. We also find hints of some of the sources
of the splits that contemporary masculinity suffers from. We
find it hard to bear ambivalence, and we want to use our reason
to decide situations once and for all. We think more easily in
terms of principles and in terms of right and wrong. This is the
way we seek to organize and control our personal relations. So,
for instance, we find it hard to accept the strength of feelings we
might have both for and against ending a relationship. We want
to think that if the decision was 'right', if we worked things out
rationally, then we should not feel all the pain of separation. We
should not feel the need to mourn a relationship we have chosen
to end. We struggle to make our emotions and feelings fit our
rational preconceptions.[10]

This is also deeply embedded in the superiority we grow up to
feel towards the emotionality and 'soppiness' of women. At some
level we can protect ourselves from being threatened by women
we are close to, because we are so assured of our superiority.
This is one aspect of men often finding it easier to be close to
women. This feeling of superiority runs deep. Possibly it is a way
of dealing with the primal betrayal of our feelings towards our
mothers. This is a way we sell ourselves. We are forced to
sacrifice our integrity so that after this it is difficult to trust our
feelings and emotions. This is a way of dealing with the hatred
we would otherwise carry for our fathers. As Freud recognizes,
'It is only in male children that we find the fateful combination
of love for the one parent and simultaneous hatred for the other
as a rival.' ('Female sexuality'). Somehow we learn to control this
hatred for our fathers through coming to identify, while at the

same time learning to disown, the feelings of love and affection we have for our mothers.

The Freudian story can easily seduce us into thinking in its own terms. It makes it difficult to show the historically specific constellation of relationships within which a particular form of masculinity is developed.[11] It is the decline of the husband's presence in the home – partly due to transformations within the labour process which have denied men the dignity and authority often identified with skilled work – which has created a situation in which a wife is as much in need of a husband as children are of a father. This encourages women to turn their attention and interest to the next obvious male – the son. In an important sense, fathers could be experienced, and could experience themselves, as dispensable. Though this will have left some men with a sense of freedom to pursue their work, at another level it helps explain the growth of the kind of jealousy that Freud is talking about.

This could well affect the intrusions that fathers make as authority figures within the family, and the tone of resentment they find themselves expressing towards their children. Often women will cease to feel so sexually interested in their husbands as they learn to discover a form of sexual satisfaction in relation to their sons. Chodorow hints at the way fathers are excluded and exclude themselves from the ongoing family relationships:

> Just as the father is often not enough present to prevent or break up the mother–daughter boundary confusion, he is also not available to prevent either his wife's seductiveness or his son's growing reciprocal incestuous impulses ... He projects his own fears and desires onto his mother, whose behaviour he then gives that much more significance and weight. (p. 105)

Though Chodorow's discussion has been important in opening up this discussion, it often remains trapped within the psychoanalytic categories themselves. This is unfortunate especially since her discussion brings us to the edge of challenging some of them.

SUPERIORITY AND GUILT

Chodorow's discussion, however, does help illuminate the ease with which, as men, we often take out our resentments on those who are closest to us. It is as if it has become almost second

172

nature for us to assume a position of superiority to women we relate to, even when we have been anxious to share domestic work and childcare. We often take up a judgemental position towards the efforts of others, with the implicit notion that we really could have done better ourselves. Somehow it becomes hard to acknowledge all the effort and attention that has gone into, say, cooking a meal or choosing presents. As men we so easily take these activities for granted so that when we do them ourselves we either turn them into an exhibition of individual skill or else squeeze them around the more central activities of our day. We can sense the deeper sources of some of this behaviour in the ways that our masculine sexual identity is established through feeling superior to women we have loving feelings for and centring ourselves in a masculine competitive world. It is as if we only know how to feel good about ourselves if we put others down.

The depths of male competition seem to resist change, even once men become aware of them. Possibly it is because our very identities are established in these realms. Since we are boys our relationships with women are used as ways of proving our esteem to other boys. This is also what makes it so difficult to give energy and attention to our personal and sexual relationships which we so easily take for granted. The deep splits which Freud identifies live on as a split between the public world of masculine identity and the private realm of relationships. According to Chasseguet-Smirgel all children must free themselves from their mother's omnipotence in order to achieve a sense of autonomy and independence.[12] Insofar as a boy achieves this liberation, he does so through his masculinity and his possession of a penis.

As Chodorow describes this process, 'His penis and masculinity both compensate for his early narcissistic wound and symbolize his independence and separateness from his mother' (p. 122). But this is to identify masculinity and independence as seeing oneself as having no needs. This involves recognizing our emotions and feelings as no part of our masculine identity which is established through an identification with our fathers in the public realm. Since our sexual feelings echo a primal loss of mother, and remind us of the guilt we feel at betrayal both of our own feelings and our relationship to her, they are often experienced as external happenings which we only with difficulty experience as deeply integrated with our personalities. We come to fear our own pleasure.

I think this helps explain the ease with which we 'cut off' from our ongoing relationships. We have learnt to compartmentalize our feelings so that we can carefully control them. But this very 'cut off' quality can hurt our developing sexual relationships and make it difficult for us to learn to take initiative and responsibility for our relationships. Often it makes our relationships incidental and our feelings unclear. Because we grow up to assume that our masculine identity has to do with our individual success and achievement in the public realm, this constantly undermines our resolve to take more initiative and responsibility in our sexual and personal relationships. Even though we are often not aware of it, we often insist on controlling the terms of relationships we are in. We get irritable if things are not done our way and we resist giving up control.

Often it is women who bring up issues in the relationship, and we find it hard to give the attention and time to resolve them. It is as if this all has to be fitted into the time we have left over from our all-important work. Then we are inevitably surprised at the intensity of the feelings our partners have held, but this only shows how out of touch we have been with the relationship as our energies and attention have been elsewhere. Sue Cartledge, in the collection *Sex and Love* shows how feminism has clearly exposed this aspect of patriarchal morality:

> As women we are brought up to be 'unselfish' and more aware of other people's needs than our own. This is the pattern on which countless women have moulded their lives. However, martyrdom is not so simple. Suppressed desires have a way of resurfacing as resentment. A women learns 'to give to others out of the well of her own unmet needs'. But the well starts to boil with fury, runs out in gullies of bitterness, dries up.
>
> 1974: When I came back I started to cry with frustration. Then I shouted at Stefan – all kinds of things came out. That we always did what *he* wanted, made love or not when *he* wanted; that I didn't have the strength of will to decide what I wanted to do, and do it .... ('Duty and desire: creating a feminist morality', p. 16)

I always seem to be surprised and shocked when this happens. I become defensive and can hear myself accusing. I recognize that something is terribly wrong, but I do not really know what to do about it. I am shaken by the fury and bitterness. I find it hard to accept that things can be that bad, though I know at some level they are. Part of me just wants to flee or withdraw. It is as if all long-term heterosexual relationships seem to be doomed in our time. For all my efforts at a more equal relationship, I have to recognize how blind and insensitive I am. It seems so easy to take our partners for granted and so hard to learn to take an active responsibility for what is going on in the relationship.

It is as if we are constantly split between a public and a private world and as if our very identity in the public world of work is constantly draining our best energies. We are scared of opening ourselves to a sense of our emotional needs since we have controlled them so tightly for so long. We fear being overwhelmed. We do not want to recognize all the frustrations we put up with daily in our work lives. We want to put a good face on things, even though at some level we know we are not being honest with ourselves. But honesty and truth have never carried much weight in the capitalist world of work.

Often we respond with anger and bitterness at demands for a more equal relationship. It is as if the denials in our own work lives are not being appreciated. As women refuse to support us emotionally and demand that we learn to do this work for ourselves our sense of masculine identity is thrown into crisis. We tell ourselves that we are putting up with everything in our work lives to support wives and children and that we are not asking for anything for ourselves. But this is part of the problem.

We are so used to denying our own needs, even to ourselves, that there is little basis upon which we could negotiate a more equal relationship. We so easily feel lost since we have no language in which to articulate this new experience and fear closer contact with other men at a time of weakness and vulnerability. We assume that others will not really want to know us. As this crisis has hit the lives of many men, relatively few have sought the support of a men's consciousness-raising group. The need for validation in another relationship with a woman has often been most pressing. Often the pain of rejection is too difficult to live with. Sometimes there is a deep feeling of bitterness and resentment towards feminism since this is blamed for the break-up of the relationship. Little is learnt.

Chapter Ten

CONCLUSION: MASCULINITY, MORALITY AND POLITICS

The reclamation of masculinity as a social and historical experience in the process of constantly being reorganized has become an urgent practical, moral and political matter. I have shown how this involves the critical engagement both with personal and emotional experience, and with the terms, philosophical and moral, in which we grasp and theorize that experience. This involves coming to terms with the quality of power in relationships, where it derives from as well as how it is experienced. This involves arguing for a distinction between power as something that people can develop within themselves and power as either domination, as in a zero sum conception, or as a kind of ever-present substance, as we find in Foucault.

Foucault has influentially argued that power emanates from everywhere and so has got away from the problems of a zero-sum conception of power. But he does it by somehow formalizing power through a conception which sees power as essentially constitutive, and thereby making it impossible to grasp the injuries that are done to individual lives. Like the structuralist theory in relation to which it has grown, it is bereft of a moral language. It fails to come to terms with the indignities and humiliations of the lives of so many who suffer from relationships of subordination. It critically fails to illuminate a sense of self-empowerment which feminism has often nourished. This allows people to talk about subverting power as domination within relationships or whatever, through the empowerment that develops through authentic individuality. This is no less crucial for men than it is for women. It involves an exploration of desires and needs. It also involves, as I have shown, that

177

understanding the different relationships we can have to language helps transform the quality of the experience of power.

EXPERIENCE, LANGUAGE AND POLITICS

Men have often reacted to the challenges of feminism with guilt. Sometimes men have been left feeling uneasy about their very sense of masculinity. Rather than respond to the theoretical and practical challenges of changing ourselves as we redefine our masculinity, it has seemed easier to adopt a negative definition of ourselves. We have felt more secure in defining ourselves as 'anti-sexist' than in clarifying what we need for ourselves. This is a limiting vision that can end up in an unhelpful attitude towards feminism as well as towards ourselves, in that it continues to expect women to define our tasks and visions for us.[1]

At another level it perpetuates a characteristic attitude in a moral culture in which it is easier for men to accept responsibility for the world, rather than focus upon individual relationships. Although it is important for men to struggle actively against sexist institutions and relationships, it is also important to work out our feelings about contraception and abortion; about childcare provisions at work; about paternity leave, and about job-sharing, rather than to find a new form for the old myth of the knight in shining white armour who struggles in the name of others. The disowning of masculinity weakens men, rather than helping to focus our feelings and thoughts.

Learning from feminism, say about the importance of consciousness-raising, can help us challenge intellectualist traditions which we often use as defences. These practices cannot be slavishly adopted; they have to be related to the specific historical and cultural experience of contemporary masculinity. Nor will this be a practice without its dangers to men used to intellectualizing our experience, rather than sharing feelings and experience more directly. But at least we can begin to own some of these difficulties we have as men. It was, after all, through consciousness-raising that women learnt of the ongoing dialectic between their experience and the categories and traditions within which this experience was to be grasped. They discovered ways in which they betrayed themselves and their experience as women in accepting the way the dominant culture

178

distorted and negated them by representing the common-sense of the culture in male categories. Women demanded that their experience as women be recognized and confirmed and be allowed to develop within its own terms. Women began to give voice and expression to their own experience, testing these meanings out with each other as they forged a language in which they could reveal and express themselves. This was how language was intitially recognized as central to women's oppression. If you deny people a language in which they can represent their history, culture and experience to themselves, you silence them.

Language had to be tested constantly against experience since language could never really be trusted if it can so easily mislead and betray. Women had learnt to give close attention to language because they had suffered at its hands. But structuralist traditions which feminists often inherited from the prevailing interpretations of Marxism have been able to subvert this newly rediscovered relationship of language to experience through insistently, if unconsciously, working to undermine whatever grip we have upon our experience. They have presented experience to us as if it were essentially an empiricist notion in which people are rendered the passive recipients of knowledge.[2] But this failed to theorize the power and insight of the experience of consciousness-raising, and often went on to present individuals as constituted through discourses that existed independently of them. It rendered people the passive creations of structures that existed independently of their making. Though a structuralist tradition promised to recognize the importance of ideology and culture, it worked to subvert some of the critical insights of feminism. Its promises were bought at a high price.

The relationship of experience to language was also an issue in sexual politics. As people attempted to live different relationships with each other, they often found themselves without a language to identify these new experiences and feelings. Relationships within the newly-formed collective living structures, that had become quite common in the early 1970s, could not be rendered visible or made intelligible within the traditional language of the family. What is more, the dominant culture continually worked to marginalize and denigrate these experiences as 'juvenile' or 'immature'. This made it hard for people to trust their own experience and to learn from attempts to live

179

different relationships. But living these relationships did bring a different experience into focus, and set up an ongoing dialectic between experience and language.

In the mid 1970s, when it seemed that women, at least, had won the right to articulate their own experience in their own terms, consciousness-raising seemed less vital. It coincided with a shift in activist politics which meant that fewer people had opportunities to engage in working-class politics. People were left without the challenge of this encounter and so without the opportunities to bring both the personal and political into their relationships. This became an abstract slogan, though still filled with promise and possibility, and for many socialists politics has become an abstract intellectual commitment, not something they had come to through attempting to live differently. But rather than this shift being admitted openly as the experience of a political generation growing up in the late 1970s and 1980s, theory came to replace experience as the basis for people's politics. Though in many ways this was similar for men and women, it was possible for women to develop a different sense of politics through their experience of consciousness-raising.

So, from the mid 1970s until the re-emergence of CND and the women's camp at Greenham Common, the turn to theory often meant a weakening of the relationship between politics and experience. The idea of trusting one's experience had lost its original meaning as experience became suspect itself. Certainly it became difficult to see how experience could be taken theoretically seriously as the basis of one's politics, even after E. P. Thompson's powerful critique *The Poverty of Theory* challenged some of the central terms in structuralist discussion. Yet Thompson looked back to an earlier political generation and was unable to appreciate the relation between experience, language and politics which had been discovered in sexual politics in the 1970s. The debate got set in misleading terms between 'humanist' and 'structuralist' interpretations of Marx, as if some ill-defined 'humanism' was the only basis upon which you could challenge the implicit rationalism of structuralism.[3]

I have wanted to argue that it is important to grasp the inadequacy of this polarity. The tendency to think in dichotomies and polarities which characterizes liberal culture, makes it hard to begin to articulate an alternative vision. I have wanted to show that challenging these polarities, which at the same time feed into a fragmentation of the self and of human experience, can be a starting point for beginning to develop such a vision. These polarities are not simply intellectual or theoretical in character; they are also the categories in terms of which our lives and our consciousness, or processes of sense-making, are organized. They are part of the way that we give meaning to our lives, and they contribute to, and distort, the quality of our lived experience.

I am not trying, then, somehow to offer a new way of itemizing emotions or emotional life, but rather am pointing to a distance from ourselves which becomes a feature of our experience in late capitalist society and is built specifically into our dominant conceptions of masculinity. I am arguing for a different kind of involvement with ourselves and others as integral to our development as socialists rather than offering an alternative 'correct' theory in polarity with what has gone before. This means recognizing that inherited traditions must themselves be grasped dialectically; we can recognize, for example, that whilst structuralist traditions have made it impossible to take seriously our emotions and desires as sources of valid knowledge, this tradition nevertheless expressed moments of truth. It has given us more scope in its conception of relative autonomy to think about the multifaceted ways in which power operates; it also, in its very rejection of the moral ground of theory, captures a truth about the prevailing ethos of our society as expressed in the 1980s in a pervasive instrumentalism, hopelessness and fatalism. If we reject its premises, we need also to account for its credibility; and it is at this point that the significance of the rationalism of our dominant traditions comes into focus.

It is still difficult to challenge 'rationalism' without being attacked for undermining the place of reason and intellect in our lives. This is where a critical exploration of the relationship between masculinity and reason could help. Certainly a reinstated rationalist tradition might appeal to women who sought respect as a person, meaning it was important not to be treated only as a body, but also as having a mind and intellect. This was an integral part of being treated as a person in her own right. But for men, this tradition is part of the problem. Even if it has sustained a powerful critical tradition, it remains, as Merleau-Ponty realized, essentially intellectualist.[4]

Structuralism, which established itself as a dominant intellectual tradition in the 1970s in France, has remained limited, as has the rationalist tradition it continued, in grasping any relationship between theory and practice. A dialectical relationship between what Marx called human sense activity and consciousness is beyond its grasp because it automatically assimilates practical activity to the conceptual categories in which it can be grasped. Rationalism has always tended to be legislative, believing that through the independent workings of reason, independent of our experience and desires, we could discern what is 'right' and 'wrong'. Such a view encourages a moralistic form of politics even on the Left with people quick to condemn people for acts which are unambiguously regarded as 'immoral' or simply 'bourgeois'. In this way the Left unwittingly sustains a morality of individual acts and so reproduces a similar framework of moral discussion, even if it seeks to condemn people for different ways of behaving.

But a structuralist tradition tends to fit more easily with the liberal relativism that has characterized liberal capitalist societies since the 1950s. It resonates more easily with this new form of common sense, arguing that our notion of 'right' and 'wrong' is constituted within Leninist or social democratic discourses. There is no way that we can appeal to any space of experience outside of these discourses without being accused of being 'essentialist'. In these post-structuralist days we are asked to be content with the idea that the struggle between different social forces is a struggle to articulate and disarticulate discourses to create a new form of alliance politics. We can only think in pragmatic terms, for instance about the success of the Nazis in gaining power in Germany. We are left without the moral basis, even, to condemn fascism.[5]

Such a tradition works to subvert our moral sense of outrage at suffering and oppression, calling it a mere 'emotional response' which just reveals our 'humanist' prejudices. Post-structuralism has damaged the moral basis of Marxism. It has sought specious support in Marx's critique of morality, which for him was a critique of a particular form of bourgeois morality which hid relations of power and subordination by presenting people as equal citizens in an equal society. With the dominance of structuralist terms of discussion, it has become difficult even to pose questions about the moral inheritance of Marxism.[6]

182

A sensitivity to the terms in which people represent their experience could have been a gain from semiology and structuralism, if it had not been followed in such uncritical ways. As it is, it has often encouraged a kind of theoretical élitism which has prevented us engaging with the contradictions in our experience. Often it tends to analyse from a distance the terms in which a certain issue is presented, rather than being able to recognize how new issues emerge in the context of people living and working differently. It can so easily subvert the dialectical relationship between language, experience and power through turning these into formal categories rather than, as Gramsci was at pains to show in the *Prison Notebooks*, keeping them as lived historical relations.

MASCULINITY, SOCIAL THEORY AND RATIONALISM

An investigation of our inherited traditions of masculinity can help subvert the hold which rationalist traditions have gained in Marxism and social theory. As men we have suffered from an identification of our masculinity with our reason. This is something we have to be continually reminded of, because we take it so much for granted. It is hardest to see those things which are closest to us. Often our sense of individual identity as men is so tied in with our sense of masculinity, that we feel deeply threatened and unsure when notions of masculinity are challenged. Sexual politics was threatening because it sought to connect our intellectuality with our personal lives. Often it is a deep fear of the personal, of vulnerability and intimacy, that unites men who would otherwise have sharp political disagreements.

It is as if our conventional political traditions and differences assume an inherited conception of masculinity as impersonal, objective, disinterested. The ideals of the scientific revolutions of the seventeenth century have become fundamental characteristics of our masculinity. We agree in our resolution to keep emotions and feelings at a distance and in our denial of them as genuine and valid sources of knowledge. This assumption, though now it is being challenged by feminism and by explorations into the nature of modern science, has organized our notion of a Western cultural inheritance. This is something Derrida has challenged recently, showing how a dominant

183

discourse of science has silenced the experience of women and ethnic groups. But his solution is a proliferation of discourses, each cutting across and subverting the assumptions of others as they bury once and for all the possibility of a universal history.[7]

What is striking is how post-structuralist work has presented itself as tolerant of difference and deeply critical of attempts of reason to speak in a universal voice, presenting its own experience as the universal experience of others. This striking shift away from discursive practices is clear in Foucault's collection of later lectures and talks, *Power/Knowledge*. His work with prisoners in Paris after the writing of *Discipline and Punish* showed that legal and juridical discourses could no longer be thought of as they were in his earlier theoretical formulations, as constituting the experience of prisoners. He saw that prisoners did not recognize themselves within this official discourse, but developed their own ways of representing their experience to themselves. Foucault's analysis can still leave us with a sense of contradiction, though more often at the level of discourses rather than the contradictions within lived experience that are often strikingly a feature of feminist writing. His last work shows that he was involved in rethinking assumptions about the self, sexuality and power that are so often taken as characterizing his work.[8] In a similar way Derrida sees a proliferation of discourses, each representing the reality and experience of a different group, without any longer hoping or thinking that these should be reconciled with one another. Reconciliation, for Derrida, is a rationalist myth that needs to be exposed. But if this helps us, for example, to see how a dominant discourse of reason works to silence the experience and voice of women, it also would seem to assume that men can, or should be able, to recognize themselves in a masculine discourse; yet Derrida leaves little space for the contradictions men feel in relation to their masculinity. We find ourselves unable to explore as hurt and damage the identification which is made between masculinity and reason.

Not only does this emphasis on discourse threaten to continue to denigrate our emotions and feelings, but it also organizes our experience in definite ways. It cripples our emotional lives as we become incapable of connecting to these parts of ourselves. It leaves our emotions and feelings, needs and desires unrecognized, and it forms them in particular ways. At some level

Derrida can recognize how a certain discourse forecloses certain possibilities for us, but he casts them in intellectualist terms. It is our lives which are crippled, not simply our understanding. But at least Derrida has encouraged a rethinking of assumptions usually taken for granted within our philosophy and social theory. Notions of masculinity should be central to such a task and we need to consider what critical assumptions are being protected if this is not appreciated.

Structuralist and post-structuralist theories have failed to illuminate contradictions within our lived experience. For one thing, these have often specifically defined themselves in opposition to the more phenomenological and historicist sympathies of Merleau-Ponty and Sartre, sometimes failing to realize how they had themselves moved away from more intellectualist interpretations of phenomenology. As they had become more sympathetic to Marx's influence, they had struggled to show that contradictions do not simply exist in our consciousness but also in our practical activities and in the relationship between the two. It is in the context of our everyday practical activities that we come to consciousness. Consciousness does not exist in an autonomous and independent realm of its own and nor does language, as different forms of a rationalist tradition have tended to assume. This means, as Wittgenstein was to realize, it is more or less significant, as is language, in the articulation of our experience.

As men, we often use language as a way of hiding ourselves and our feelings. It can so easily be used as a way of distancing ourselves from our experience, though sensitive psychoanalytic practice shows it can also be used to bring us back into contact with ourselves. But this is to question the existence of a vantage point outside our everyday practical activities and relationships, a point from which language can be understood as somehow 'constituting' our 'experience' and sense of individual identity. This gives language a more significant place than it often has in our lives and, as I have tried to show, betrays a central understanding in Wittgenstein's later works. This could itself remind us of Marx's idea that the meaning of our language can only be discovered if it is grounded in our activities and relationships. Language itself is often an elaboration of gestures which young children have already learnt to make. Language shifts the terms in which communication takes place but it does not bring it into existence.

Even though Derrida has helped people to value differences, rather than to subsume different experiences, it remains difficult to break the cultural pressure to make our life fit our theories. This should have been one of the lessons of the late 1960s but it has taken on new intellectualist forms. An underlying critical assumption about the essentially 'humanist' nature of ideas of self or individual identity, has made it impossible to relate these notions to our lived experience, since 'experience' itself has been rendered an inadmissible category. So as our theoretical discussions seem to take a step towards the concerns of sexual politics, we often find that its inherited theoretical language has become strangely depersonalized.

The structuralist identification that thoughtlessly tends to be made between 'experience' and 'empiricist' dismisses at a theoretical stroke any recognition of a tension between our experience and our language, that is, it brushes aside a central gain of consciousness-raising. If Althusser had not initiated such a crude dismissal of Lukàcs he could have learnt from his writings on issues of method in Marx in *History and Class Consciousness*, that empiricism involves accepting the categories in which our experience initially presents itself as a sufficient basis for our theorization. But women could have learnt long ago from the practice of consciousness-raising, that this would have been to accept essentially masculine definitions of their experience. This meant judging themselves in terms which were not their own and inevitably led women to betray significant aspects of their experience. This insight proved impossible to sustain within a structuralist tradition that seemed to offer so many dazzling opportunities for theoretical development. But it is important to realize that a price has been paid.

Since women often describe an experience of being overwhelmed by their emotions and feelings, they might keenly welcome a stress on reason and intellect which can offer more control and self-determination. But for men who have been brought up to identify so directly with our minds, it can be equally important to stress the independent existence of feelings and emotions as sources of knowledge and understanding. We have to be suspicious of turning feelings and emotions into

mental-states which happens as much within analytical philosophy as it does within a French rationalist tradition. This is a
move which subsumes different dimensions of our experience
under a single category of mind, and makes it impossible to
acknowledge the different levels to our experience – the mental,
the bodily, the emotional and the spiritual. At best, our conception of personal identity remains essentially intellectualist.
This promises the control of our minds over the rest of our
experience which has been deeply cherished within masculine
ideals of self-control ever since the beginnings of different
traditions of modern philosophy with Descartes.

FEMINISM, MEN AND EXPERIENCE

Consciousness-raising made it possible to theorize a relationship
between consciousness, experience and power. So, for instance,
traditional marriage relationships in which women feel grateful
for their husband's work can invalidate women's feelings of
anger. Women can feel they have no right to get angry within a
culture which makes us feel we need reasons for our feelings, or
else they should do their best to control them and keep them to
themselves. Women can be made to feel they have to suppress
these feelings. But in suppressing feelings we are suppressing
parts of ourselves, though Foucault's *A History of Sexuality* makes
it almost impossible to register this kind of point since it is
assumed to depend upon a naturalistic conception of feelings.
Here I would want to talk of *suppression*, not simply of difference.

I have shown some of the cultural sources for the common
notion that feelings have to be justified, before we can allow
ourselves to acknowledge and express them. Women have learnt
through consciousness-raising that they are not alone in these
feelings and that they can learn from them about the workings
of a relationship of power and subordination that has so often
been presented as a relationship of loving equality. They have
also recognized it is not simply the fault of individual men,
though they insist men have to change themselves if the relationship is to be recognized on more equal terms.

Women learnt to assert the validity of their emotional expressions, their bodily experiences and their own thoughts and
intuitions. In this way they extended and broadened their

187

experience. If they were to be respected in their own right as persons, then these different dimensions of experience had to be given proper recognition and acknowledgement. In learning to question the common masculine charge that they were being 'emotional' or 'irrational', women have refused to justify themselves in the terms of men. Rather they have learnt to empower themselves through asserting and valuing those very aspects of the historical experience of women that men have so often ridiculed and spurned.

It is important not to simplify the differences which have emerged within feminism, most strikingly between socialist feminism and radical feminism, cut across by a difference between a theoretical feminism which has looked towards structuralist work, and a movement of ecological feminism which has been stronger in the United States. The writings of Susan Griffin powerfully represent the ideas of this ecological movement. Such a distinction between varieties of feminism is useful in illuminating ideas of the 'natural' and 'nature'.[9] Because women's subordination has always been justified as 'natural', as part of the order of things that we only tamper with at our peril, feminism developed with a deep suspicion of arguments from nature or the natural as essentially legislative or as directed to uncovering a single and abiding truth.

But this impulse, however well grounded it was originally, became confused when rendered within the neat structuralist distinctions that seemed to be making similar points. So the 'natural' is often opposed to the 'socially and historically constructed'. In a similar way sex is seen as part of the 'natural' which comes to be seen as the 'biological' and gender is seen as a radically separated discourse which is socially and historically constituted. We find our discussions split into separate and autonomous realms when many of the interesting questions seem to straddle, if not question, these categorizations. We discover intellectual distinctions coming to have an existence and reality of their own independent of the problems and contradictions in the experience of men and women they are supposed to illuminate. But this is because this connection, so vital to consciousness-raising, has been lost, as any talk of 'experience' has been identified with an appeal to nature and so with an appeal to a non-discursive realm.

When we think about masculinity and the identification of male identity with reason we see that this has historically involved a process of separation from our natures. We discover that our notions of 'reason' have been developed in fundamental opposition to nature, to emotions and desires. For men this has meant an attenuated sense of our lived experience as we discover we have been systematically estranged from our bodies and from our emotional lives. It is as if we exist as disembodied minds able to produce arguments for our behaviour, but unable to share what we feel and experience about a situation. This rationalism even invaded feminist debates on nature and the natural. This has created a fundamental fragmentation in masculine experience.

At some level this has turned men against themselves, willing to judge ourselves harshly if our experience does not fit the rational plans we have set ourselves. We come to fear the revelations of a nature we have so long controlled and suppressed. We suspect that if we come into more contact with our feelings of anger, resentment and disgust, these feelings will surely overwhelm us. It would only confirm our deepest cultural fears that we are unloveable anyway, because we inherit a nature that is evil and can only be used to good if it is carefully controlled. I have shown how this is the way we prove ourselves as men, though at another level we fear that if others knew what we were 'really like' they would not want to have anything to do with us. But these are issues we keep far from the surface of our consciousness as we do our best to live out the ideals we have set for ourselves. An inherited identification of masculinity with reason fully legitimates this strategy. But at another level we sense that we give relatively little of ourselves a full expression.

A post-structuralist tradition has left us in a bind. It can offer us a critical grasp of our inherited culture, but it places our own experience and relationships at a safe distance. If this has not been Derrida's intention, it has often been the consequence of his work. It renders it impossible to apprehend what it means for men to be out of touch with themselves, or estranged from their lived somatic experience. We would be open to a theoretical challenge of 'essentialism' or 'humanism', and the problems we experience in living more equal relationships with partners would be made to seem insubstantial, even unreal. In this way we are led to replace an experiential, historical and personal process of consciousness-raising with an intellectual exercise of deconstruction.

The era of philosophical and cultural exploration into the roots of a Western tradition we so often take for granted, has often cost us our place in this process, as it threatens to turn our politics into an intellectual commitment, thereby removing it from the task of transforming our relationships. We risc continuing a deeper inheritance of rationalism, at the very moment we are supposedly subverting it.

We threaten what can be learnt from consciousness-raising if we accept an intellectual critique of the very category of experience. This is especially true for men who often have such a tenuous grasp of their experience. Often it has been the antagonism to nature, to emotions, feelings and desires that has set men so firmly against ourselves. We have to refuse the false oppositions of so much structuralist theory while we can learn from its recognition of the fragmentation of individuality not to reinstate a false sense of our integrity as individuals. We should not think that a solution can be discovered at the level of consciousness. It will involve a transformation of relationships of power and subordination.

The sense of existing in pieces is familiar to many men who often experience themselves quite differently at work and at home. But we require a theoretical illumination of the contradictions that seem to be pulling masculinity apart precisely because our minds seem to have so little connection to our bodies; because our sexuality seems disconnected from our love; because our language seems to get in the way of our intimacy. This is part of a broader crisis which involves the challenges of feminism for men to be more emotionally involved and present in relationships, and the challenging of everyone to the treatment of masculinity as if it were a biological category which is somehow given for all time. This idea of masculinity as biologically given has been the assumption, if not the intention, underpinning much feminist writing on men. But this involves being able to illuminate contradictions in the historical experience of masculinity and not simply in our ideas about it.

I have tried to show that such an exploration includes coming to understand how traditions which have been the dominant radical challenge to bourgeois morality have often unwittingly developed on an infrastructure of moral identity and perception which itself has roots in the development of capitalism. Critically this includes the notion that there is a ground, in reason, from which competing claims can be equally assessed and validated. This continues and reinforces a separation of ideas from lived reality. It is this separation which is mystifying particularly in that it sustains men's propensity to speak on behalf of everyone. It is rather the case that the belief in such a ground has been characteristic of men's particular experience.

This should help make clear the importance of people defining for themselves the character and form of the oppression they suffer. This involves a radically different conception of morality from what has often prevailed on the Left. I have shown how it is built upon a critical grasp of experience as opposed to being organized around a conception of duty.

As I have argued before, within a liberal moral culture, morality is closely identified with reason. It was Kant's ethical writings which secured this identification and separated considerations of morality from nature, from the satisfaction of needs, emotions and desires. Since we inherit an identification of masculinity with reason, there is a strong connnection between masculinity and our sense of morality. This tends to reinforce our claims, as men, to speak in the interests of all since we speak with the voice of morality and morality is supposed to be universal if it is anything. Marx remained trapped within these hopes of universalism. He looked to the proletariat not simply to redeem itself, but to serve as a universal class able to bring about the emancipation of humanity in general. This has tended to make socialism too much of a male creed, as others are supposed to hold back in the secure knowledge that their emancipation is in secure hands. This dream has faded. Feminism has helped develop a different sense of politics. Feminism is not just a challenge to men, but an example of breaking masculine hegemony which identifies reason, masculinity and universality, even for men. Feminists have learnt that people have to do things for themselves because it is only each oppressed group which can define the character and form of the oppression it suffers.

Marx's critique of bourgeois morality has often been read as a critique of morality in general. His writings have been used to denigrate the place of moral considerations, as if they inevitably serve to legitimate existing relations of power and subordination. Certainly Marx doubted whether a moral critique of capitalist relations could itself organize people to transform these relations. Rather we had to look at historical forces which were capable of challenging capitalist relations. But this could include a moral critique which developed a closer relationship between experience and moral theory as part of social transformation. Within a Leninist tradition, however, history became interpreted to mean whatever served to enforce the power of the proletariat, and whatever brought the revolution closer was to be deemed 'moral'. This denigrated morality by turning it into an instrument of power that could so easily be manipulated. It enshrined a conception of morality as duty to the revolution, which within the Soviet Union, so often became a subordination to the needs of production.[10]

Though issues of masculinity were rendered invisible, such a process of subordination could even exploit the traditional connection between male dignity and work that had been central for the organization of capitalist production. But with the de-skilling of the labour process with the introduction and rationalization of assembly-line production, work has been less able to sustain masculine identity. Simone Weil saw this as a debasement of working people, as money became the only incentive to work and as trade unions increasingly came to represent the wage-demands of men in secure employment, while failing when it came to the conditions of women and immigrant workers. Weil was one of the few who have been concerned to rework the moral inheritance of Marxism.

Since the idea of Marxism as a theory of productive forces had gained a new currency within Anglo-American writing at least, and since this has always undermined the moral character of so much of Marx's writing, it is worth including Weil's words from *Oppression and Liberty*:

The recognition of the fact that the capitalist system grinds down millions of men only enables one to condemn it morally; what constitutes the historic condemnation of the system is the fact that, after having made productive progress possible, it is now an obstacle in its way. The essential task of revolutions

192

consists in the emancipation not of men but of productive forces. As a matter of fact, it is clear that, as soon as these have reached a level of development high enough for production to be carried out at the cost of little effort, the two tasks coincide; and Marx assumed that such was the case in our time. It was this assumption that enabled him to establish a harmony, indispensable to his moral tranquility, between his idealistic aspirations and his materialistic conception of history. ('Critique of Marxism', p. 43)

Even though Weil's interpretation of Marx often remains within a narrow framework of economic determinism, she is able to touch crucial moral issues that seem only to have sharpened with time.[11]

Within a structuralist tradition we witness a similar distinction between the 'moral' and the 'structural' as if we are condemned to think of morality as the transmission of eternal values. We mention morality only to turn our backs on it. It allows us to turn away from morality conceived in terms of individual values, towards a consideration of social practices which help constitute, say, our sense of 'right' and 'wrong'. So we can think critically for example about legal institutions and the ways they work with social security to define and enforce conceptions of 'right behaviour'. Structuralist notions provide powerful critical modes of analysis, but of an amoral form which leaves us thinking about interventions in a range of social practices bereft of any moral criteria upon which such an intervention can be made. Often we are left sneering about moral considerations as if these take us away from the 'political' tasks at hand.

As so often before, a rationalist tradition has left us with a critical language of analysis but with no way of connecting to the contradictions in people's everyday experience. This has been brought out sharply in the England of the 1980s when the intellectual language has remained radical but distant, and Thatcherism has been able to take the moral initiative. Intellectual discussion remains mesmerised, unable to connect with the misery and suffering produced with mass unemployment. It seems to deliver us to a safe space in which we can continue talking to each other, and it happens despite our best intentions. As the theory itself knows only too well, misery, like desire, comes into existence through a particular set of discourses. But if this helps us focus upon the organization of social practices, it does so at the cost of our connection to lived experience. Experience enters as an incidental anecdote with little connection with the analysis at hand.

We have to acknowledge the workings of our inherited moral traditions before we can break with them. If we make an intellectual break, however lucid and radical this is, we often reproduce the assumptions of liberal morality in our experience and relationships. This has been reinforced by structuralist theory which has made us less sensitive to the personal because it sustains a tradition in which reason is the only source of dignity. It cannot validate the fullness of our experience, since we can only think well of ourselves to the extent that we are rational – right thinking. This has made it crucial to have the 'correct analysis', even if this is only tenuously connected to a political practice.

We find it hard to validate our different capacities and abilities since these are presented back to us as intellectual categories, ways we organize our perceptions and structure our experience of the social world. It is at this deeper level of felt experience that we are unwittingly sustaining cultural definitions of masculinity. We render invisible the damage done to the development of our emotional, intuitive and spiritual capacities as we identify so closely with our reason. We reproduce a relationship of domination within ourselves, as we are taught to listen to a voice of reason that shuts out the echoes of our imaginations, desires, emotions and feelings. We squeeze ourselves so that we can fit the mental images we have created for ourselves. We condemn ourselves harshly if we cannot live up to these high standards of 'correct behaviour' we have set for ourselves. Morality becomes indistinguishable from moralism.

We need to rediscover a moral voice which is no longer moralistic and judgemental. As I have argued, we so easily resent others if we think they are not making the same sacrifices and denials we are, a resentment that Nietzsche saw at the heart of Christian morality. When we question our inherited conceptions of masculinity we are challenging moral traditions which have identified masculinity with moral superiority. Men are supposed to have principles while women have only feelings and emotions. By questioning reason as the only source of dignity, men are beginning to refuse this opposition between reason and nature. We are not simply looking to recover the moral significance of our feelings of compassion, kindness and caring for others but we are looking for a different framework for our moral discussion.

This is to refuse a bourgeois tradition which is built upon the split between reason and nature, a tradition in which we learn to condemn parts of ourselves. We have inherited a distorted vision of our humanity in which we would have greater moral worth if we were not so influenced by our natures. This is the way I have shown men to be fundamentally divided against ourselves, learning to despise our sexual feelings as indications of a brutish nature. I have argued that, as feminists realized for themselves, the liberalization of attitudes has often rendered pain invisible, as men pretend to live out conceptions of themselves which have very little reality in their experience. This makes it crucial to maintain a dialectic between our experience and the conceptual terms in which we would seek to know it.

As men we are only publicly assured of dignity if we identify with our reason. We learn to despise our softer feelings as 'feminine'. We put these at a distance from ourselves, making little sense of Jung's insight that we have to recognize them as integral parts of ourselves. It is not only that we think of reason as the only source of valid knowledge; it is also that it becomes the only capacity we have to guarantee our humanity. It not only affects our understanding, but influences the formation of our capacities and their relationships with each other. I have shown how, as men, it is often very difficult for us to *accept* our feelings and desires, as we are often trapped into constantly proving ourselves. This means living constantly in the future as we do our best to achieve our targets: we are constantly planning. The present is a moment we continually evade. We become tense and anxious when we have to settle into it. Often it is from these tensions and contradictions in our lived experience that we can begin to realize how little is the relation we have with ourselves as men.

195

LIBERALISM, IDENTITY AND EMOTIONAL LIFE

Our liberal moral traditions set men against themselves as we identify with our reason and separate ourselves from our emotional lives. The very universalism of our rationalist tradition impersonalizes our experience, so that moral action also becomes universal in character. We tend to think of reasons as impersonal and this can blind us to the specific historical and cultural traditions we inherit. Whether we are men or women, black or white, working class or middle class, these differences are deemed incidental when it comes to considering the character of moral action. This enduring feature of liberal moral culture makes it difficult to accept that, though we exist as individuals, we do not thereby cease to exist in our gender, class or ethnic identities.

This universalizing pressure, which is to 'free' our experience from these 'partial identifications', separates people from a continuing sense of class or ethnic identity, and, in the end, compromises their individuality. Relating to others as 'individuals', even if we are working with the best egalitarian intentions not to discriminate against people because of their race, class or gender, we are unwittingly negating them as we refuse to acknowledge a shared history and culture. It is more than simply a matter of the ways we treat others; it involves us in a social process which impersonalizes our experience as we remove ourselves and others from sustaining any connection with our historical and cultural roots. Because we see this identification with a universal culture as freedom from the inhibiting habits and traditions of a group or class, setting individuals free to make decisions for themselves, it is hard to identify the damage we can be doing at the same time.

So a tradition of moral rationalism can remove us from our class, sex or racial histories, as well as from our emotions, feelings and desires. Not only are we offered 'freedom' at the cost of weakening our sense of connectedness with others, but we are also left with little connection to our own natures, needs and desires. We can neither root ourselves in our history and culture, nor in our experience. The structuralist tradition has reinforced this tendency towards an impersonalization of experience through its refusal to recognize issues of identity and

196

experience: class, sex and race are treated as modes of class-ification or organization of perceptions, rather than as lived historical experiences. While this has made us aware of assumptions about gender or class, it has also made it difficult to appreciate people's relationships to their gender or ethnic identities. Again this goes back to its distorting grasp of what goes on in consciousness-raising, whether it be in relation to gender, class or ethnicity.

To break into this self-reinforcing circle of rationalism and its self-denying moralism, we need to value a slow and gradual process of consciousness-raising in which people begin to re-organize perceptions they have of themselves. This can lead to understanding our experience and histories in quite different terms. It is a process of learning which is not simply intellectual in character. It can so often involve personal and emotional transformations as we begin to relate differently to ourselves. In this way it challenges the traditional organization of academic knowledge. We are forced to recognize the pull of different kinds of knowing.

Marxist theory has been too ready to dismiss liberal moral theory as 'individualistic' without really understanding how it organizes our experience of ourselves, with the consequence that its own transformative power is limited. If it is true that a liberal moral tradition works to individualize our moral con-sciousness through organizing itself around providing reasons for individual moral action, we should understand this limiting definition of morality, in the process of transforming it. We should not simply be thinking of replacing a 'moral' conscious-ness with a 'political' analysis. That reinforces the very frag-mentation of morality and politics which liberal theory fosters. Rather we should seek to explain the weakness of our inherited moral traditions in accounting for the moral significance of relations of power and subordination.

Liberal moral theory works to individualize our moral experi-ence through presenting it as an individual quest to prove our moral worth. This sets morality into a competitive framework which can turn salvation into an individual moral goal. The invisible presence of masculinity is at work here, with its valuing of independence and self-sufficiency. We become suspicious of the help or care of others, as if these automatically detract from the moral worth of our actions. I have tried to show how we end up doing things for ourselves, fearing the emotional dependency of relationships. This creates an inequality in our emotional and sexual relationships as we fear intimacy and find it hard to make ourselves vulnerable to others. We are ready to give support, but fearful of showing our needs lest they prove overwhelming and destructuve.

Liberal moral culture has built upon a Christian tradition in which we assume ourselves to be individually free to relate to others in any way we choose. We learn that it is always possible to abstract from the social relations of power and subordination to treat others with respect as equal human beings. This powerful tenet of liberal theory makes it difficult to understand the workings of power and subordination. We treat them as incidental because we think of moral relations as personal relations in which we are always free to treat others as equals. It assumes that we determine our lives and that our actions are the outcome of reason.

In this tradition, personal change is based on will and determination, which enable us to be the people we want to be. It is this aspect of moral rationalism that Freud and psychoanalytic work can help challenge. Often the Left has echoed a simplistic moral psychology which has explained human action in terms of interests and voluntaristic change. It depends upon an appeal to duty and will to draw people away from acting out of self-interest. Consequently socialist politics so often builds upon an ethic of self-denial. What is more, it assumes a split between personal change and political change in which the person is often denigrated.

Feminism has brought the personal and the political into relation with each other. In this way it has challenged basic assumptions of a liberal moral culture. What is more it has given a way of healing the split between morality and politics. Equal relations can no longer be established through taking up an attitude of equal respect towards others, but involve a transformation of material relations of housework and childcare. We are not equally free to live moral lives. The autonomy of morality which underpins liberal moral theory has been challenged. But so have attempts within Marxist theory to reduce morality to politics. Equal relations have to do with the quality of our relations and with the freedom to develop our different capacities as free and equal human beings, as well as with issues of distributive justice.

The terms of our moral and political discussion need to shift if they are honestly to reflect these understandings. Respect for a person no longer simply means being ready to acknowledge that others have an equal right to their own opinions. Nor is it simply a matter of the attitudes we take up towards others in our personal relations. Rather it involves a transformation of relations of power and subordination so that people have equal possibilities to exercise their capacities. But this also involves a challenge to the liberal assertion that people are already free to develop their abilities and potentialities. It is not only women who are denied this freedom; the vision itself is flawed. It is not only that women have been suppressed, but that their suppression embodies the splitting off of areas of experience and the denial of a range of capacities and understandings. This is all part of channelling our very sense of freedom and morality in a rationalistic direction. This has refused dignity to our emotional lives, to our feelings, to our imaginations, to our bodies. This is something women have learnt for themselves. They were told they existed as equals, but they have learnt from the experience of themselves as denigrated.

So as women themselves realized, it was not simply a matter of changing through an act of will, or even of living differently in relationships. We needed to learn from Freud as well as from Marx, though they could not be brought together easily. The structuralist attempt to bring Freud in as an analysis of our inner lives, while Marx continued to provide a framework for our 'outer lives' has been as dismal as the mechanical attempts of Reich and Fromm in an earlier generation. It is misplaced to relate them as theoretical systems each with their own object of study. It is the very categories they take for granted that will need to be reworked and tested within a new historical and cultural experience. We cannot assume that the academic boundaries we know, even when they are the categories of 'Marxism' and 'psychoanalysis', will be sustained. This as is true of reworking masculinity as it was in feminist theory.

We have to start with a sense of the difficulties and problems that men are facing in their attempts to live differently, rather than with theoretical conceptions alone. But this is not to assume our experience exists in a space untouched by theory. Our lives and experience are shot through with philosophical and moral assumptions, but when we question the identification of masculinity with reason we are already questioning a deep assumption in our moral and political traditions. This means coming to terms with our personal histories, as Freud realized, as much as coming to look openly and honestly at our issues in relationships with both men and women. For equality has to do with the quality of our relationships, not simply with good intentions. We have to be ready to share the reality of our experience, rather than shy away from any such notion.

But as we touch these issues, we have to face embarrassment and unease, since we can no longer leave ourselves out of account. This is difficult for men, since we are brought up with very little connection to ourselves in this way. This is a challenge not only to our inherited theoretical and political traditions and the organization of academic knowledge and political practices, but also to ourselves. As we change ourselves, learning to value the insights of consciousness-raising and a new process of transformation through therapy as part of socialist understanding, new problems will come into focus. As we redefine our masculinity, we will discover our own traditions, history and culture.

NOTES

CHAPTER ONE: INTRODUCTION

1 There is a problem with talking in terms of a masculinist theory, because feminist writers such as Ehrenreich and English use the term 'masculinism' to refer to a particular form of male supremacy that emerged through and in opposition to patriarchy with the development of capitalism. It carries inherently-oppressive implications, and so is not a sort of companion term for 'feminism'. This still leaves an issue about how best to characterize the nature of theory that seeks to illuminate men's contradictory relation to an experience and culture supposedly made in their image. This is an aspect of the very invisibility under consideration.

2 The connection between emotions and feelings and our inherited liberal conceptions of freedom, respect and justice is discussed more fully in Victor Seidler's *Kant, Respect and Injustice: The Limits of Liberal Moral Theory*. An illuminating discussion of the place of emotions and feelings in Kant's ethical theory is provided in Lawrence Blum's *Friendship, Altruism and Morality*.

3 For introductory reading into the basis of structuralism, see Jonathan Culler's *Saussure* and Frederic Jameson's *The Prison House of Language*. For a fuller critique of these and other Althusserian positions, see my 'Trusting ourselves: Marxism, human needs and sexual politics' in *One-Dimensional Marxism*, Simon Clarke *et al*, and E. P. Thompson's wide-ranging essay, 'The poverty of theory' in *The Poverty of Theory, and Other Essays*.

4 A useful introduction to these movements of French thought, giving some historical grasp of their development in relation to phenomenology, existentialism and Marxism, is provided by Vincent Descombes in *Modern French Philosophy*. Foucault's development is illustrated in the collection of his writings, *Power/Knowledge*, edited by Colin Gordon.

5 A significant discussion of these issues has been focused by responses to John Rawl's *A Theory of Justice*. See Charles Taylor's 'The nature and scope of distributive justice', and the concluding chapter to my

Kant, Respect and Injustice: The Limits of Liberal Moral Theory.
6 Sheila Rowbotham's *Dreams and Dilemmas* is a stimulating collection of her feminist writings that illuminates some of the tensions developing in the period. See also *Conditions of Illusion: Papers from the Women's Movement*, ed. Sandra Allen, Lee Sanders and Jan Wallis.
7 Through focusing on issues of masculinity and reason, we move close to the heart of Weber's *The Protestant Ethic and the Spirit of Capitalism*. This is something that David Morgan briefly discusses in 'Men, masculinity and the process of sociological enquiry' in *Doing Feminist Research*, ed. Helen Roberts.

CHAPTER TWO: REASON

1 The connection between a reformulated masculinity and the seventeenth-century scientific revolution is suggestively drawn in Brian Easlea, *Science and Sexual Oppression*, particularly Chapter 3. It is also made in B. Ehrenreich and D. English, *For Her Own Good*.
2 The identification of civilization with reason is reflected upon in T. Adorno and M. Horkheimer's *Dialectic of Enlightenment*. It is also a significant theme in M. Horkheimer's *Eclipse of Reason*, which explores the connection of a narrowed conception of reason and rationality to particular forms of individuality.
3 Descartes' vision of philosophy as a mirror of nature is illuminated historically in Richard Rorty's lucid *Philosophy and the Mirror of Nature*. For an introduction to Descartes' thought, see Jonathan Rée, *Descartes*, and Bernard Williams, *Descartes: The Project of Pure Enquiry*.
4 The place of women within this philosophical conception of reason is usefully traced in Genevieve Lloyd's *Men of Reason*. See also Susan Moller Okin's *Women in Western Political Thought*, Helen Kennedy and Susan Mendus' *Women in Western Political Philosophy*, and Jean Grimshaw, *Feminist Philosophers*.
5 The idea that oppressed or subordinate groups learn to deal with different realities, knowing that their experience is often at odds with the vision of objective reality held by those with power over their lives, is thoughtfully discussed in Jean Baker Miller's *Towards a New Psychology of Women*.
6 It is still difficult to recognize and so take responsibility for Auschwitz seeing it as in part an outgrowth of a culture and science which we all share, rather than as liberalism has tended to do, as a breakdown of Western liberal values and traditions. Susan Griffin has taken some steps towards this in *Pornography and Silence*, opening up connections that are left invisible within traditional academic boundaries. It is also part of the significance of Claude Lanzmann's film *Shoah* which reasserts the connection between past and present by insisting that we treat the destruction of European Jewry as part of our lives.
7 Simone Weil argues that, in continuing to teach our children to

admire the Roman values of power and greatness, we are continuing unwittingly to reproduce values that Hitler was himself seeking
to emulate. It is only in questioning these values and concerns that
we make good the defeat of Hitler. This remains a challenging
notion. Simone Weil's work is being given a belated recognition.
Her challenge to both liberalism and orthodox Marxism has cut
across the polarities of much recent social and political theory. See
Lawrence Blum and Victor Seidler's *A Truer Liberty: Simone Weil and
Marxism*.

8 This Marxist vision of universality is challenged by Walter Benjamin
in his 'Theses on the philosophy of history' in *Illuminations*. It was
part of his complicated relationship with the Frankfurt School. This
is well documented in Susan Buck-Morss's brilliant study, *The
Origin of Negative Dialectics*, which explores the relationship of
Adorno to Benjamin.

9 Without making specific connections to issues of masculinity, Fritjof
Capra's *The Turning Point* is a useful introduction to the shifts in our
forms of knowledge and experience brought about by the movement towards mechanistic conceptions of the natural world. For a
fuller grasp of some of these shifts within science, see *The Meta-
physical Foundations of Modern Science*. Whitehead's *Science and the
Modern World* is very useful to place some of these changes in a
broader historical context.

10 See my 'Reason, desire and male sexuality' in *The Cultural Construc-
tion of Sexuality*, ed. Pat Caplan. For a useful introduction to
Foucault's work there is Alan Sheridan's *Michel Foucault: The Will to
Truth*.

11 The connection of masculinity with an autonomous form of reason
has had a significant impact on the shaping of men's moral
experience which has too readily been universalized to form a norm
against which women have been found lacking. It is part of the
challenge of Carol Gilligan's *In A Different Voice* to show how both
Freud and Piaget were controlled by an essentially masculine vision
of moral experience. I have argued that this is most systematically
present in Kant's ethical writings in my *Kant, Respect and Injustice*.

12 The idea of the inner child is present in different forms in much
psychoanalytic work. See, for instance, D. W. Winnicott *The Child,
the family and the Outside World* and Francis Wicks *The Inner World of
Childhood*. Some of these issues are reflected upon in Alice Miller's
The Drama of the Gifted Child and in *For Your Own Good*, where she
shows the extraordinary pain and psychological suffering inflicted
on children under the guise of conventional child-rearing and
pedagogy.

13 Sheila Rowbotham's *Woman's Consciousness/Man's World* brought out
the tensions and contradictions for women living in a man's world.
She also appreciated that it was a problem for many men, but it has
taken many years for men to explore a language that could
illuminate their experience of masculinity. It is always easier to

assume that, especially in the 1980s, the broader political questions have left the issues of identity, experience and power behind in the consciousness-raising of the 1970s, or else been adequately subsumed within a theoretical discourse.

CHAPTER THREE: SEXUALITY

1 A useful theoretical exploration of psychoanalytic work bearing on these themes is provided by Nancy Chodorow in *The Reproduction of Mothering*. This argues that boys actually suffer from the discontinuity in their relationship with their mothers, in a way that influences their capacities for intimate and caring relationships.

2 The early writing of the women's movement reflects upon some of these experiences. See, for instance, the collection edited by Michelene Wandor *The Body Politic* and Sheila Rowbotham's *Dreams and Dilemmas*.

3 Some of the connections between Kantian ethics and an identification of masculinity and reason are briefly explored in my 'Fathering, authority and masculinity' in *Male Order: Unwrapping Masculinity*, ed. R. Chapman and J. Rutherford. They are also discussed by Susan Mendus in 'Kant: an honest but narrow-minded bourgeois?' in *Women in Western Political Thought*, ed. Ellen Kennedy and Susan Mendus. It is also a theme in Jean Grimshaw's *Feminist Philosophers: Women's Perspectives on Philosophical Traditions*.

4 This is usefully discussed by Brian Easlea in *Science and Sexual Oppression*, chapter 3. It is also an important theme in Carolyn Merchant's *The Death of Nature*.

5 The notion of possessive individualism separated from any direct connection with issues of masculinity is explored by C. B. Macpherson's classical study, *The Political Theory of Possessive Individualism: Hobbes to Locke*. It is also a continuing theme of his *Democratic Theory: Essays in Retrieval*. The notion of political atomism is also usefully clarified by Charles Taylor's essay 'Atomism' in his *Philosophy and the Human Sciences. Philosophical Papers 2*.

6 The hidden nature of men's dependency in their relationships with women is a central theme in Susie Orbach and Louise Eichenbaum's attempts to develop a feminist form of psychoanalytic theory. See, for instance, *What Do Women Want?* and *Understanding Women: A Feminist Psychoanalytic Approach*.

7 The issues that emerge around friendships between men are illuminatingly explored by Stuart Miller in *Friendships Between Men*

8 A deep grasp of personal and political development is provided by Susan Griffin in her *Made From This Earth*. It warns us against simplistic classifications, which were an abiding difficulty in this period.

9 Some of the tensions and contradictions in the politics of this period have been shared by Mike Hales in *Living Thinkwork*, and written up somewhat abstractly by Nigel Young in *An Infantile Disorder? The*

Crisis and Decline of the New Left. A feel for those days, at least within
what was loosely labelled the libertarian Left, is given by Allison Fell
in *Every Move You Make.* The particular context I was involved with
was in East London, for a time within the setting of a group called
'Big Flame'. A sense of its politics can be gained from its journal,
Revolutionary Socialism. There were many different groups active in
this period, but few drew their inspiration from libertarian developments within the Italian Left, particularly from Lotta Continua.

10 I have explored some of these connections in 'Trusting ourselves:
   Marxism, human needs and sexual politics' in S. Clarke *et al, One-
   Dimensional Marxism.*

11 Some attempt to illuminate what it was like to grow up as girls in the
   1950s is given in Liz Heron's *Truth, Dare or Promise.* There are also
   some helpful insights into this period in Sheila Rowbotham's
   Woman's Consciousness/Man's World.

12 For some useful reflections on the relationship of masculinity to
   Judaism, see the special edition of *Changing Men,* 'Issues in gender,
   sex and politics', ed. Harry Brod, Spring 1987. Feminist writing has
   made some of these connections visible for women. See, for instance,
   Nice Jewish Girls: A Lesbian Anthology, ed. Evelyn Torton Beck.

13 Some of the early writing of the Women's Liberation Movement can
   help restore some of the tensions of this period. See, for instance,
   The Body Politic, ed. Michelene Wandor.

14 Some sense of the ideas that were current in this period is given in
   the Red Collective's *The Politics of Sexuality in Capitalism* and also in
   Eli Zaretsky's *Capitalism, the Family and Personal Life.*

15 Some of the developments are discussed in a way that makes clear
   their movement towards a structuralist framework within Jeffrey
   Weeks' *Sexuality and its Discontents* and his *Sexuality.* A similar
   movement is apparent in Juliet Mitchell's work: see, for instance,
   Women: The Longest Revolution.

16 A useful introduction to situationist writing is given in *Leaving the
   Twentieth Century.* In the 1980s, the writings of Debord and Vainigger
   have again become available and are again emerging as a significant
   influence, partly due to an interest in Baudrillard's work. See, for
   instance, his *The Mirror of Production.*

17 Jeffrey Weeks seems to come close to recognizing some of these
   difficulties, though his thinking remains firmly within a structuralist
   framework. As he writes:

> The critique of existentialism which underpins this work has been
> very useful in casting light on hidden but controlling assumptions,
> and in opening up the sexual field to new questions, about
> history, power, meanings, diversity, choice and so on. (p. 113).

But he also agrees with Foucault that recent liberation movements
'suffer from the fact that they cannot find any principle on which to
base the elaboration of the new ethics' ('On the genealogy of ethics:
an overview of work in progress' in Paul Rabinow (ed.) *The Foucault*

Reader, p. 343) and that we are left bereft of ways of thinking about the place of sex in our individual lives. This is not a minor question, as Weeks acknowledges, for 'at its heart, is the old, old question of ethics, of how we should live', p. 113, *Sexuality*. I argue, through a sharing of experience, that this has to be our starting point and that the very silencing of these concerns within a structuralist framework indicates, for all its power, the ways that it remains flawed.

18 See the illuminating discussion of these tensions in Lawrence Blum's *Friendship, Altruism and Morality*. See also my *Kant, Respect and Injustice*. For Kant's writings on relationships between the sexes see the *Anthropology*.

19 A useful discussion of this theme is provided by Erich Fromm in *The Fear of Freedom*, chapters 2 and 3, R. H. Tawney's *Religion and the Rise of Capitalism*, and Max Weber's *The Protestant Ethic and the Spirit of Capitalism*.

20 A useful introduction to this aspect of Cartesianism is provided by Fritzjof Capra in *The Turning Point*, though it fails to make explicit the implications for our inherited traditions of masculinity.

21 This understanding of the emotional life of the body is a critical insight of Reich. Its significance for social theory is yet to be grasped, though Foucault, who remains deeply critical of Reich, goes some way in introducing the regulation of the body as a crucial mechanism of power. For a critical assessment of Foucault's challenge to the notion of repression, see my 'Reason, desire and male sexuality' in *The Cultural Construction of Sexuality*, ed. Pat Caplan. For an appreciation of Reich's relationship to Freud, see Reich's *The Function of the Orgasm* and the illuminating biography on Reich by Myron Sharaf, *Fury on Earth*.

22 Issues of friendship and relationship are cogently discussed in *Sex and Love*, Sue Cartledge and Joanna Ryan (eds). A pathbreaking study in the exploration of relationships between women is Lillian Faderman, *Surpassing the Love of Men: Romantic Friendship and Love between Women from the Renaissance to the Present*.

23 An ambivalence about how to understand 'the personal is political' as a challenge to liberal assumptions exists in Mary Midgeley and Judith Hughes' *Women's Choices* and Janet Radcliffe Richards' *The Sceptical Feminist*.

CHAPTER FOUR: CONTROL

1 Some attempt to connect Marxism to issues of masculinity is made by Jeff Hearn in *The Gender of Oppression*, and by Bob Connell in *Gender and Power*. For a useful feminist assessment, see *Feminist Politics and Human Nature* by Alison Jaggar.

2 A historically sensitive discussion of privacy is given by Barrington Moore in *Privacy*. It is also a theme in Jean Bethke Elshtain's *Public Man, Private Woman*.

3 Some of these connections are explored in Brian Easlea's *Witch*

Hunting, Magic and the New Philosophy and Barbara Ehrenreich and Deirdre English's *For Her Own Good*.

4 The Protestant conception of individuality is discussed by Erich Fromm in *Fear of Freedom* and by Reinhold Neibuhr in *The Nature and Destiny of Man*, chapter 3, 'Individuality in modern culture'.

5 The relationship of masculinity to principles and rules is illuminated in Carol Gilligan's study, *In A Different Voice*. It draws upon the work of Nancy Chodorow in *The Reproduction of Mothering*.

6 See Freud's discussion in *Civilization and its Discontents* and the discussions this provoked in Reich's *The Function of the Orgasm* and Herbert Marcuse's *Eros and Civilisation*. For a structuralist reading of these issues which presents a useful historical account, see Jeffrey Weeks' *Sexuality and its Discontents*.

7 The form of relationship to our emotional lives is barely thought about within a modern philosophical tradition in which rationalism has been dominant. It is partly because the tradition has assimilated Spinoza into a rationalist tradition that it has been difficult to appreciate his significant questioning of emotional life. At some level he remains an important source for Freud's work. There are also unexplored connections with the direction of thought we find in the later Wittgenstein. Some attempt to open up discussion of Hume and Spinoza in this regard is made by Jerome Neu, *Emotion, Thought and Theory*.

8 John Stuart Mill's *Autobiography* is a startling reminder that intellectual development can be quite independent of the develoment of our emotional lives. This point is developed by Susia Orbach and Luise Eichenbaum in *The Psychology of Women*.

9 A useful introduction to Lukàcs' writings is provided in A. Arato and P. Breines' *The Young Lukàcs and the Origin of Western Marxism*. An understanding of Lukàcs' political and intellectual development is provided by Michael Lowy in *Georg Lukàcs – from Romanticism to Bolshevism*. An understanding of the relationship of phenomenology and Marxism is provided by Lucien Goldmann in *Lukàcs and Heidegger*.

10 A political understanding of psychoanalysis is usefully explored by Jean Baker Miller in *Towards a New Psychology of Women*. See also Anne Foreman, *Femininity as Alienation* and the collection of essays, *Capitalism and Infancy*, ed. Barry Richards.

11 A useful introduction to the theorization of sexual relations is provided by Mike Blake in *Human Sexual Relations*.

12 Useful historical background to the culture of this period is provided by Elizabeth Wilson's *Only Half Way to Paradise: Women in Post-War Britain, 1945–1968*.

13 Steven Lukes' *Marxism and Morality* attempts to clarify the relationship, through exploring what he takes to be a central paradox in Marx's relationship to morality. Partly because of the status of moral theory within a structuralist tradition, this remains a relatively unexplored issue. The recent influence of orthodox interpretations

of Marx within analytic philosophy has set a different but equally constraining framework for these issues. Some of these views are discussed by Richard Miller in *Analysing Marx: Morality, Power and History.*

14 Some of these developments are discussed in my 'Trusting ourselves: Marxism, human needs and sexual politics' in *One-Dimensional Marxism*, Simon Clarke *et al.*

15 A richer and more exploratory discussion of forms of individualism has been a feature of sexual politics and moral theory in the 1980s. See, for instance, *Reconstructing Individualism: Autonomy, Individuality and the Self in Western Thought*, ed. Thomas Heller, Morton Sosna and David Wellbery.

16 A grasp of some of the internal developments of feminism and a sense of how it learnt from the Black Power movement is provided in Sheila Rowbotham's *Dreams and Dilemmas.*

17 See the articles by Nancy Chodorow, 'Toward a relational individualism: the mediation of self through psychoanalysis' and Carol Gilligan, 'Remapping the moral domain: new images of the self in relationship' in *Reconstructing Individualism*, ed. Thomas Heller *et al.*

18 Reich's continuing allegiance to some of Freud's early insights into sexuality and libido is made clear in *Reich Speaks of Freud*. It is also clarified in Myron Sharaf's biography, *Fury on Earth: A Biography of Reich.*

19 It is difficult to recognize the significance of Reich's work and the bodily-oriented therapies he encourages within a structuralist theoretical tradition that dismisses his work as a form of 'biologism' or 'essentialism'. It is threatening to a form of intellectualism that insists on controlling the body and emotional life as part of the control of nature through an autonomous idea of culture.

20 The connection between language and expression is given one of its clearest formulations in the modern period in Herder's writings. An illuminating introduction is provided by Isaiah Berlin in *Vico and Herder*. It does not have to assume, as structuralist-inspired work has falsely supposed, a unified and harmonious conception of the person. It can as effectively illuminate the fragmentations, displacements and painful silences that so often inform our inherited masculinities.

21 The significance of the Growth Movement as a challenge to orthodox psychoanalysis deserves careful analysis. It has been too easily dismissed and trivialized for its early excesses and anti-intellectualism. It has opened up a fresh concern for the quality of experience and relationship. For a useful introduction to the gestalt work of Fritz Perls, see *In and Out of the Garbage Can* and *Gestalt Therapy Verbatim.*

22 For a useful guide to a whole range of practices, see Sheila Ernst and Lucy Goodison *In Our Own Hands*, which grew out of a collective experience in Red Therapy. It helps to bring out some of

the hopes and tensions that lie within these methods. Some of these broader political issues are reflected upon in relation to developing a feminist psychoanalytic practice in *Living with the Sphinx*, ed. Sheila Ernst and M. Maguire.

23 I have discussed Foucault's writings on sexuality in 'Reason, desire and male sexuality' in Pat Caplan (ed.) *The Cultural Construction of Sexuality*.

CHAPTER FIVE: CHANGE

1 Central notions in Althusser's conception of Marxism are developed in his set of essays entitled *For Marx*. I have tried to draw out some of the ambiguities, especially in his conception of ideology which is supposed to help us restore a sense of ideology as a lived relation, rather than simply as a false set of mystifying ideas, in 'Trusting ourselves: Marxism, human needs and sexual politics' in *One-Dimensional Marxism*, ed. Simon Clarke *et al.*

2 A grasp of the significance of the notion of 'possessive individualism' for assumptions maintained within a liberal moral culture can be found in C. B. Macpherson, *The Theory of Possessive Individualism*. Help in relating the tradition to the experience of women can be found in Susan Moller Okin, *Women in Western Political Thought*.

3 For a reassessment of the place of emotions and feelings within Kant's moral theory, and so also for a critical orientation towards an identification of morality with reason, see Lawrence Blum, *Friendship, Altruism and Morality*. See also Bernard Williams' discussion, 'Persons, character and morality' in *Moral Luck*, which can help us think about the notions of personal identity and personal change which are often implicit within liberal moral theory. There is also a useful analytical discussion focusing on Hegel's critique of some of these prevailing assumptions in Kantian moral theory, in Charles Taylor, *Hegel and Modern Social Theory*.

4 Gramsci's notion of hegemony is discussed in *Prison Notebooks*. Often, understanding of Gramsci's ideas has been hampered because they have been interpreted within an already accepted Althusserian reading of Marx. This obviously makes it difficult to understand the significance of Hegel in Gramsci's discussions of Marxism and so in his discussion of the relationship between state and civil society. Such misinterpretation guides some of the otherwise useful contributions to Chantal Mouffe, *Gramsci and Marxist Theory*. Carl Boggs' useful *Gramsci's Marxism* does not help on the critical issue of hegemony, since it gets trapped by a notion of hegemony as the transmission of dominant values and so makes it difficult to grasp the workings of social relations of power and subordination.

5 A useful assessment of some of the free-school literature of the late 1960s and early 1970s is found in Allen Graubard's *Free the Children*. For an analysis more grounded in the English situation, see M. Young and G. Whitty, *Society, State and Schooling*.

6 Though Michel Foucault's account of the growth of insanity in the age of reason in the sixteenth and seventeenth centuries, *Madness and Civilization*, is not related to a particular conception of masculinity, I think such a reworking could usefully be made. This could be related to the suggestive account in Brian Easlea, *Science and Sexual Oppression*, which briefly deals with the relationship of masculinity to the development of sickness in the seventeenth century.

7 See Kant's *The Groundwork to the Metaphysics of Morals*, and *The Moral Law*. See also Ernst Cassirer, *Kant, Rousseau, Goethe* and Jeffrie Murphy's brief discussion of Kant's political theory in *Kant's Philosophy of Right*.

8 Libertarian politics or the late 1960s and early 1970s tended to assume that people should only work politically from their own situation, since this was the only basis upon which you would be taking similar risks with the people you were organizing with and so be able to relate in a situation of rough equality. This encouraged an interest in community politics and a suspicion of traditional Left involvement in industrial struggles, since these often involved setting yourself up in typical Leninist fashion, as somehow knowing what is best for others to struggle around. We felt we could avoid this invidious situation without limiting ourselves to 'struggling around our own situation', however important we took this to be as a starting point for political activity.

9 Big Flame was an activist group which started in Liverpool in 1969 around a community-based newspaper, and which developed into a series of 'base-groups' which organized around particular sectors of class struggle. It developed a kind of libertarian politics which was initially influenced by the extensive theory and experience of *Lotta Continua* in Italy. In this way it brought to bear different revolutionary traditions, in its attempts to develop a practice suitable to the changed conditions of modern British capitalism. Reading the journal *Revolutionary Socialism* gives you some idea of its development. It has retained an ambiguous relationship with a Leninist tradition.

10 Experience in the Fords group helped question a traditional distinction between 'economic' and 'political' consciousness which clearly defined a role for political organizers. We learned how changes in the labour process, especially with assembly-line production, had fundamentally questioned many people's attitudes towards work, as well as traditions of political organizing. It was partly because some of the distinctions between different grades of workers no longer had a basis in the organization of production, but were maintained as part of management's command structure, that more egalitarian demands were made in the generation of intense class struggle sparked in 1968 in France and Italy.

11 The East London group split from Big Flame nationally because of its decision to adopt a more conventional democratic centralist form of organization which would see itself developing around an agreed

line articulated in a reorganized national newspaper. We thought this direction was deeply at odds with the forms of organizing we had learned about in East London and with what we had learned from feminist theory and practice. It was easy to submerge the significant political differences in suggesting we were more concerned with local issues and with sexual politics. Similar issues have emerged for socialist theory and practice with the publication of *Beyond the Fragments* by Sheila Rowbotham, Lynne Segal and Hilary Wainwright.

12 There is a broad literature relating to the Growth Movement, little of which has been taken seriously on the Left. For a very useful introduction to Wilhelm Reich's work see David Boadella's *Wilhelm Reich: The Evolution of his Work*. And for a useful collection of articles which shows the development of bodily-oriented therapies, see David Boadella (ed.), *In the Wake of Reich*. For a useful introduction to Alexander Lowen's work see his *Bioenergetics*; for Kellerman's work, *Your Body Speaks its Mind*; for Perls' work, *Gestalt Therapy Verbatim*. For a critical overview of different methods, see Joel Kovel, *A Complete Guide to Therapy*. And for a sense of the ways these methods were redefined within the experience of Red Therapy because of the insights of feminism and radical politics, Sheila Ernst and Lucy Goodison, *In Our Own Hands – A Book of Self-Help Therapy* and the pamphlet *Red Therapy*.

13 Juliet Mitchell's *Psychoanalysis and Feminism* was important in promoting a particular view of the relationship between psychoanalysis and feminism, one which drew upon Lacan's reading of Freud. This encouraged an enormous interest in Lacan but it tended to ignore the critiques of Lacan's interpretation of the unconscious which were already significant in France, such as Deleuze and Guatari, *Anti-Oedipus* and the significance of Luce Irigaray's work with whom an interview has been translated in *Ideology and Consciousness* No. 1 as 'Women's exile'. Juliet Mitchell's book also served to promote a misleading critique of Reich's writing which became dismissed as 'biologistic' and so foreclosed serious critical attention of different ways in which Marxism and psychoanalysis had been related to each other. It is only with the break-up of the rationalist Althusserian reading of Marx in the early 1980s that these easy dismissals are being more generally reconsidered.

14 Reich was concerned to develop a notion of mass psychology and to consider methods for the prevention of neurosis. This was clear, for instance, in his *Mass Psychology of Fascism*. The individualism which the Growth Movement often shares with traditional psychoanalysis has made this aspect of Reich's work difficult to develop, though in many ways it is most crucial.

15 See, for instance, a useful discussion in Anne Foreman's *Femininity as Alienation* and Jean Baker Miller, *Towards a New Psychology of Women* and *Psychoanalysis and Women*. A related discussion has also been stimulated by Nancy Chodorow's *The Reproduction of Mothering*.

See, for instance, the review by Joanna Ryan in *Revolutionary Socialism* No. 6.

16 See, for instance, Douglas Holly (ed.), *Education or Domination*.

17 The tendency to dismiss different forms of individualism as 'bourgeois' before we distinguish between them has damaging consequences for the development of socialist theory. This is something that Simone Weil recognizes in her *Oppression and Liberty*. It is also something Max Horkheimer helps us with in his *Eclipse of Reason*. Thompson also recognizes this in his 'Open letter Leszek Kolakowski' in his *Poverty of Theory*.

18 See Max Weber's *The Protestant Ethic and the Spirit of Capitalism*. See also Erich Fromm's *Fear of Freedom*, Chapters 2 and 3.

19 See Wilhelm Reich's discussion of his break with Freud in the early sections of *The Function of the Orgasm*. See also his *Reich Speaks of Freud*.

20 See, for instance, the studies in Reich's *Character Analysis*. To situate this work within his overall development, see David Boadella, *Wilhelm Reich: The Evolution of his Work* and Myron Sharaf, *Fury on Earth: A Biography of Reich*.

21 Jean-Paul Sartre, *Anti-Semite and Jew*. See also his essay entitled 'The itinerary of a thought' in *Between Existentialism and Marxism*.

22 Our sense of the relationship between Marx and Hegel gets disorganized through Althusser's reading of Marx in *For Marx*. It might turn out that the notion of the proletariat as a 'universal class' which Althusser also tends to reproduce is an aspect of the Hegelian inheritance within Marxist work which needs to be critically evaluated, especially when it leaves us with a unitary notion of the 'proletariat'.

23 Some of the ideas are developed in a fragmented way in Marx's *Critique of the Gotha Programme*. There is a useful discussion of bourgeois conceptions of freedom and equality in Galvano Della Volpe. *Rousseau and Marx*.

24 See, for instance, Sheila Rowbotham's 'Women's liberation and the New Politics', reprinted in *The Body Politic* and her *Woman's Consciousness/Man's World*. To understand how some of these ideas took hold in the emerging Black Power movement see, for instance, *The Autobiography of Malcolm X* and George Jackson's *The Soledad Brothers*. Similar ideas have found a voice in the writings of Steve Biko and the Black Consciousness movement in South Africa.

25 Thinking about this crucial issue of human needs in Marxism and psychoanalysis is helped by Agnes Heller's *The Theory of Human Need in Marx*. This is something I discuss in 'Trusting ourselves: Marxism, human needs and sexual politics' in *One-Dimensional Marxism*, Simon Clarke *et al.*

26 See the brief opening discussion in Simone Weil's *The Need for Roots*. Some useful introduction to her work is given in George Abbot White (ed.), *Simone Weil: Interpretations of a Life*. For those who want to relate her to radical politics see the essay in the collection by Staughton Lynd on 'The first New Left ... and the third'.

27 This is something that the experience of sexual politics can give us a living sense of. The underlying objectivism in Russell Jacoby's *Social Amnesia* makes it difficult to use his otherwise invaluable historical account of the relationship of Marxism to psychoanalysis, to understand the significance of feminism and sexual politics in this ongoing discussion. Fortunately this was something Herbert Marcuse himself came to appreciate at the end of his life, though too late to reformulate some of the Frankfurt School's assumptions. See his 'Failure of the New Left?' and the discussion in the *New German Critique*, No. 18, Fall 1979.

28 Towards the end I think Lacan's attempt to see the unconscious as structured according to a logic of its own can, somewhat paradoxically, too easily assimilate our unconscious lives to a pre-existing rationalist framework. I think that both Reich and Jung have crucial insights which need to be more assimilated within socialist theory and practice.

29 See my discussion in 'Men and feminism', *Achilles Heel* No. 2, and the special issue of *Achilles Heel* given over to the issue of 'Masculinity and Violence', *Achilles Heel* No. 5.

30 In the late 1970s a gap opened up between developments in Marxist theory and the theorization of ongoing political practice. It was partly through developments within Marxist theory that people developed an intellectual interest in Freud, partly through Althusser's indebtedness to Lacan. The two forms of this theoretical appropriation tended to reinforce each other. Only relatively recently has this theoretical dominance been challenged, partly through an acknowledged crisis in Marxist theory and socialist practice and partly through the experience of feminist therapy and sexual politics. This is not to deny the usefulness of a structuralist tradition in questioning the dominance of heterosexual and patriarchal assumptions, even if it questions its ability to develop a theoretical understanding of personal change. For instance, Michel Foucault's influential discussion in his *A History of Sexuality* Vol. 1 has usefully questioned a blanket notion of repression, but only at the price of suggesting that our elaborate talk about sexuality stretching back to the Victorians, far from being any sign of sexual displacement, means that somehow we do not live in a sex-denying culture. This is to allow a theory of language to replace a theory of sexuality.

31 This is one of Adorno's crucial insights that he developed in his essay 'Sociology and psychology', *New Left Review*, 46 and 47, 1968.

32 I was struck by the number of people I had met in therapy groups who had considerable political experience in radical politics. In some way people were drawing upon a notion of experienced truth that had originally been prompted in radical politics. This is not to suggest many people remained revolutionaries. For a useful antidote to this idea read Michael Rossman, *New Age Blues*.

33 See, for instance, Sheila Rowbotham and Jeffrey Weeks, *Edward Carpenter and Havelock Ellis: Socialism and the New Life*; Stephen Yeo's

interesting 'A new life: the religion of socialism in Britain 1883–1896' in *History Workshop*. No. 4: pp. 5–56 (Autumn 1977); and David Fernbach's *The Spiral Path*.

34 See Martin Jay's essay 'The Jews and the Frankfurt School' in *New German Critique* No. 19, pp. 137–49. See also Adorno and Horkheimer, *Dialectic of Enlightenment* and Susan Buck-Morss, *The Origins of Negative Dialectics: Theodor W. Adorno, Walter Benjamin and the Frankfurt Institute*.

CHAPTER SIX: IDENTITY

1 Sexual politics is constantly struggling against its own forms of moralism – against taking up a 'holier than thou' position towards others. It has constantly moved people away from their own experience into an analysis that so often within a structuralist tradition assumed a life of its own. We learn to think of the 'self' as an abstraction whose reality is lived out exclusively in relation to externalized structures. Often our insight and feeling just slip away.

2 Within a utilitarian culture it can become difficult to draw any meaningful distinction between needs and wants. This is usefully reflected on by Alvin Gouldner in Chapter 3 of *The Coming Crisis of Western Sociology*. It is also a theme in Michael Ignatieff's *The Needs of Strangers*.

3 An interesting structuralist discussion of human needs is provided by Kate Soper in *On Human Needs*.

4 See for instance some of the discussions brought together in *The Unhappy Marriage of Marxism and Feminism*, ed. Lydia Sargent (London: Pluto Press, 1981). See also *The Curious Courtship of Women's Liberation and Socialism* by Batva Weinbaum and *Is the Future Female?* by Lynne Segal.

5 Some useful discussions of collective living in the 1960s and 1970s are given in *Co-ops, Communes and Collectives* ed. John Case and Rosemary Taylor, and in *They Should Have Served That Cup of Coffee* ed. Dick Cluster. For a more general understanding of the development of the New Left in the United States, see W. W. Breines' *The Great Refusal: Community and Organization in the New Left, 1962–1968*.

6 Images of political activism are usefully explored by Sheila Rowbotham *et al* in *Beyond the Fragments*.

7 Wittgenstein in *Culture and Value* suggests some connections between this way of thinking and a minority status connected to being Jewish within a Christian culture. I am only beginning to come to terms with this.

8 Some discussion of the relationship of politics to therapy is found in Stephen Frosh, *The Politics of Psychoanalysis*, and less directly in Peter Fuller's *Art and Psychoanalysis* and *Images of God*.

9 Men's ambivalent relationship towards dependency is a theme in Susie Orbach and Louise Eichenbaum's work. It is also a theme in Lilian Rubin's *Intimate Strangers*.

10 A useful introduction to Benjamin's writing is provided for by the collection *Illuminations*, with an introduction by Hannah Arendt.

CHAPTER SEVEN: LANGUAGE

1 The relationship of rationalism to our inherited conceptions of personal identity is illuminated in the early part of Sartre's *Anti-Semite and Jew*. This is also usefully explored in Della Volpe's *Rousseau and Marx*.

2 This awareness of a loss of personal power associated with a denial of Jewish identity is explored by Freud. See the discussion of Freud's relationship to Judaism in David Bakan's *Freud and the Jewish Mystical Tradition*. This is also a theme in Marthe Roberts' *From Oedipus to Moses*.

3 It has taken time for some of these connections to surface, only for me to recognize how they were part of the anti-Semitic writing of Otto Weininger's influential *Sex and Character*. This work seemed to have a lasting influence on Wittgenstein, and part of his own reflections on Jewishness brought together in *Culture and Value* are a response to it. It is more difficult to know what this meant for him later in his life.

4 Sociological work that offers some kind of passing illumination into the connections between self-respect, male identity and class is provided by Richard Sennett and Jonathan Cobb in *The Hidden Injuries of Class*. It remains a significant model for qualitative research.

5 A useful introduction to Foucault's work is provided by Alan Sheridan's *Michel Foucault: The Will to Truth*. For some sense of the scope of work stimulated by Foucault, see for instance Roy Porter's *A Social History of Madness*. For a more general assessment, see *Foucault A Critical Reader*, ed. David Couzens Hoy.

6 The influence of Cartesianism was a significant theme in Richard Rorty's stimulating *Philosophy and the Mirror of Nature*.

7 A useful collection of articles focusing on some of the implications of this conception of the body is provided by Ted Polhemus in *Social Aspects of the Human Body*. See also the useful discussion by Oliver Sachs in *A Leg to Stand On*. For a feminist reading of these issues, see Kim Chernin *Womansize*.

8 The idea of perception as a source of knowledge within a Western philosophical tradition is usefully explored by M. Merleau-Ponty in *The Phenomenology of Perception*.

9 This rationalist conception of the relation between knowledge and action is usefully explored by Stuart Hampshire in *Thought and Action*. It is thoughtfully, if briefly, questioned by Iris Murdoch in her essay 'The idea of perfection' in *The Sovereignty of Good*.

10 For a useful introduction to Wittgenstein, see Norman Malcolm, *Ludwig Wittgenstein: A Memoir*, and for an understanding of Wittgenstein's philosophical development, Norman Malcolm's

Nothing is Hidden. For a warning against particular misreadings of his work see Stanley Cavell's *Must We Mean What We say?*.

11 Dale Spender's work on language has been critically discussed by Debbie Cameron in *Feminism and Linguistic Theory* and by Lynne Segal in *Is the Future Female?*.

12 An understanding of Gramsci's insights into the relationships between language and power has been difficult to reach since his writings, initially translated in the late 1960s and 1970s, were often interpreted within a tradition of structuralist Marxism, that was then dominant. His work can be more usefully appropriated as a challenge to this tradition of work. See for instance 'The study of philosophy' in Part 3 of *The Prison Notebooks*.

13 A useful critical introduction to structuralist accounts of language is provided by Frederick Jameson in *The Prison House of Language*.

14 See, for instance, David Silverman and Brian Torrode's *The Material Word*, which is otherwise a useful, if difficult, introduction to this kind of work.

15 With the dominance of Kant within an Enlightenment vision, it has been harder to appreciate the significance of the counter-Enlightenment which, within a liberal moral culture, is too easily discounted as 'irrational' or 'reactionary'. Wittgenstein's questioning of the Cartesian tradition might come to be seen as placing him closer to the writings of Herder in his challenge to Kant. See for instance the illuminating essay by Isaiah Berlin, 'Herder and the Enlightenment' in *Vico and Herder*. Too narrow a grasp of the philosophy of language has led to minimizing some of the broader implications of his work. This is suggested as much by David Pears in the concluding chapter to his *Wittgenstein* by M. O. L. Drury in *The Danger of Words*.

16 The relationship of freedom to individuality is discussed by Alan Ryan in *J. S. Mill* and Isaiah Berlin in 'John Stuart Mill and the ends of life' in *Four Essays on Liberty*

CHAPTER EIGHT: STRENGTH

1 The idea that our emotions have to be 'rational' before they can be expressed, involves a form of control in relation to our emotional lives that is reflected in a rationalist philosophical tradition. Wittgenstein's discussion of 'Private languages' in the *Philosophical Investigations* is a challenge to those assumptions and to the character of relationships they foster.

2 A useful discussion of the formation of gender identity is provided by Nancy Chodorow in *The Reproduction of Mothering*. For the development of Freud's work see *Three Essays on the Theory of Sexuality*. For a presentation of this development within a broadly structuralist framework, see Jeffrey Weeks' *Sexuality and its Discontents* and Juliet Mitchell's *Psychoanalysis and Feminism*.

3 See, for instance, Jeffrey Weeks' *Coming Out: Homosexual Politics in*

Britain from the 19th Century to the Present, and *Sex, Politics and Society: The Regulation of Sexuality since 1800*.

4 For a stimulating, if difficult, discussion of this issue of 'private language', see the early part of Stanley Cavell's *The Claims of Reason*. See also the useful discussion in Norman Malcolm's *Nothing is Hidden* (Oxford: Blackwell's 1986).

5 For a useful introduction to the early developments of Simone Weil's thought, see her *Lectures in Philosophy*. For a more general introduction to her work, see Richard Rees, *Simone Weil: A Sketch for a Portrait* and Dorothy Tuck McFarland *Simone Weil*.

6 The identification of masculinity with independence and self-sufficiency has deep sources within the possessive individualism we inherit within a liberal moral culture. This is discussed by C. B. Macpherson in *The Political Theory of Possessive Individualism* and connected to issues of masculinity in my *Kant, Respect and Injustice*.

7 See, for instance, Dennis Altman, *Homosexual: Oppression and Liberation* and David Fernbach, *The Spiral Path: A Gay Contribution to Human Survival*. For Lesbianism, see Lillian Faderman, *Surpassing the Love of men*, E. M. Ettorre *Lesbians, Women and Society* and D. G. Wolfe, *The Lesbian Community*.

8 For interesting, if in some sense limited, work on the male role, see J. Pleck and J. Sawyer, *Men and Masculinity* and J. Pleck, *The Myth of Masculinity*.

9 For reflections on men's relationship to work, see *Achilles Heel* No. 4 (1980) on *Men and Work*. See also the interesting discussion in Richard Sennett's *The Fall of Public Man* and Richard Sennett and Jonathan Cobb's *The Hidden Injuries of Class*.

10 For some useful discussion into the changing character of youth culture see, for instance, Dick Hebdidge *Subcultures: The Meaning of Style*, and Phil Cohen 'Subcultural conflicts and the working-class community', in *Working Papers in Cultural Studies*, No. 2 Spring 1972. Paul Willis' *Learning to Labour* opens up connections in relation to identity, class and masculinity.

11 See, for instance, Ernesto Laclau *Politics and Ideology in Marxist Theory* and the more recent Chantal Mouffe and Ernesto Laclau, *Hegemony and Socialist Strategy*.

12 Some of the implications of this for the nature of depression that can afflict so many men is drawn out by Dorothy Rowe, *Depression*. See also her *Construction of Life and Death*.

CHAPTER NINE: INTIMACY

1 A useful introduction to a form of family therapy that can be sensitive to some of these issues is provided by Robin Skynner and John Cleese in *Families and how to survive them*. See also the article by Terry Cooper.

2 An attempt to connect Marxism with issues of masculinity has been made by Jeff Hearn in *The Gender of Oppression*. See also the discussion in Bob Connell's *Gender and Power*.

3 The nature of this aspect of oppression is clearly presented in Sheila Rowbotham's *Woman's Consciousness/Man's World* and by Jean Baker Miller in *Towards a New Psychology of Women*.

4 See Mill's illuminating *Autobiography*, which still reveals some of the tensions within our inherited rationalist conception of masculinity, which brought him to a nervous breakdown.

5 A useful discussion of some of these contradictions is provided by Sue Cartledge and Joanna Ryan's *Sex and Love: New Thoughts on Old Contradictions*. See also Sheila Ernst and M. Maguire, *Living with the Sphinx: Papers from the Women's Therapy Centre*.

6 See the discussion by Andy Moye in *The Sexuality of Men*, ed. Martin Humphreys and Andy Metcalf. Part of this chapter appeared as 'Fear and intimacy' in that collection.

7 This is an aspect of the pioneering work into men's sexuality that has been carried out by Terry Cooper and Rex Bradley in 'Spectrum', London. It has drawn on the work of Stanley Kellerman. See, for instance, *The Body Speaks Its Mind*, and *Somatic Reality*.

8 Some useful insights into these questions of forms of responsibility and control can be gained from Carmen Claudin-Urondo, *Lenin and the Cultural Revolution*, Richard Gombin *The Radical Tradition* and Sheila Rowbotham *Dreams and Dilemmas*.

9 Freud's paper, 'Some psychical consequences of the anatomical distinction between the sexes' is preprinted in the Penguin Library of his work, in a volume entitled *Sexuality*.

10 This identification of morality with principles conceived by reason alone is confirmed by Carol Gilligan's *In A Different Voice*. She shows that we have tended to idealize the moral experience of men, so turning it into a norm against which a different women's experience of care and concern within relationships has often been diminished and denied.

11 The relationship of authority within the family to historically specific forms of masculinity is something the Frankfurt School were aware of. See, for instance, Adorno and Horkheimer, *Aspects of Sociology*. See also *The Fatherless Society*.

12 Chasseguet-Smirgel's interesting developments in psychoanalytic theory are available in *Female Sexuality*. See also *The Ego Deal* and *Creativity and Perversion*.

CHAPTER TEN: CONCLUSION: MASCULINITY, MORALITY AND POLITICS

1 This tendency to produce a negative conception of masculinity, as if it is masculinity itself that cannot be redeemed or changed, is a difficulty in much anti-sexist men's writing, as it is with some radical feminist writing on men. See, for instance, the otherwise useful collection, *For Men Against Sexism*, ed. John Snodgrass. It is a tendency of thought within radical feminism that Lynne Segal's *Is the Future Female?* challenges. It helped define the vision that informed the publication of *Achilles Heel* in England.

2 Some of the difficulties of identifying all references to experience with a tradition of empiricism were drawn attention to by E. P. Thompson's essay 'The poverty of theory' in his *The Poverty of Theory and Other Essays*.

3 Some sense of how structuralism has shifted the terms of discussion so that issues of the relationship of identity, power and experience could only be conceptualized as aspects of a 'theory of the subject' can be gained from *Language and Materialism* by Rosalind Coward and John Ellis. The journal *Ideology and Conscious* and *M/F* were significant in developing this form of work which in its arrogance marginalized others as 'essentialist' or 'humanist'. Slogans had replaced thought.

4 See the discussion in M. Merleau-Ponty's *Phenomenology of Perception*. A useful introduction to his work is provided by Sonia Kruks *The Political Philosophy of Merleau-Ponty*.

5 An emphasis on the articulation of discourses has fostered a discussion of political alliances which would bring together the new social movements without really grasping the nature of the challenge they individually make to our inherited conceptions of politics. It is as if language provides us with a strangely neutral framework within which powerful intellectual and political differences seem to be dissolved. For instance, see Ernesto Laclau and Chantal Mouffe, *Hegemony and Socialist Strategy*.

6 This has fostered an orthodox interpretation of Marx in which moral language is taken to be specific to particular modes of production so that a language of justice and morality cannot be invoked as a challenge to capitalist social relations. See, for instance, Allan Wood, *Karl Marx*. For a more fruitful, if limited, attempt to pose questions about the moral inheritance of Marxism, see Steven Lukes' *Morality and Marxism*. See also how Simone Weil raises some of these issues within her critique of orthodox Marxism in *Oppression and Liberty*. See the discussion in L. Blum and V. Seidler, *A Truer Liberty: Simone Weil and Marxism*.

7 One of Derrida's major works is *Of Grammatology* which has a useful introduction by Gayatri Spivak. For an introduction to the ideas informing deconstruction see D. C. Wood, 'An introduction to Derrida' in *Radical Philosophy* No. 21 (Spring 1979). See also D. Norris, *Marxism and Deconstruction*.

8 Some of the tensions in Foucault's work are already apparent in the collection *Power/Knowledge*, ed. Colin Gordon. He seems to be working with quite a different approach in his last work on sexuality. As Weeks has acknowledged, 'Foucault, in taking us through the arts of existence in the ancient world, is asking us to reflect on the ways of life that would be valid for us today' *Sexuality*, p. 114.

9 For a useful introduction to different forms of feminist theory see *Feminist Politics and Human Nature* by Alison Jaggar. See also Hester Eisenstein's *Contemporary Feminist Thought* and N. Keohane *et al*, *Feminist Theory*.

10 Significant questions were raised about this problem in the early years of the Soviet Union. See, for instance, Wilhelm Reich *The Sexual Revoltuion* and Emma Goldman, *Living My Life*.
11 See Weil's early writings recently translated by McFarland and Van Ness as *Simone Weil: Formative Writings 1929–1941*. See also Lawrence Blum and Victor J. Seidler, *A Truer Liberty: Simone Weil and Marxism*.

BIBLIOGRAPHY

Adorno, T. W. and Horkheimer, M. (1974), *Aspects of Sociology*, London: Heinemann.

Allen, S., Sanders, L. S. and Wallis, J. (1974), *Conditions of Illusion: Papers from the Women's Movement*, Leeds: Feminist Books Ltd.

Althusser, Louis (1971), *Lenin & Philosophy and Other Essays*, London: New Left Books.

———— (1970), *For Marx*, London: New Left Books.

Altman, Denis (1971), *Homosexual: Oppression and Liberation*, New York: Outerbridge & Dienstfrey.

Bakan, David (1958), *Sigmund Fred and The Jewish Mystical Tradition*, New York: Schocken.

Beck, Evelyn Torton (1982), *Nice Jewish Girls; A Lesbian Anthology*, Watertown, USA: Persephone Press.

Benjamin, Walter (1970), *Illuminations*, London: Fontana Books.

Berlin, Isaiah (1968), *Four Essays on Liberty*, Oxford: Oxford University Press.

———— (1976), *Vico and Herder*, New York: Random House.

Blum, L. (1980), *Friendship, Altruism and Morality*, London: Routledge & Kegan Paul.

Blum, L. and Seidler, V. (1989), *A Truer Liberty: Simone Weil and Marxism*, London: Routledge.

Boadella, David (1976), *In the Wake of Reich*, London: Coventure.

———— (1973), *Reich: the Evolution in his Work*, London: Vision.

Boggs, Carl (1976), *Gramsci's Marxism*, London: Pluto Press.

Brake, Mike (1982), *Human Sexual Relations: Towards a Redefinition of Sexual Politics*, London: Penguin Books.

Breines, Wini (1982), *The Great Refusal: Community & Organisation in the New Left 1962–68*, New York: Pioneer.

Buck-Morss, Susan (1977), *The Origin of Negative Dialectics*, Brighton: Harvester Press.

Cameron, Deborah (1986), *Feminism and Linguistic Theory* London: Macmillan.

Caplan, Pat (1988), *The Cultural Construction of Sexuality*, London: Tavistock.

221

Capra, Fritjof (1982), *The Turning Point: Science, Society and the Rising Culture*, London: Wildwood House.

Cartledge, S. and Ryan, J. (1983), *Sex and Love: New Thoughts on Old Contradictions*, London: The Women's Press.

Case, J. and Taylor, R. (1979), *Co-ops, Communes and Collectives*, New York: Pantheon.

Cavell, Stanley (1968), *Must We Mean What We Say?*, New York: Scribners.

———— (1979), *The Claims of Reason*, Oxford: Oxford University Press.

Chapman, R. and Rutherford, J. (1988), *Male Order: Unwrapping Masculinity*, London: Lawrence & Wishart.

Chasseguet-Smirgel, J. (1970), *Female Sexuality*, Michigan: Ann Arbor, University of Michigan Press.

———— (1987), *The Ego Ideal*, London: Free Association Books.

———— (1985), *Creativity and Perversion*, London: Free Association Books.

Chernin, Kim (1983), *Womansize: The Tyranny in Slenderness*, London: The Woman's Press.

Chodorow, Nancy (1978), *The Reproduction of Mothering: Psychoanalysis and the Sociology of Gender*, Los Angeles: California University Press.

Claudin-Urondo, C. (1971), *Lenin and the Cultural Revolution*, Brighton: Harvester Press.

Cluster, Dick (1979), *They Should Have Served That Cup of Coffee*, Boston: South End Press.

Cobb, J. S., and Sennett, R., *Hidden Injuries of Class*, Cambridge: Cambridge University Press.

Connell, Bob (1986), *Gender and Power*, Oxford: Polity Press.

———— (1984), *Which Way Is Up?*, London: Allen & Unwin.

Coward, R. (1984), *Female Desire: Women's Sexuality Today*, London: Paladin.

Coward, R. and Ellis, J. (1977), *Language and Materialism*, London: Routledge & Kegan Paul.

Della Volpe, Galvano (1978), *Rousseau and Marx*, London: Lawrence & Wishart.

Derrida, Jacques (1974), *Of Grammatology*, Baltimore: John Hopkins Press.

Descombes, Vincent (1980), *Modern French Philosophy*, trans. L. Scott-Fox and J. M. Harding, Cambridge: Cambridge University Press.

Drury, M. O'L. (1973), *The Danger of Words*, London: Routledge & Kegan Paul.

Easlea, Brian (1980), *Witch-Hunting, Magic and the New Philosophy*, Brighton: Harvester Press.

———— (1982), *Science and Sexual Oppression*, London: Weidenfeld & Nicolson.

Ehrenreich, B. and English, D. (1979). *For Her Own Good*, London: Pluto Press.

Eisenstein, Hester (1984), *Contemporary Feminist Thought*, London: Unwin Paperbacks.

Eisenstein, Zillah (1979), *Capitalist Patriarchy and the Case for Socialist Feminism*, New York: Monthly Review Press.
Ernst, S. and Goodison, L. (1981), *In Our Own Hands*, London: The Women's Press.
Ernst, S. and Maguire, M. (1981), *Living with the Sphinx: Papers from the Women's Therapy Centre*, London: The Women's Press.
Ettorre, E. M. (1980), *Lesbians, Women and Society*, London: Routledge & Kegan Paul.
Faderman, Lillian (1980), *Surpassing the Love of Men: Romantic Friendship and Love between Women from the Renaissance to the Present*, London: Junction Books.
Fell, Alison (1984), *Every Move You Make*, London: Virago Press.
Fernbach, David (1981), *The Spiral Path*, London: Gay Men's Press.
Foreman, Ann (1977), *Femininity as Alienation*, London: Pluto Books.
Foucault, Michel (1979), *The History of Sexuality: An Introduction*, London: Allen Lane.
———— (1978), *Discipline and Punish*, London: Penguin Books.
———— (1980), *Power/Knowledge: Selected Interviews and Other Writings*, ed. Colin Gordon, Brighton: Harvester Press.
———— (1984), *The Foucault Reader*, ed. Paul Rabinow, New York: Pantheon Books.
———— (1967), *Madness & Civilization*, London: Tavistock.
Freedman, E. *et al* (1985), *The Lesbian Issue: Essays from Signs*, Chicago: University of Chicago Press.
Freud, Sigmund (1905), *Three Essays on the Theory of Sexuality*, London; Hogarth Press.
Fromm, Erich (1942), *Fear of Freedom*, London: Routledge & Kegan Paul.
Frosh, Steven (1987), *The Politics of Psychoanalysis*, London: Macmillan.
Giddens, Anthony (1977), *Studies in Social and Political Theory*, London: Hutchinson.
Gilligan, C. (1982), *In a Different Voice: Psychological Theory and Women's Development*, Cambidge, Mass: Harvard University Press.
Goldmann, Emma (1982), *Living My Life*, New York: Gibbs M. Smith.
Goldmann, Lucien (1980), *Lukàcs and Heidegger*, London: Routledge & Kegan Paul.
Gombin, Richard (1978), *The Radical Tradition*, London: Methuen.
Gouldner, Alvin (1970), *The Coming Crisis of Western Sociology*, London: Heinemann.
Gramsci, A. (1971) *Selections from the Prison Notebooks*, ed. and trans. by O. Hoare and G. Nowell-Smith, London: Lawrence & Wishart.
Graubard, Allen (1972), *Free the Children*, New York: Vintage Books, Random House.
Griffin, S. (1980), *Pornography and Silence*, London: Women's Press.
———— (1982), *Made from this Earth*, London: The Women's Press.
Grimshaw, J. (1987), *Feminist Philosophers*, Brighton: Harvester Press.
Hales, Mike (1980), *Living Thinkwork*, London: CSE Books.
Hampshire, Stuart (1965), *Thought and Action*, London: Chatto & Windus.

223

Hearn, Jeff (1986), *The Gender of Oppression*, Brighton: Harvester Press.
Hebdige, D. C. (1979), *Subcultures: The Meaning of Style*, London: Methuen.
Heller, Agnes (1976), *The Theory of Human Need in Marx*, London: Allison & Busby.
Heller, Thomas, Sosna, Morton *et al* (1986), *Reconstructing Individualism: Autonomy, Individuality and the Self in Western Thought*, Stanford: Stanford University Press.
Heron, Liz (1985), *Truth, Dare or Promise: Girls Growing Up in the Fifties*, London: Virago.
Hirschman, A. (1979), *The Passions and the Interests*, Princeton NJ: Princeton University Press.
Holly, Douglas (ed.), (1974), *Education or Domination*, London: Arrow Books.
Horkheimer, Max, (1947), *The Eclipse of Reason*, New York: The Seabury Press.
Horkheimer, Max & Adorno, Theodore W. (1973), *The Dialectic of Enlightenment* (trans. John Cumming) London: Allan Lane.
Humphries, M. and Metcalf, A. (1985), *The Sexuality of Men*, London: Pluto Press.
Ignatief, M. (1984), *The Needs of Strangers*, London: Chatto & Windus.
Jackson, George (1971), *The Soledad Brothers: The Prison Letters of George Jackson*, London: Jonathan Cape, and Penguin Books.
Jacoby, Russell (1976), *Social Amnesia*, Brighton: Harvester Press.
Jaggar, Alison (1983), *Feminist Politics and Human Nature*, Brighton: Harvester Press.
Jameson, F. (1976), *The Prison House of Language*, Princeton: Princeton University Press.
Kellerman, Stanley (1975), *The Body Speaks its Mind*, New York: Simon & Schuster.
——————— (1979), *Somatic Reality*, Berkeley, California: Center Press.
Kennedy, E. and Mendus, S. (1987) *Women in Western Political Philosophy*, Brighton: Harvester Press.
Keohane, N. and Rosaldo, M. (1982), *Feminist Theory*, Brighton: Harvester Press.
Kruks, Sonia (1981), *The Political Philosophy of Merleau-Ponty*, Brighton: Harvester Press.
Laclau, Ernesto (1977) *Politics and Ideology in Marxist Theory*, London: Verso, New Left Books.
Laclau, E. and Mouffe C. (1985), *Hegemony and Socialist Strategy*, London: Verso.
Laing, R. D. (1960), *The Divided Self*, London: Tavistock.
——————— (1968), *The Politics of Experience*, London: Penguin Books.
Lloyd, Genevieve (1986), *Men of Reason*, London: Methuen.
Lowen, Alexander (1963), *The Betrayal of the Body*, London: Collier Macmillan.
——————— (1976), *Bioenergetics*, London: Penguin Books.

Lowy, Michael (1979), *Georg Lukàcs – From Romanticism to Bolshevism*, London: New Left Books.

Lukàcs, Georg (1971), *History and Class Consciousness*, London: The Merlin Press.

Lukes, S. (1984), *Marxism and Morality*, Oxford: Oxford University Press.

McFarland, Dorothy (1983), *Simone Weil*, New York: Frederick Ungar.

McRobbie, A. and Nava, M. (1984), *Gender and Generation*, London: Macmillan.

MacPherson, C. B. (1962), *The Political Theory of Possessive Individualism*, Oxford: Oxford University Press.

———— (1973), *Democratic Theory: Essays in Retrieval*, Oxford: Oxford University Press.

Malcolm, Norman (1958), *Ludwig Wittgenstein: A Memoir*, Oxford: Oxford University Press.

———— (1986), *Nothing is Hidden*, Oxford: Blackwells.

Marx, Karl (1962), *Critique of the Gotha Programme*, SW 2, Moscow: Foreign Languages Publishing House.

Marx, Karl (1977), *Selected Writings*, ed. David McLellan, Oxford: Oxford University Press.

Merchant, Carolyn, (1980), *The Death of Nature*, New York: Harper and Row.

Merleau-Ponty, M. (1962), *Phenomenology of Perception*, London: Routledge & Kegan Paul.

Midgley, M. and Hughes, J. (1983), *Women's Choices: Philosophical Problems facing Feminism*, London: Weidenfeld & Nicolson.

Mill, J. S. (1971), *Autobiography*, ed. J. Stillinger, Oxford: Clarendon Press.

Miller, Alice (1981) *The Drama of the Gifted Child*, London: Faber & Faber.

———— (1983), *For Your Own Good*, London: Faber & Faber.

Miller, Jean Baker (1976), *Towards a New Psychology of Women*, Boston: Beacon Press.

Miller, Richard (1984), *Analysing Marx*, Princeton: Princeton University Press.

Miller, Stuart (1983), *Friendship Between Men*, London: Gateway.

Mitchell, Juliet (1984), *Women: The Longest Revolution*, London: Virago.

———— (1975), *Psychoanalysis and Feminism*, London: Penguin Books.

Mitchell, J. and Rose, J. (1982), *Feminine Sexuality*, London: Macmillan.

Moore, Barrington (1984), *Privacy: Studies in Social and Cultural History*, New York: Pantheon Books.

Mouffe, Chantal (1979), *Gramsci and Marxist Theory*, London: Routledge & Kegan Paul.

Murdoch, I. (1970), *The Sovereignty of Good*, London: Routledge & Kegan Paul.

Neibuhr, Reinhold (1964), *The Nature and Destiny of Man*, New York: Scribners.

Neu, Jerome (1977), *Emotion, Thought and Therapy*, London: Routledge & Kegan Paul.

Perls, Fritz (1969), *Gestalt Therapy Verbatim*, Moab Uttar: Real People Press.

Pleck, Joseph (1981), *The Myth of Masculinity*, Boston: MIT Press.

Pleck, Joseph and Sawyer, J. (1974), *Men and Masculinity*, New Jersey: Prentice-Hall.

Plummer, Kenneth (1981), *The Making of the Modern Homosexual*, London: Hutchinson.

Polhemus, Ted (1978), *Sexual Aspects of the Human Body*, London: Penguin Books.

Porter, Roy (1987), *A Social History of Madness*, London: Weidenfeld & Nicolson.

Rawls, John (1971), *A Theory of Justice*, Cambridge, Mass: Harvard University Press and Oxford University Press.

Red Collective (1978), *The Politics of Sexuality in Capitalism*, London: Red Collective and Publications Distribution Cooperative.

Ree, Jonathan (1974), *Descartes*, London: Allan Lane.

Rees, Richard (1966), *Simone Weil: A Sketch for a Portrait*, Oxford: Oxford University Press.

Reich, Wilhelm (1942), *The Function of the Orgasm*, New York: Farrar, Strauss & Giroux.

———— (1970), *The Mass Psychology of Fascism*, New York: Farrar, Strauss & Giroux.

———— (1972), *Reich Speaks of Freud*, London: Souvenir Press.

Reiche, R. (1970), *Sexuality and Class Struggle*, London: New Left Books.

Richards, Barry (1984), *Capitalism and Infancy*, London: Free Association Press.

Roberts, Helen (ed.) (1981), *Doing Feminist Research*, London: Routledge & Kegan Paul.

Roberts, Marthe (1976), *From Oedipus to Moses: Freud's Jewish Identity*, London: Litman Library, Routledge & Kegan Paul.

Rorty, Richard (1979), *Philosophy and the Mirror of Nature*, Oxford: Blackwells.

Rossman, Michael (1979), *New Age Blues or the Politics of Consciousness*, New York: E. P. Dutton.

Rowbotham, Sheila (1973), *Woman's Consciousness/Man's World*, London: Penguin Books.

———— (1983), *Dreams and Dilemmas*, London: Virago.

Rowbotham, S. and Weeks, J. (1978), *Socialism and the New Life: Edward Carpenter & Havelock Ellis*, London: Pluto Books.

Rowbotham, S., Segal, L. and Wainwright, H. (1979), *Beyond the Fragments*, London: The Merlin Press.

Rowe, Dorothy (1982), *The Constructions of Life and Death*, London: Wiley.

———— (1983), *Depression*, London: Routledge & Kegan Paul.

Rubin, Lillian (1985), *Intimate Strangers*, London: Fontana.

Ryan, Alan (1984), *J. S. Mill*, London: Routledge & Kegan Paul.
Sachs, Oliver (1984), *A Leg To Stand on*, London: Gerald Duckworth.
Sandel, Michael (1983), *Liberalism and the Limits of Justice*, Cambridge: Cambridge University Press.
Sargent, Lydia (ed.) (1981), *The Unhappy Marriage of Marxism and Feminism*, London: Pluto Books.
Sartre, J.-P. (1948) *Anti-Semite and Jew*, London: Secker & Warburg.
———— (1974), *Between Existentialism and Marxism*, trans. John Mathews, London: New Left Books.
Sayers, J. (1986), *Sexual Contradictions*, London: Tavistock.
Segal, Lynne (1986), *Is The Future Female?*, London: Virago Books.
Seidler, V. J. (1980), 'Trusting ourselves: Marxism, human needs and sexual politics' in S. Clarke, Seidler *et al. One-Dimensional Marxism*, London: Allison & Busby.
———— (1986), *Kant, Respect & Injustice: The Limits of Liberal Moral Theory*, London: Routledge & Kegan Paul.
Sennett, Richard (1978), *The Fall of Public Man*, New York: Vintage, Random House.
Sennett, R. and Cobb., J. (1970), *The Hidden Injuries of Class*, New York: Vintage Paperacks.
Sharaf, Myron (1983), *Fury on Earth: A Biography of Wilhelm Reich*, New York: St Martin's Press/Marek.
Silverman, D. and Torrode, B. (1980), *The Material Word*, London: Routledge & Kegan Paul.
Skynner, Robin and Cleese, John (1983), *Families and How to Survive Them*, London: Methuen.
Smart, Barry (1986), *Michel Foucault*, London: Ellis Horwood/Tavistock.
Snodgrass, Jon (1977), *For Men Against Sexism*, New York: Times Change Press.
Soper, Kate (1981), *On Human Needs*, Brighton: Harvester Press.
Taylor, Charles (1985), 'Atomism' and 'The nature and scope of distributive justice' in *Philosophy and the Human Sciences, Philosophical Papers 2*, Cambridge: Cambridge University Press.
Thompson, E. P. (1978), *The Poverty of Theory and Other Essays*, London: The Merlin Press.
Volpe, Galvano (1978), *Rousseau and Marx*, London: Lawrence & Wishart.
Weeks, Jeffrey (1977), *Coming Out: Homosexual Politics in Britain*, London: Quartet.
———— (1981), *Sex, Politics and Society: The Regulation of Sexuality since 1800*, London: Longmans.
———— (1985), *Sexuality and its Discontents*, London: Routledge & Kegan Paul.
———— (1986), *Sexuality*, London: Ellis Horwood, Tavistock Publications.
Weil, S. (1958), *Oppression and Liberty*, London: Routledge & Kegan Paul.
———— (1978), *Lectures on Philosophy*, Cambridge: Cambridge University Press.

————— (1986), *Formative Writings*, ed. D. McFarland and Van Ness, London: Routledge & Kegan Paul.

Weinbaum, Batva (1978), *The Curious Courtship of Women's Liberation & Socialism*, Boston: South End Press.

Weininger, Otto (1906), *Sex and Character*, London: Heinemann.

White, George Abbot (1981), *Simone Weil: Interpretations of a Life*. Boston: University of Massachusetts Press.

Whitehead, A. N. (1987), *Science and the Modern World*, London: Free Association Books.

Wicks, Francis G. (1977), *The Inner World of Childhood*, London: Coventure.

Williams, Bernard (1978), *Descartes: The Project of Pure Enquiry*, Brighton: Harvester Press.

Willis, Paul (1977), *Learning to Labour*. London: Saxon House (Gower).

Wilson, Elizabeth (1980), *Only Half Way to Paradise: Women in Post-War Britain 1945–1968*, London: Tavistock Publications.

————— (1977), *Women and the Welfare State*, London: Tavistock Publications.

Winnicott, D. W. (1957), *The Child and the Outside World*, London: Tavistock.

————— (1964), *The Child, the family and the Outside World*, Harmondsworth: Penguin.

Wittgenstein, Ludwig (1963), *Philosophical Investigations*, Oxford: Basil Blackwell.

————— (1980), *Culture and Value*, trans. Peter Winch, Oxford: Blackwells.

Wolfe, D. G. (1979), *The Lesbian Community*, San Francisco: University of California Press.

Wood, Allen (1983), *Karl Marx*, London: Routledge & Kegan Paul.

Young, Nigel (1977), *An Infantile Disorder? The Crisis and Decline of the New Left*, London: Routledge & Kegan Paul.

Young, M. and Whitty, G. (1977), *Society, State & Schooling*, Surrey: The Falmer Press.

Zaretsky, Eli (1976), *Capitalism, the Family and Personal Life*, London: Pluto Press.

NAME INDEX

229

SUBJECT INDEX

action, goal-oriented/instrumental 7,
9–10, 58
animals 14–5, 38, 127; nature 80, 97;
wants/desires 129
Auschwitz 16

Big Flame group 82, 84, 93–4
Black movement 5, 74, 100
bodily experience/feelings/movement
58, 77, 84, 87, 97, 102, 104, 116
body, as a machine/instrument 39–40,
44–5, 48, 65, 129–30, 161

Campaign for Nuclear Disarmament
(CND) 180
capitalist market/social order 46;
consumer capitalism 34; and desire/
emotion/need 15, 33, 87; and the
individual 121; and masculine
identity 45, 192; and Protestantism/
Protestant ethic 26, 100
Cartesian dualism/rationalism/
tradition 123, 129, 131, 154
children 127; as closer to nature
14–15
Chinese revolution 37
Communist Manifesto 99
consciousness-raising 3, 11–12, 17–18,
42–3, 51–2, 54–5, 61, 68, 77–8,
80–1, 104, 122, 146, 170, 186–8,
190, 197, 200
control 55–6, 62–3, 66, 77; as external
66–7; as domination 44, 48–9, 64–5,
70, 161; false sense of 118; see also
language, men's relation to, power
of men, and self-control
counter-hegemonic culture 79

desire, opposed to reason 4, 6, 18;
individual 132; and morality 67,
70–2; and sexuality 22; and wants,
as animal 129; see also emotions,
feelings, needs

emotions, and feelings 10, 52, 71; as
animal 97; denied as sources of
knowledge 16–20, 37, 66, 89, 127;
and desires 10, 77; domination of
7–8, 44, 48–9, 70; as externally
produced 24, 50; and language
63–4, 81, 137; and men and
individuality 133; as private in Marx
45; and reason 2, 13, 15, 37–8, 50;
as reasonable/rational 144, 171; as
socially constructed 36; and
therapy, see feelings and therapy; as
weakness 157; see also
fragmentation, and self-control
empiricism/empiricist tradition 9, 51,
59
Enlightenment 3–5, 12, 44, 46, 128, 164
equality 55, 57, 60, 75–6, 116–17,
200; of opportunity 126
ethnicity, and identity 16, 99–101,
124–6, 184; see also being Jewish
examples 11
experience, individual/personal 1–2,
4, 10, 51; in Foucault 19

fascism 16, 182
fear, of the father 170–2; of intimacy/
the personal 52, 161–3, 198; as
weakness 157
feelings 33–6, 38; and activism 83;
and desires as threats to self-control

231